Prediction in Criminology

SUNY Series on Critical Issues in Criminal Justice
Edited by Donald Newman and Gilbert Geis

Prediction in Criminology

Edited by DAVID P. FARRINGTON
AND
ROGER TARLING

State University of New York Press

Published by
State University of New York Press, Albany

©1985 State University of New York

For information, address State University of New York Press, State University Plaza, Albany, N.Y., 12246

Library of Congress Cataloging in Publication Data

Main entry under title:

Prediction in criminology.

(SUNY series on critical issues in criminal justice)
1. Criminal justice, Administration of—United States—Statistics—Forecasting.
2. Criminal justice, Administration of—Canada—Statistics—Forecasting. 3. Criminal justice, Administration of—Great Britain—Statistics—Forecasting. I. Farrington, David P. II. Tarling, Roger. III. Series.
HV9950.P73 1985   364'.028   84-16447
ISBN 0-88706-004-8
ISBN 0-88706-003-X (pbk.)

Contents

Preface

Prediction has always been an important topic in criminology. Prediction instruments have been used extensively to aid criminal justice decisionmakers, most notably in selecting prisoners for parole. Current uses of prediction methods include the identification of offenders for a policy of "selective incapacitation" and the identification of dangerous offenders. Prediction methods are also used to evaluate different kinds of penal treatments and to assess the likely effects of penal policy changes on the criminal justice system. As a by-product of this substantive research, a good deal of attention has been paid to the statistical and methodological issues involved in constructing sound prediction instruments.

Although the prediction literature is vast, the books, reports, and articles that have been produced have always been rather specific, focusing narrowly on one area of application, such as parole or dangerousness. The aim of this book is to bring together papers that discuss a wide variety of applications of prediction research in criminology that should be of concern to policymakers, practitioners, academics, and researchers. The collection includes works from the United States, Canada, and Great Britain and should, therefore, be of considerable interest to a wide international audience. The book stresses both the methodology of prediction research and the substantive findings, and it includes an extensive introductory review of the literature to set the specific applications in context.

Predictions of future offending, whether made implicitly or explicitly, are bound to influence criminal justice decisionmaking for some time to come. In the interests of justice, those predictions should be made as explicitly and as accurately as possible. We hope that this book will contribute to these ends.

David P. Farrington
Roger Tarling

May 1983

List of Contributors

Tony Black, Psychology Department, Broadmoor Hospital, Crowthorne, Berks, England.

R. Gordon Cassidy, School of Business, Queen's University, Kingston, Ontario, Canada.

John B. Copas, Department of Statistics, Birmingham University, England.

J. Eric Cullen, Psychology Department, Aylesbury Youth Custody Center, Aylesbury, Bucks, England.

David P. Farrington, Institute of Criminology, Cambridge University, England.

Don M. Gottfredson, School of Criminal Justice, Rutgers University, Newark, New Jersey, U.S.A.

Stephen D. Gottfredson, Department of Criminal Justice, Temple University, Philadelphia, Pennsylvania, U.S.A.

Gillian Hill, Institute of Criminology, Cambridge University, England.

John A. Perry, Central Statistical Office, London, England.

Sheila Speirs, Young Offender Psychology Unit, Home Office Prison Department, London, England.

Penny Spinks, Psychology Department, Broadmoor Hospital, Crowthorne, Berks, England.

Roger Tarling, Home Office Research and Planning Unit, London, England.

David Thornton, Young Offender Psychology Unit, Home Office Prison Department, London, England.

William L. Wilbanks, Criminal Justice Department, Florida International University, Miami, Florida, U.S.A.

Leslie T. Wilkins, Research Professor (Emeritus), School of Criminal Justice, State University of New York, Albany, New York, U.S.A.

I
Introductory Section

CHAPTER 1

Criminological Prediction: An Introduction

DAVID P. FARRINGTON AND ROGER TARLING

SUMMARY

This chapter reviews a number of applications of prediction methods in criminology: selective incapacitation; dangerousness; delinquency; evaluation of penal treatments and parole; bail, police, and institutional decisions; and the prediction of rates (for example, of imprisonment) using mathematical or computer models. It also reviews several basic issues of concern to those involved in prediction in criminology: selection and measurement of predictor and criterion variables; combining predictors; measuring predictive efficiency; shrinkage; and some ethical issues.

INTRODUCTION

A criminological prediction study investigates the extent to which one or more criterion measures (for example, measures of delinquent or criminal behavior) can be predicted by one or more measures of other factors operating at an earlier time (predictors). Most studies are concerned with predicting which persons in a convicted group will be reconvicted in the future; some studies aim to predict which persons in an unconvicted group will be convicted in the future. Other researches are interested in predicting other criterion measures, such as the likelihood of persons released on bail failing to attend court, the likelihood of persons in prison attempting to escape, length of sentences likely to be given, or time likely to be served in prison. Finally, other prediction studies deal not with individuals so much as with predicting future rates—of arrests or imprisonment, for example—especially in the light of future demographic or penal policy changes.

All of these kinds of research are represented in this book. Most chapters (3, 4, 5, 9, and the primarily methodological 11 and 12) focus on methods for predicting reconvictions of ex-prisoners, former mental patients, or probationers. Chapter 8 discusses the prediction of delinquency in an unconvicted group, and chapters 6 and 7 examine other criterion measures (absconding and self-injury in institutions). Finally, chapter 10 describes a model of a criminal justice system that can be used in predicting the effects of penal policy changes.

This book predominantly focuses on multivariate prediction and on how best to select and combine predictor variables into a composite measure (a prediction table or risk groups). It does not consider univariate or clinical prediction studies to any extent. In prediction research, the values of the predictor variables should be recorded at some time earlier than those of the criterion ones, so that knowledge of the criterion variables cannot bias the measurement of the predictors. This requirement was not fulfilled in some famous prediction studies (for example, Glueck and Glueck, 1950). Even where the values of the predictor variables were recorded beforehand, it is usual for the data to be extracted and coded and for multivariate predictions to be made retrospectively. Most researchers wish to draw conclusions about the accuracy of prospective prediction, and it may be that prospective longitudinal researches are essential for this (for a review of such studies in criminology, see Farrington, 1979).

Most criminological studies emphasize explanation rather than prediction, although the two are not mutually exclusive and there is sometimes only a fine dividing line between them. Correlational or cross-sectional studies, for example, comparisons of arrest rates and crime rates to investigate general deterrence, clearly should not be considered predictive. However, researches designed to investigate the independent effects of a number of explanatory variables on some criterion or dependent variable recorded some time later could in some sense be regarded as predictive. Such researches will not be reviewed here unless they are concerned with the accuracy of prediction. For example, Farrington and Morris (1983) used regression techniques to investigate which variables were independent predictors of sentence severity and of reconviction. Their research is not regarded as a prediction study because the authors did not attempt to derive a composite predictive measure or to report the accuracy of their predictions. (Their investigation established that, after controlling for other factors, the sex of the defendant had no influence on the severity of the sentence or the likelihood of reconviction.)

Prediction research has mainly been carried out in an attempt to assist persons in the criminal justice system who have to make decisions. For example, it should be helpful to provide information about the predicted likelihood of reoffending for parole board members, about the predicted likelihood of escaping for institutional staff, and about the predicted likelihood of failing to attend court for prosecutors and judges. Changes in penal policy should not be made in the absence of predictions about their likely effects. This introductory chapter reviews some of the uses of prediction methods in criminology, to set the scene for the more detailed descriptions that follow.

AREAS OF APPLICATION

Selective Incapacitation

One of the most recent applications of prediction research is the work of Greenwood (1982) on selective incapacitation, the latest of a series of studies concerned with the penal aim of incapacitation. Interest in incapacitation increased in the mid–1970s after the well-known reviews of Martinson (1974) in the United States and Brody (1976) in England suggested that rehabilitation as a penal aim was not being achieved by existing treatment measures. This controversial conclusion was essentially confirmed by a National Academy of Sciences panel in an impressive, methodologically sophisticated review (Sechrest, White, and Brown, 1979).

Incapacitation research has primarily focused on estimating the number of crimes prevented by mandatory sentences of incarceration for certain categories of detected offenders. This estimation process requires detailed knowledge about criminal careers, research in which has also increased greatly in the last ten years. The conclusions reached in incapacitation research have varied considerably, depending on the methods used (for example, measuring offending by official records or self-reports) and on the assumptions made about the proportion of crimes committed by undetected offenders.

As an example, Van Dine, Dinitz, and Conrad (1977), using official records, concluded that a mandatory five-year prison sentence following all felony convictions would prevent only 4 percent of recorded violent crimes. On the other hand, Petersilia and Greenwood (1978), also using official records, argued that such a sentence would decrease violent crime by about one-third. In a self-report study, Peterson, Braiker, and Polich (1980) estimated that the release of all state prisoners would lead to an increase in armed robberies of 22 percent, in burglaries of 6 percent, and in auto thefts of 7 percent. The results and methodological problems of incapacitation research have been reviewed in Blumstein, Cohen, and Nagin (1978), Brody and Tarling (1980), and Cohen (1983).

The increasing interest in incapacitation has coincided with the development of career criminal prosecution programs in many jurisdictions of the United States. These aim to concentrate prosecution resources on serious, repeat offenders, to increase their conviction rates and average periods of incarceration (see, for example, Greenwood, 1980). However, none of the jurisdictions reviewed by Chelimsky and Dahmann (1980) used quantitative predictions of future criminal activity, which these authors considered to be a key element in translating targeted prosecution into crime-reduction effects.

This leads us to Greenwood (1982), who wished to develop a method of predicting which offenders committed offenses at high rates while they were in the community. On the basis of a self-report study with incarcerated offenders, Greenwood proposed a prediction score based on seven variables:

1. incarceration for more than half of the two-year period preceding the most recent arrest;
2. a prior conviction for the crime type that is being predicted (burglary or robbery);
3. a juvenile conviction prior to age 16;
4. commitment to a state or federal juvenile facility;
5. heroin or barbiturate use in the two-year period preceding the current arrest;
6. heroin or barbiturate use as a juvenile;
7. employment for less than half of the two-year period preceding the current arrest.

Each person was scored 0 or 1 according to the presence or absence of each item, leading to a prediction score between 0 and 7 for each offender. Greenwood showed how these prediction scores were related to crime rates. For example, the median annual offense rate for burglary for Californian prisoners was 1.4 for those scoring 0 or 1 on the scale, 6.0 for those scoring 2 or 3, and 92.9 for those scoring 4 or more. Greenwood argued that decisionmakers acting on the basis of incapacitation should be more selective: predicted high-rate offenders should receive longer prison sentences, while predicted low-rate offenders should receive shorter ones. If a penal policy of this kind were adopted, he estimated that, in California, it would be possible to achieve a 15 percent reduction in the robbery rate together with a 5 percent reduction in the incarcerated population.

This kind of a policy option is likely to prove very attractive to legislators, prosecutors, judges, and prison administrators. Previous incapacitation research on mandatory sentences has inevitably involved impractically large increases in prison populations. For example, the mandatory five-year sentences considered by Petersilia and Greenwood (1978) would have led to a prison-population increase of 450 percent. Selective incapacitation's promise of a decrease in the crime rate together with no increase in the incarcerated population seems too good to be true.

Unfortunately, it probably is. Greenwood's (1982) prediction research suffers from many of the problems ignored by the Gluecks (1950) more than thirty years before. For example, it is entirely retrospective and has no validation sample. In many ways it is much more sophisticated than that of the Gluecks, and Greenwood is aware of many of the problems raised by his prediction methodology. It is to be hoped that his prediction device can be validated prospectively. For the moment, quoting this recent example shows how prediction in criminology continues to be an important topic. Further information relevant to incapacitation is presented in the chapter by Farrington.

Dangerousness

The area of criminology where there has been perhaps most discussion about prediction in recent years is dangerousness or violent behavior. In the United States, Monahan (1981) has recently reviewed the prediction of violent behavior, while in England Floud and Young (1981) have not only reviewed the literature on dangerousness but also proposed a new sentence for a new legal category of dangerous offenders. Discussions about dangerousness seem likely to continue for some time, at least in England (see, for example, *British Journal of Criminology,* 1982; Hinton, 1983).

Unfortunately, this topic is of rather limited interest here, because most of the concern has been with clinical rather than statistical prediction. Some of the arguments about overprediction of violence, or high false-positive rates (see Bottoms, 1977; Monahan, 1978), will be discussed below in the section on measuring predictive efficiency. Some of the most thoughtful methodological contributions to the dangerousness debate have been made by Gordon (1977, 1982). For example, Gordon has estimated that patients held in secure mental hospitals under American dangerousness statutes were among the most dangerous one in 1,000 of the population, and has pointed out the difficulty of predicting in relatively homogeneous populations.

Perhaps because of the belief in the impossibility of predicting dangerous behavior (or in the undesirability of incarcerating people on the basis of such predictions), there has been comparatively little effort to select and combine variables into a predicted dangerousness scale. The best-known such scale is probably the legal dangerousness scale of Cocozza and Steadman (1974), based on four items (a juvenile record, the number of previous arrests, previous convictions for a violent offense, and the severity of the commitment offense). However, this scale does not seem to have been adequately constructed or validated.

There have been some sophisticated attempts to predict dangerous behavior of ex-mental patients, and two are reviewed in this book (see the chapters by Black and Spinks and by Copas). In England, Walker and McCabe (1973) devised a points score to predict reconvictions, and Soothill, Way, and Gibbens (1980) showed how well it predicted serious sex or violent offenses in another hospital sample. Another analysis of predicting reconvictions was carried out by Payne, McCabe, and Walker (1974) in one of the first prediction studies using logistic regression. Finally, Steadman and Morrissey (1982) used discriminant analysis in predicting assaults in hospitals and in the community. It is surprising that more attempts have not been made to predict dangerous or violent behavior using multivariate techniques.

Predicting Delinquency

The work of the Gluecks (1950) is perhaps the best-known prediction research in the history of criminology. The Gluecks compared 500 institutionalized male delinquents with 500 unconvicted boys who were in ordinary schools, had cooperative parents, and were not known to have committed any minor offenses. The two groups were said to be matched on age, IQ, national origin, and residence in underprivileged areas and were studied at an average age of 14–15. The Gluecks developed a prediction table based on five factors: the discipline of the boy by the father, the supervision of the boy by the mother, the affection of the father for the boy, the affection of the mother for the boy, and the cohesiveness of the family. Each boy was scored on each item according to the percentage of those in his category who were delinquents. For example, if the discipline of the boy by the father was rated as overstrict or erratic and 72.5 percent of boys in that category were delinquents, 72.5 would be added to the boy's prediction score.

The scores on this scale ranged from 116 to 414, and the discrimination of delinquents from nondelinquents seemed remarkable. Of those (52) boys scoring 400 or more, 98.1 percent were delinquents, while of those (172) scoring 150 or less 97.1 percent were nondelinquents. The Gluecks advocated that their prediction device (the Glueck Social Prediction Table) should be used to identify potential delinquents at the time of school entrance (age 6), and this proposal reached the White House in 1970 but was fortunately rejected. According to *Psychiatric News* (October 21, 1970), a Dr. Hutschnecker sent a report to President Nixon stating that "9 out of 10 delinquents could have been correctly identified at the age of 6" and "suggesting mass testing of all 6 to 8-year-old children."

Contemporary commentators immediately perceived the difficulties surrounding the Gluecks' research. For example, Anderson (1951) was probably right in saying that "this book would be substantially improved if chapter 20 on the Prediction of Delinquency had not been written." Among the most obvious problems were the following:

1. the delinquents and nondelinquents were extreme groups;
2. the high proportion of delinquents in the study (50 percent) made it easier to predict delinquency than is true in the general population (see West and Farrington, 1973, p. 134);
3. the interviewers may well have been biased by having knowledge of who was, or was not, a delinquent;
4. relationships at age 14–15 would not necessarily hold for measures at age 6;
5. the absence of a validation sample meant that there was heavy capitalization on chance in deriving the prediction table.

Unfortunately, the work of the Gluecks led to the discrediting of prediction in general and predicting delinquency in particular for many criminologists, despite the fact that there were a number of validation studies that showed that the Glueck Social Prediction Table did have some predictive power. This was shown, for example, by Havighurst et al. (1962), Craig and Glick (1963), Hodges and Tait (1963), Trevvett (1965), and Feldhusen, Thurston, and Benning (1973). The table even seemed to have some validity in Czechoslovakia (Veverka, 1971), but it was not impressive in Australian follow-up studies by Dootjes (1972) and Loftus (1974).

Since 1950, almost the only attempts to predict delinquency using multivariate methods have been carried out by psychologists and have been based on questionnaires. A common method has been to derive a delinquency prediction scale from an existing questionnaire, adding up items to make a simple points score. Occasionally, a scale has been constructed in one sample and validated in another. Questionnaires used in delinquency prediction include the Minnesota Multiphasic Personality Inventory (Hathaway and Monachesi, 1957; Hathaway, Monachesi, and Young, 1960; Briggs, Wirt, and Johnson, 1961), the Eysenck Personality Questionnaire (Putnins, 1982), the Jesness Inventory (Graham, 1981), and the Bristol Social Adjustment Guide (Stott, 1960, 1964).

The volume of criticism by criminologists (for example, Kahn, 1965; Venezia, 1971; Weis, 1974) suggests that the prediction of delinquency is almost a taboo area. In this book, one of the most famous prediction researchers, Wilkins, states that he does not approve of it. There has been little research on delinquency prediction using modern predictive techniques (for exceptions, see Feldhusen, Aversano, and Thurston, 1976; Wadsworth, 1978). It seems to us that it is desirable to carry out methodologically adequate research on delinquency prediction, if only to aid in the verification of delinquency theories. To this end, the chapter by Farrington in this book investigates how well delinquency can be predicted using different prediction techniques.

Parole Prediction

Most of the advances in the use of prediction methods in criminology have occurred in the area of parole prediction, and prediction methods have had their greatest policy influence on parole procedures. One of the most famous and earliest prediction studies in criminology was carried out by Burgess (1928). In this study each person was given a score of 0 or 1 on each predictor, depending on whether the parole-violation rate of persons in the same category was less than or greater than average. Ohlin (1951) further developed this method in parole research by scoring each person +1, 0, or -1 on each of a number of predictors, depending on whether the value of the variable was associated with an above-average, average, or below-average success rate. Unlike Burgess, Ohlin included in his prediction scores only those variables which were the most closely associated with the criterion (12 out of 27); he suggested (p. 112) that predictors that were closely associated with other predictors might be eliminated to "avoid over-weighting any one aspect of the parole picture." More sophisticated methods of selecting and combining predictors, most of which were first used in parole research, are reviewed later in the section on combining predictors.

Decisions made by the United States Parole Board are influenced by a Burgess-type points prediction score (the Salient Factor Score) prepared for each prisoner and developed by D. M. Gottfredson et al. (1975). Prisoners accumulate points on this nine-item scale if they have: had no prior convictions; had no prior incarcerations; had their first commitment at age 18 or older; had a commitment offense not involving auto theft; never had parole revoked; no history of drug dependence; completed twelfth-grade education; been employed for at least six months during their last two years in the community; and a plan to live with a spouse and/or children upon release. Hoffman and Beck (1976) showed that the Salient Factor Score was a valid predictor of parole success in a new sample of prisoners.

In an attempt to reduce disparity in parole decisions, Gottfredson, Wilkins, and Hoffman (1978) developed guidelines for parole board members based on their recent paroling practice. The average time served by any prisoner before release was to depend partly on the seriousness of the offense and partly on the Salient Factor Score. This varied from 6–10 months for a high SF score and a less serious offense to 55–65 months for a low SF score and a more serious offense. Parole board members could use their clinical judgment to make a decision outside the guidelines, but if they chose to do so they would have to show reason. In an analysis of about 6,000 decisions, the authors found that only about 16 percent were outside the guidelines. Furthermore, M. R. Gottfredson (1979) showed that when parole decisions about time served were made with the guidelines, they were less disparate than were the original judicial decisions about sentence lengths. (Attempts have also been made to develop guidelines for sentencing: see Wilkins et al., 1978, and Hewitt and Little, 1981.)

A Burgess-type prediction device also has some influence in the English parole system. The English prediction score was constructed by Nuttall et al. (1977) and based on 16 variables covering the offender's previous criminal history (the type of offense committed, the number of previous convictions and previous prison sentences, the interval at risk since the last conviction, the age at first conviction) and also the offender's age, marital status, living arrangements, and employment history. Offenders were given points according to the category in which they fell, at a rate roughly of 1 point (+ or -) for every 5 percent difference between the reconviction rate of their category and the overall reconviction rate.

This prediction score proved to be an excellent predictor of reconviction. When the total number of offenders was divided into construction and validation samples, it was found that there was no shrinkage of predictive efficiency between them (see the section on shrinkage below). Furthermore, Sapsford (1978) showed that this score was a good predictor of reconviction in a later sample of released prisoners. The English parole system is essentially a two-tier one, with a prisoner's case being considered first by a Local Review Committee covering his prison and then by the National Parole Board. Prediction scores are considered at both these stages, and they also influence whether a prisoner progresses from the first stage to the second. For example, according to Nuttall et al. (1977), if the Local Review Committee unanimously decided that the prisoner was unsuitable for parole, he was rejected if his predicted probability of reconviction within two years was 51 percent or greater (or 35–50 percent or greater for a prisoner convicted of an offense involving violence, drugs, or arson). On the other hand, if his predicted probability was less than 35 percent (or 35-50 percent or greater for a prisoner convicted of a less serious offense), his case was passed to the National Parole Board for consideration.

Sophisticated parole prediction research has been carried out in many countries, from Gottfredson and Ballard (1964) in the United States to Challinger (1974) in Australia and Nuffield (1982) in Canada. As will be pointed out in the section on combining predictors, Burgess-type points scores have usually proved to be the most satisfactory prediction devices. This book includes a recent investigation of parole prediction by Gottfredson and Gottfredson and some views by another famous pioneer in this field, Wilkins. It also includes a report by Wilbanks on a classic parole prediction study which has been referred to in standard books (for example, Gottfredson, Wilkins, and Hoffman, 1978; Greenberg, 1979) but has never before been published. Finally, the chapter by Hill reviews a topic of considerable interest to parole board members: the extent to which behavior and other factors measured in an institution add to predictions of recidivism that can be made at the time of the sentence.

Evaluation of Penal Treatments and Parole

Prediction scores have often been used in research evaluating the effects of different penal treatments. One of the methodological problems faced in this type of research is how to disentangle the effects of the treatments from those of the kinds of people who receive them. The best way of ensuring that comparable people receive different treatments is to assign the people at random to the treatments. However, because of ethical, legal, and practical problems, randomized experiments in criminology are often difficult to arrange (for a review, see Farrington, 1983). The major alternative method is matching, but it is difficult to match people simultaneously on more than a small number of factors. It is more feasible to match people on prediction scores or to evaluate treatments according to differences between predicted and actual reconviction rates (for example). The advantages of these kinds of designs have been discussed by Clarke (1976). In randomized experiments, prediction scores can be very useful in checking the success of the random assignment in producing comparable groups (see Kassebaum, Ward, and Wilner, 1971).

Mannheim and Wilkins (1955) were perhaps the first to use prediction techniques in evaluating penal treatments. They compared reconviction rates of open and closed institutions within different risk categories and found that the open institutions had consistently lower reconviction rates. Uusitalo (1972) repeated this research in Finland, but found no difference there between open and closed institutions. Cockett (1967) used the difference between predicted and actual reconviction rates in evaluating the success of an experimental regime in one institution in comparison with six others, and Bottoms and McClintock (1973) used a similar method in a before-and-after comparison of two regimes in one institution. Farrington and Nuttall (1980) also used the difference between predicted and actual reconviction rates as a measure of institutional effectiveness and found a high negative correlation (- 0.76) between overcrowding and effectiveness in an analysis of 19 prisons.

Prediction scores have also been used in the evaluation of parole. Nuttall et al. (1977) compared observed and expected reconviction rates for prisoners released on parole and those released at the expiry of their sentences and found no evidence that parole had any effect on reconviction. This method has some similarities to that used by Waller (1974), whose project is not considered a prediction study. Waller carried out a stepwise multiple regression analysis to investigate which factors were independently related to arrest; he reported that whether offenders were paroled or discharged had an effect over and above other variables, with parole associated with low arrest rates.

Prediction scores can also be used in studying interactions between types of treatment and types of offenders. An interaction might be demonstrated if the relationship between treatment and recidivism was different in different risk groups. However, such interactions have rarely appeared. For example, Walker and McCabe (1973) reported that after-care was associated with a lower probability of reconviction in all risk groups, and Gottfredson, Gottfredson, and Garofalo (1977) concluded that time served was not related to parole success in any risk group.

There are obvious methodological problems in evaluation research using prediction scores, the main one being that offenders are not equivalent on all possible variables. Offenders with the same prediction score may differ not only on variables that are not measured but even on the variables that make up the prediction score, and these differences may be responsible for observed differences in outcome. As Simon (1971) pointed out, offenders may be allocated to open or closed institutions on the basis of factors not included in case records. Another problem is that the prediction table may lose its efficiency as time goes by. Analyses of changes over time are rather problematical. For example, Little (1962) used the Mannheim-Wilkins (1955) prediction device to conclude that, over time, English borstals were receiving progressively worse risks on average and that they were becoming less successful in any given risk category. This kind of analysis really requires reconstruction and revalidation of the prediction device.

Other Prediction Techniques for Individuals

There have been many other examples of the use of prediction techniques for individuals. Predictions can aid or have aided many of the criminal justice decisions reviewed by Gottfredson and Gottfredson (1980): decisions to report a crime, to call the police, to arrest a suspect, to release on bail, to charge a suspect; and correctional decisions such as level of custody, treatment program, academic program, and work assignment. The studies of bail decisions are especially interesting. For example, Gottfredson (1974) attempted to predict failure to appear in court and arrests while on bail using the well-known VERA scale (which was not derived in defensible prediction research) and an empirically derived scale. His study included not only offenders released on bail and thought suitable for release but also offenders released on bail despite being thought unsuitable. He found that the VERA scale had rather low predictive power, while his empirically derived prediction device suffered considerable shrinkage. More recently, Goldkamp (1978a, 1978b) has reviewed the literature on bail decisionmaking and carried out a further prediction study.

Prediction methods have been used to assist police decisions. For example, Eck (1979) described research designed to predict which cases were most likely to be solved. He argued that the overall proportion of cases solved could be increased if a case-screening prediction device was used to allocate police resources. Eskridge (1983) used a prediction device to help police officers identify potential suspects in connection with burglaries. From the characteristics of a burglary, he used discriminant analysis to predict the probability that the offender was male, over 21, alone, and so on.

As examples of institutional prediction research, Cowden and Pacht (1967) attempted to predict institutional and postrelease adjustment, and Potter (1981) tried to predict whether a juvenile needed to be housed in secure accommodation. Sapsford and Smith (1979) showed that the predictors of sentence length were different from the predictors of time served, suggesting that parole decisions were not merely resentencing. Other examples of institutional prediction research can be found in the chapter by Hill, Thornton and Speirs, and Cullen.

Predicting Rates

The major rates researchers have tried to predict are crime rates and imprisonment rates. Some of this research is merely extrapolative, stating what would happen if present trends persisted. This applies, for example, to the research on prevalence by Christensen (1967) in the United States, Christiansen and Jensen (1972) in Denmark, and Farrington (1981) in England. The more interesting prediction research for our purposes involves the use of some kind of mathematical or computer model.

Most of the criminal justice system models derive from the pioneering work of Blumstein and Larson (1969), who devised the original JUSSIM model. This is essentially an interactive computer program that specifies how offenders flow through the different elements of the system: through police, courts, corrections, and parole, for example. It assumes that the system parameters are independent of each other and of flow rates and that they do not change over time. The user can enter data from his or her own criminal justice system and use the model to predict the effects of changes in any element. JUSSIM 2 takes account of the feedback of recidivists into the system, and JUSSIM 3 additionally incorporates a crime-generation process and a victim-generation process taking account of characteristics of offenders and victims (see Blumstein and Koch, 1980). The chapter by Cassidy in this volume gives details of CANJUS, a model of the Canadian criminal justice system, which has not previously been published. Work is currently in progress on a model of the English criminal justice system (Butler, 1982).

Several researchers have combined mathematical models with demographic forecasts to predict future crime rates (Fox, 1978) or imprisonment rates (Blumstein, Cohen, and Miller, 1981). Miller (1981) was concerned to predict the impact of determinate sentencing on prison populations and, as he pointed out, these kinds of predictions should ideally be taken into account before legislation is enacted. As another example of the use of mathematical models, Zeeman et al. (1977) and Smith (1980) attempted to predict the occurrence of prison riots from events leading up to them.

One of the best reviews of criminal justice system models was provided by Chaiken et al. (1975). An interesting class of models they describe are the patrol car allocation models. Again, these are essentially interactive computer programs. The user inputs such information as the area of a precinct, its expected call rate, its average service time, and the patrol car response speed. The user can specify performance standards and the model will then predict what is needed (for example, in the way of the number of patrol cars, the number of patrol officers, and the availability of officers at specified times) to achieve them. These kinds of mathematical or computer models for system predictions seem likely to increase in future.

BASIC ISSUES

The Predictors

A number of basic issues are common to most prediction research in criminology. The first is how to select and measure predictor variables. In most studies (see, for example, the review by Pritchard, 1979), the choice of predictors is determined primarily or exclusively by what is available in existing case records. This seems unsatisfactory. Vold's (1949, p. 452) comment of more than thirty years ago is still relevant: "The most discouraging thing about the whole field of prediction in criminology is the continued unreliability and general worthlessness of much of the so-called 'information' in the original records. Opinions, hearsay, and haphazardly recorded judgments still constitute the bulk of any parole file." Similar comments were made recently by Wilkins (1980).

Case records have a number of other disadvantages in addition to their subjectivity and the fact that, in general, their information is recorded for administrative and not research purposes. There tends to be a rather unsystematic, incomplete coverage of points of interest, and the cases on which information is missing are rarely a random sample of all cases. As an example, Mannheim and Wilkins (1955) based their multiple regression analysis on only those cases where there was no missing data on their selected predictors and found that doing so reduced their sample from 720 to 385. Furthermore, the 385 included had a much higher success rate (57.5 percent) than the 335 excluded (31.3 percent). In some ways, the exclusion of cases is the most defensible method of dealing with the problem of missing data, but it has the disadvantage that the analysis can be based on an unrepresentative subset of the data. Other researchers have dealt with missing observations by replacing each one with the modal or median value of the variable, but this introduces error of another sort.

Ideally, predictor measures should be chosen on theoretical grounds, according to what is expected to predict the criterion (see, for example, Dean, 1968). Interpretations are made easier if each empirical variable measures one theoretical construct. Analyses are made easier if each predictor is normally distributed and measured on an interval scale, but categorical measures are more common. It is desirable to investigate the form of the relationship between each predictor and the criterion, since nonlinear relationships can cause problems. Also, it is desirable to try to establish the reliability and validity of all predictor measures. It may be that advances in prediction will be made only when these kinds of measurement problems are taken more seriously and overcome.

It seems plausible to suggest that predictions would be improved if information from several different sources was used. It may then be possible to overcome the errors inherent in any one source. Very few prediction studies have compared the efficiency of predictions derived from different data sources, although Beverly (1964) concluded that case records combined with home background information predicted better than case records alone. Gough, Wenk, and Rozynko (1965) showed that the ability of a base expectancy score (based largely on current and previous offenses and age) to predict parole violation was hardly improved at all by the addition of personality-test data, and similar results were reported by Gendreau, Madden, and Leipciger (1980). It would be interesting to establish whether case records, home background information, and psychological tests identified the same or different potential recidivists. More research on different kinds of predictors is clearly needed.

The Criterion

Most criminological studies involving individual predictions use official records of offending as the major criterion variable. This raises all kinds of problems. For example, the likelihood of a conviction or a parole violation depends not only on the behavior of the offender but also on the behavior of persons in the criminal justice system. For example, Lerman (1975) reanalyzed data from the Community Treatment Project (Palmer, 1971), making a sharp distinction between offenses known to the police and the reactions of California Youth Authority personnel and parole agents to these offenses. He found that there was no difference in offending between the experimental and control groups, but that the experimental group was far less likely to suffer revocation of parole or incarceration as a consequence of offending. This shows the desirability of separating offending behavior from discretionary reactions to offending.

Self-report and victim surveys of offending suggest that official records are only the tip of an iceberg. It is desirable to have multiple measures of offending (see, for example, Waldo and Chiricos, 1977), so that the biases and errors in each can be detected and allowed for to some extent. There are problems with legal categories of crime, which may not adequately reflect the behavior that occurred (for example, because of plea bargaining). Also, police forces may vary in their efficiency of reporting to central record-keeping systems (Steer, 1973).

The criterion variable in most prediction studies is the occurrence of one or more convictions within a specified time period. However, there can be a considerable delay between committing an offense and being convicted of it and between the date of the conviction and the date on which the conviction can be found in an official record (Kleinman and Lukoff, 1981). Therefore, short follow-up periods of up to two years are likely to miss a number of offenses because of these administrative delays. Kantrowitz (1977) argued that it was possible to predict eventual parole violation rates at an early stage and therefore that short follow-up periods could be used. However, in some studies (Jesness, 1971; Dunlop, 1974; Waldo and Griswold, 1979), conclusions after a short follow-up have been changed after a longer-term follow-up.

The most commonly used criterion variable in criminological prediction studies is the simple official delinquent/nondelinquent or recidivist/nonrecidivist dichotomy. More complex measures have been used, taking account of frequency, seriousness, time to the first offense (Gottfredson and Ballard, 1965), or rate of offending per unit time at risk (Harris, Kaylan, and Maltz, 1981). As in the case of the predictors, it is desirable to have criterion variables that are reliable and valid. Any measure based on official records, however cleverly it is constructed, is going to be susceptible to all the well-known problems of record-keeping. Therefore, future researchers should attempt to supplement official records by more valid and more direct measures of offending (for example, observational measures: see Buckle and Farrington, 1984).

Combining Predictors

One of the concerns of this book centers on how to select a subset of the predictor variables and combine them into a composite predictor in order to maximize predictive efficiency. The composite predictor often takes the form of a prediction table (also called an "experience table" or a "base expectancy table"), which divides the sample into different risk groups with different probabilities of offending. It is important to note that statistical predictions are made for groups and not for individuals.

The selection and combination of predictors is based on the belief that a composite variable will predict a criterion more accurately than will a single predictor. This is not necessarily true; success depends on the theoretical links between the predictors and the criterion. If only one construct *A* causes the construct *Y*, which is being measured by the criterion, then a combination of predictors will predict the criterion more efficiently only if it provides a more accurate measure of A than any single predictor. On the other hand, if constructs A, B, and C jointly cause Y, then a combination of measures of A, B, and C should predict better than a single measure of, say, A. Strictly speaking, theoretical analyses should guide not only the choice of predictors to measure but also their combination.

On the basis of the classic works by Meehl (1954) and Sawyer (1966), it seems that prediction by statistical methods is more efficient than clinical prediction. However, the primary use of statistical prediction in the criminal justice system is to guide the essentially clinical decisions by such persons as parole board members. It is important to investigate whether clinical prediction informed by statistical prediction is better than statistical prediction alone. In agreement with this, Gibbens (1965) showed that predictions of success or failure after leaving institutions made by psychiatrists guided by the Mannheim-Wilkins prediction table were superior to those based on the table alone.

The simplest method of combining predictors is the points score ascribed to Burgess (1928) and detailed above. The Glueck method, using percentages as weightings, has also been described above. These techniques have been criticized for their lack of statistical justification and for not allowing sufficiently for the intercorrelations between factors. For example, Wilkins and MacNaughton-Smith (1964) said that they were "intolerably crude and inadequate," "have been discredited by many writers and are only mentioned for their historical importance." Researchers were castigated for not using more "advanced" methods (for example, see Thurston, Benning, and Feldhusen, 1971).

These kinds of criticisms led to the use of least-squares multiple regression techniques by such researchers as Kirby (1954) and Mannheim and Wilkins (1955) in the 1950s. Kirby used a discriminant function analysis, but with a dichotomous criterion variable this is mathematically equivalent to multiple regression. However, there are some obvious problems in applying multiple regression techniques to criminological data, and these have been summarized by Palmer and Carlson (1976). For example, the underlying statistical assumptions are violated by dichotomous dependent variables. Interaction effects cause problems when the number of predictors is relatively large and can be investigated systematically only when the analysis is theoretically guided. On the other hand, it has been argued (Beverly, 1964) that interaction effects are rare in criminological data.

Disquiet with multiple regression led in the 1960s to the use of hierarchical clustering techniques, such as configural analysis (Glaser, 1962), predictive attribute analysis (Wilkins and Mac-Naughton-Smith, 1964), and automatic interaction detector analysis (Schumacher, 1974). These techniques essentially aim to classify a heterogeneous population into homogeneous subgroups. They do not require such restrictive assumptions about the nature of the variables as is typical of multiple regression and hence are more suitable for use with criminological data. However, they are undoubtedly somewhat arbitrary and difficult to justify statistically.

Dissatisfaction with both multiple regression and predictive attribute analysis led to the use of loglinear and logistic techniques in the 1970s (see, for example, Payne, McCabe and Walker, 1974; Solomon, 1976). These methods are statistically justifiable and applicable to the kinds of categorical data typically collected in criminology. Unfortunately, despite hopes that "logistic regression will prove to be a better competitor [to Burgess] than linear regression has been in the past" (Larntz, 1980, p. 68), there is little evidence of its superiority as yet.

Comparisons of methods of selecting and combining predictors, in most cases using parole data, have usually shown that it is difficult to exceed the efficiency of the simple Burgess points score in a validation sample. An early comparison of the Burgess and Glueck methods (Ohlin and Duncan, 1949) showed that they were quite similar in predictive efficiency, which is not surprising in the light of Kirby's (1954) reported 0.9 correlation between them. Gottfredson and Ballard (1965) then showed that multiple regression and the Burgess method produced quite similar results, and La Brie (1970) reported that the Glueck method and multiple regression were quite similar (although he did not have a validation sample). Ward (1968) compared the Burgess and Glueck methods and multiple regression and found that multiple regression was slightly superior.

Moving on to the methods of the 1960s, Babst, Gottfredson, and Ballard (1968) reported that configural analysis and multiple regression worked about equally well, and Simon (1971) discovered that predictive attribute analysis, multiple regression, and the Burgess method were about equally efficient. Simon's English comparison was replicated in Australia by Challinger (1974) and in Canada by Nuffield (1982). Both found that, if anything, a Burgess-type points score was the best. It has sometimes been argued that the more sophisticated techniques would fare better with larger construction samples (Kirby, 1954) but there is no evidence of this. Babst, Gottfredson, and Ballard (1968), with a construction sample of over 3,000, did not find multiple regression superior to configural analysis.

Little is known as yet about the efficiency of the loglinear/logistic methods of the 1970s in comparison with earlier methods. Van Alstyne and Gottfredson (1978) compared the Burgess technique with a loglinear method and reported that the Burgess technique was superior. However, Fuchs and Flanagan (1980) argued that they had failed to collapse the data over nonrelevant variables and hence spread the sample over too many cells for a valid analysis. One of the aims of this book is to provide more information about the relative efficiency of different methods of selecting and combining predictors. The chapter by Tarling and Perry gives a more detailed exposition of the methods and extends the research of Simon (1971) to include comparisons with logistic regression and automatic interaction detector analysis. The chapters by Gottfredson and Gottfredson, Wilbanks, and Farrington also include systematic comparisons of prediction techniques.

Measuring Predictive Efficiency

It is unfortunate that there are no widely accepted methods of measuring predictive efficiency, as this makes it difficult to compare results obtained in different studies. The choice of statistical technique to measure predictive efficiency depends on the nature of the predictor and criterion variables being compared. Usually, both are dichotomous. If a prediction score is derived, a cutoff point is chosen and all persons on one side of it are regarded as predicted offenders while those on the other side are regarded as predicted nonoffenders. This dichotomy reflects the type of decisions usually facing persons in the criminal justice system, such as parole board members: should the offender be released or kept in prison? The criterion variable, of course, is usually whether the person is arrested (or convicted) or not.

When both predictor and criterion are dichotomous, researchers are often concerned with the rate of false positives, or with the percentage of predicted offenders who do not turn out to be actual offenders. As mentioned above, a great deal of the discussion about dangerousness has concentrated on this problem, leading to the argument that dangerousness cannot be predicted. However, as Gordon (1977) pointed out, researchers should also be concerned about the false-negative rate, or the percentage of predicted nonoffenders who become actual offenders. The reverse percentages are also interesting—for example, the percentage of actual offenders who were predicted offenders and the percentage of actual nonoffenders who were predicted offenders. Stott (1960) used the terms *selectivity* to describe the percentage of predicted offenders who become actual offenders and *range* to describe the percentage of actual offenders who were predicted offenders. Different conclusions may be indicated by considering different percentages, so it is usually desirable to present the complete 2 × 2 table.

The extent to which a false positive really is false depends on the correctness of theoretical models of behavior. For example, imagine that each prisoner can be ordered on an underlying dimension of "recidivism potential," which is probabilistically related to actual recidivism. In other words, persons with a high recidivism potential have a high probability of being reconvicted. Imagine also that recidivism potential can be measured accurately and that some cutoff point is chosen so that all prisoners whose recidivism potential is greater than a certain value are predicted to be recidivists. Because the occurrence of recidivism depends essentially on unpredictable or chance factors, some prisoners with high recidivism potential will not be recidivists. However, providing that the actual probability of recidivism in any group is similar to the predicted probability of recidivism, the prediction could have been accurate. To call someone with high recidivism potential who does not become a recidivist a false positive implies that the prediction was mistaken, but this is not necessarily true. As Gordon (1982) pointed out, the determination of false positives often presupposes an all-or-none model of the underlying process (here, recidivism potential).

The simplest measure of predictive efficiency is the percentage of predictions that do not coincide with actual outcomes. However, such a measure is greatly influenced by the base rate of the outcome (for example, the proportion of released persons who become actual recidivists). Consider the study by Wenk, Robison, and Smith (1972), who concluded that violence could not be predicted. Violence was defined as a recorded violent offense within 15 months of release from a juvenile facility, and it had a prevalence of 2.5 percent. If every person in this study had been predicted to be nonviolent, 97.5 percent of the predictions would have been correct. These kinds of considerations led Ohlin and Duncan (1949) to propose the proportionate reduction in error (calculated by comparing errors obtained with a prediction instrument and errors obtained with the base rate alone) as an index of predictive efficiency. In their research, 40.1 percent of parolees were violators and 32.5 percent of the predictions made by their Burgess-type instrument were incorrect, so the proportionate reduction in error was 19 percent (40.1 minus 32.5, then divided by 40.1). However, this method gives equal weight to all kinds of incorrect predictions.

If both the predictor and the criterion are dichotomous, the best summary statistic might be the ϕ correlation, derived from χ^2, which measures the strength of the association and, unlike χ^2, does not increase linearly with sample size. One disadvantage with the ϕ correlation is that its maximum value is not necessarily 1.0, but depends on the marginal totals. Another problem is that it is less meaningful to criminal justice system decision makers than are percentages.

Predictions derived from combinations of variables are usually not dichotomous but a series of ordered categories or almost continuous values. For the purpose of measuring predictive efficiency, it is undesirable to dichotomize, as doing so results in a loss of information. There are a variety of measures for summarizing the strength of the relationship between an ordered scale and a dichotomy. The χ^2 has the disadvantage that it merely measures deviation from chance expectation and is insensitive to any ordering of risk groups. Given that the risk groups are usually in a definite order, γ would seem to be more suitable, especially as its sampling distribution can be calculated (Goodman and Kruskal, 1963).

A more commonly used statistic in the prediction literature is the mean cost rating proposed by Duncan et al. (1953). In their study, *cost* refers to the proportion of successes who are identified as failures and *utility* refers to the proportion of failures who are identified as failures. Duncan and his co-workers discussed the construction of cost-utility curves relating, for all possible cutoff points, the cost at a given cutoff point to the utility at that point. The mean cost rating is proportional to the area between this curve and the diagonal cost = utility curve, which corresponds to zero predictive power or chance expectation. The main disadvantage with the mean cost rating is that its sampling distribution is unknown, making it impossible to test its statistical significance.

The cost-utility curve of Duncan et al. is quite similar to the Receiver Operating Characteristic (ROC) curve used in many fields of psychology (see Swets, Tanner, and Birdsall, 1961). The ROC curve was first used in criminology by Fergusson, Fifield, and Slater (1977). In the delinquency context, the ROC curve shows the relationship at all possible cutoff points between the proportion of delinquents who were predicted and the proportion of nondelinquents who were predicted. Under the assumptions of interval scales and normal distributions, it is possible to derive a quantity d', from the ROC curve. In the delinquency case, d' would be an index of the separation of the distribution of delinquents' scores from the distribution of nondelinquents' scores and hence of the efficiency of the prediction instrument.

If the criterion is dichotomous and the predictor is continuous, the biserial or point-biserial correlations can be used. The biserial correlation should be used where it can be assumed that there is a continuous variable underlying the dichotomy, which seems reasonable in criminological prediction. The point-biserial correlation could be used if the dichotomy was truly discrete. Another possibility is to compare the scores of the two groups (for example, recidivists and nonrecidivists) using such statistics as the Pearson r or Student's t (if the scores are measured on an interval scale) or Kendall's τ or the Mann-Whitney U (for ordinal scales).

The various measures of predictive efficiency have been discussed in some detail by Simon (1971). Some are known to be mathematically related. For example, Lancucki and Tarling (1978) showed that the mean cost rating was related to Kendall's τ, and Tarling (1982) extended this analysis to demonstrate relationships between these two measures, the area under the ROC curve, and the Goodman-Kruskal γ. It is hoped that these papers will encourage the use of more standardized and comparable measures of predictive efficiency.

It would be desirable for researchers to publish complete tables showing the combined predictor against the criterion, or cumulative success and failure curves. This would be useful not only to researchers but also to criminal justice system decisionmakers, who may be more interested in the prediction of small extreme groups than in overall measures of predictive efficiency. If cutoff points have to be chosen, having at one's disposal the complete curves could be useful in determining them. For example, if both kinds of successful predictions could be assigned a certain social benefit and both kinds of unsuccessful predictions could be assigned a certain social cost, these social costs and benefits could be used to determine an optimal cutoff point for criminal justice decisions.

Shrinkage

The estimate of predictive efficiency in the sample used to construct a prediction instrument (the construction sample) will always be too high. This is because all statistical measures of association have a sampling distribution about the population value, with the result that the value of (for example) the product-moment correlation in a sample will be greater or less than its value in the whole population. In selecting predictors that have the highest correlations with the criterion in a (construction) sample, there will be a tendency to select predictors with sample correlations higher than their population correlations. This means that the sample measure of predictive efficiency will be greater than the corresponding population measure of predictive efficiency.

It is essential to obtain an unbiased estimate of the population predictive efficiency. There are a number of ways of achieving this, but the simplest and most common is to apply the prediction instrument to a different sample of people (the validation sample) and to measure its predictive efficiency in this sample. The decrease in predictive efficiency between the construction and validation samples is called "shrinkage." Greenberg (1979, p. 183) outlined a quantitative measure of the amount of shrinkage, running from 0 to 1, and the chapter by Copas in this book is concerned with predicting the likely degree of shrinkage in advance.

It is common to divide a total sample at random into two halves and to use one half for construction and the other half for validation. Unfortunately, the shrinkage between these two samples is not necessarily an accurate guide to the shrinkage between the construction sample and a later validation sample. It is difficult to predict the extent to which prediction instruments can be generalized over time, place, and samples without having some underlying theory of the effects of the predictors on the criterion and some idea of boundary conditions within which the theory holds. If a prediction instrument is to be used in criminal justice decisionmaking, it is essential that the sample from which it is derived is drawn from the population on which it is to be used. This requirement would not be met, for example, if an instrument were derived from persons released on bail and applied to persons being considered for bail.

Shrinkage seems to be more of a problem with the more sophisticated statistical techniques than with the cruder Burgess and Glueck measures. The more sophisticated techniques are more sensitive and use more of the data in the construction sample, but the problem seems to be that the extra amount of data used is essentially error variance, which is different in the validation sample. The most successful predictions tend to be those obtained using simpler methods. For example, Nuttall et al. (1977) derived an impressive prediction instrument based on giving 1 point for each 5 percent difference in reconviction rates, as described earlier. The mean cost rating was .50 in the construction sample and .56 in the validation sample (both of which contained 1,138 released prisoners). To give some idea of the success of the prediction in the validation sample, 89.1 percent of the 138 men with the highest scores were reconvicted, in comparison with 3.7 percent of the 107 with the lowest scores. This level of prediction seems useful for many criminal justice purposes.

Ethical Issues

The ethical issues in prediction will not be discussed in detail here, although some are reviewed in the chapter by Wilkins. Many criminologists are concerned about the labeling or stigmatizing effects of being predicted as a delinquent or a recidivist, especially if this prediction is followed by some attempt at prevention or treatment and especially when the predictions are applied to unconvicted people. Venezia (1971) was expressing a popular view when he stated that preventive intervention should be based on current needs rather than predicted future behavior, and an American Psychological Association (1978) task force recommended that psychologists should be cautious in making predictions about criminal behavior for use in decisions to imprison or release. More research is needed on the extent to which different kinds of predictions have stigmatizing or other undesirable effects.

Another problem centers on the kinds of variables that can be taken into account in a prediction instrument used in the criminal justice system. For example, if race is a good predictor of reconviction, should judges explicitly take race into account in their sentencing decisions and sentence differentially according to race? Most people would not like the idea of racial discrimination in the criminal justice system, but it may be present in an implicit rather than explicit fashion. As Monahan (1981, p. 41) stated, "why should courts worry about whether the Constitution permits sex or age to be used in an actuarial prediction table for parole release when they can just get a psychiatrist or psychologist to 'launder' both these factors into a prediction based on 'clinical expertise'?"

Some ethical issues can be viewed in terms of social costs and social benefits. In proposing special protective sentences for dangerous offenders, Floud (1982, p. 219) argued that "we have to make a moral choice between competing claims: the claim of a known individual offender not to be unnecessarily deprived of his liberty; and the claim of an innocent (unconvicted) unknown person (or persons) not to be deprived of the right to go about their business without risk of grave harm at the hands of an aggressor." Floud talked about the "redistribution of risk" between these people, and it may be that criminological prediction can be justified by reference to these kinds of social costs and social benefits.

CONCLUSIONS

A repeated theme of this introductory review is that prediction research in criminology needs to be theoretically guided. Theoretical considerations should guide the choice of predictors, the choice of criteria, and methods of selecting and combining predictors into a prediction instrument. Also, there is a pressing need for better methods of measuring predictors and criteria and for the use of multiple measures. What is measured should not be determined by what is available but by what is theoretically desirable and by considerations of validity and reliability.

There is also a need for more research on mathematical methods of selecting and combining predictors. It is implausible to suggest that it is impossible to improve on the predictive efficiency of a simple Burgess-type points score, although it may be that improvements will be conditional on advances in measurement. In the interests of comparing studies, it is desirable to publish complete prediction tables and to reach agreement on indices of predictive efficiency. In addition, there needs to be more research on the generalizability of prediction instruments over time and place.

Most research on prediction in criminology so far has concerned parole prediction. There is a need for more prediction research in other areas. For example, in the case of sentencing, it would be very helpful for judges to be told, for each class of offender and offenses, the probability of achieving any given penal aim with any given sentence. There is also a need for more systems research. As argued earlier, changes in penal policy should not be made without first predicting their effects, preferably using mathematical or computer models. Also, prediction methods should be used more in estimating the adequacy of competing criminological theories.

Prediction methods assume continuity in behavior and/or environment. How much continuity actually exists is an important question needing further investigation. It will, of course, never be possible to predict offending with 100 percent accuracy. However, predictions of future offending are bound to influence criminal justice decisionmaking for some time to come. In the interests of justice, those predictions should be made as accurately as possible. We hope that this book will contribute to this end.

REFERENCES

American Psychological Association (1978). Report of the task force on the role of psychology in the criminal justice system. *American Psychologist* 33:1099–1113.

Anderson, J. E. (1951). Review of *Unraveling Juvenile Delinquency. Journal of Criminal Law, Criminology, and Police Science* 41:745–48.

Babst, D. V.; Gottfredson, D. M. ; and Ballard, K. B. (1968). Comparison of multiple regression and configural analysis techniques for developing base expectancy tables. *Journal of Research in Crime and Delinquency* 5:72–80.

Beverly, R. F. (1964). *Base expectancies and the initial home visit research schedule.* Sacramento: California Youth Authority, Research Report 37.

Blumstein, A.; Cohen, J.; and Miller, H. D. (1981). Demographically disaggregated projections of prison populations. In *Research in Public*

Policy Analysis and Management, ed. J. Crecine, vol. 1. Greenwich, CT: JAI Press.

Blumstein, A.; Cohen, J.; and Nagin, D., eds. (1978). *Deterrence and incapacitation.* Washington, DC: National Academy of Sciences.

Blumstein, A., and Koch, G. G. (1980). A prolegomenon for a macro model of criminal justice planning. In *Indicators of crime and criminal justice*, ed. S. E. Fienberg and A. J. Reiss. Washington, DC: Government Printing Office.

Blumstein, A., and Larson, R. (1969). Models of a total criminal justice system. *Operations Research* 17:199–232.

Bottoms, A. E. (1977). Reflections on the renaissance of dangerousness. *Howard Journal* 16:70–96.

Bottoms, A. E., and McClintock, F. H. (1973). *Criminals coming of age.* London: Heinemann.

Briggs, P. F.; Wirt, R. D.; and Johnson, R. (1961). An application of prediction tables to the study of delinquency. *Journal of Consulting Psychology* 25:46–50.

British Journal of Criminology (1982). Special number on dangerousness. Vol. 22, no. 3.

Brody, S. R. (1976). *The effectiveness of sentencing.* London: Her Majesty's Stationery Office.

Brody, S., and Tarling, R. (1980). *Taking offenders out of circulation.* London: Her Majesty's Stationery Office.

Buckle, A., and Farrington, D. P. (1984). An observational study of shoplifting. *British Journal of Criminology* 24:63–73.

Burgess, E. W. (1928). Factors determining success or failure on parole. In *The workings of the indeterminate-sentence law and the parole system in Illinois*, ed. A. A. Bruce, A. J. Harno, E. W. Burgess, and J. Landesco. Springfield, IL: Illinois State Board of Parole.

Butler, S. (1982). Mathematical modelling of the criminal justice system. *Home Office Research Bulletin* 14:16–20.

Chaiken, J.; Crabill, T.; Holliday, L.; Jaquette, D.; Lawless, M.; and Quade, E. (1975). *Criminal justice models.* Santa Monica, CA: Rand Corporation.

Challinger, D. (1974). A predictive device for parolees in Victoria. *Australian and New Zealand Journal of Criminology* 7:44–54.

Chelimsky, E., and Dahmann, J. (1980). The Mitre Corporation's national evaluation of the career criminal program. *Journal of Criminal Law and Criminology* 71:102–06.

Christensen, R. (1967). Projected percentage of U.S. population with criminal arrest and conviction records. In *Task Force Report: Science and Technology*, ed. President's Commission on Law Enforcement and Administration of Justice. Washington, D.C.: Government Printing Office.

Christiansen, K. O., and Jensen, S. G. (1972). Crime in Denmark—A statistical history. *Journal of Criminal Law, Criminology, and Police Science* 63:82–92.

Clarke, R. V. G. (1976). Cross-institutional designs and their place in evaluating penal treatments. In *Evaluation research in criminal justice.* Rome: United Nations Social Defense Research Institute.

Cockett, R. (1967). Borstal training: A follow-up study. *British Journal of Criminology* 7:150–83.

Cocozza, J. J., and Steadman, H. J. (1974). Some refinements in the measurement and prediction of dangerous behavior. *American Journal of Psychiatry* 131:1012–14.

Cohen, J. (1983). Incapacitation as a strategy for crime control: Possibilities and pitfalls. In *Crime and justice,* ed. M. Tonry and N. Morris, vol. 5. Chicago: University of Chicago Press.

Cowden, J. E., and Pacht, A. R. (1967). Predicting institutional and postrelease adjustment of delinquent boys. *Journal of Consulting Psychology* 31:377–81.

Craig, M. M., and Glick, S. J. (1963). Ten years' experience with the Glueck Social Prediction Table. *Crime and Delinquency* 9:249–61.

Dean, C. W. (1968). New directions for parole prediction research. *Journal of Criminal Law, Criminology, and Police Science* 59:214–18.

Dootjes, I. (1972). Predicting juvenile delinquency. *Australian and New Zealand Journal of Criminology* 5:157–71.

Duncan, O. D.; Ohlin, L. E.; Reiss, A. J.; and Stanton, H. R. (1953). Formal devices for making selection decisions. *American Journal of Sociology* 58:573–84.

Dunlop, A. B. (1974). *The approved school experience.* London: Her Majesty's Stationery Office.

Eck, J. E. (1979). *Managing case assignments.* Washington, DC: Police Executive Research Forum.

Eskridge, C. W. (1983). Prediction of burglary. *Journal of Criminal Justice* 11:67–75.

Farrington, D. P. (1979). Longitudinal research on crime and delinquency. In *Crime and Justice,* ed. N. Morris and M. Tonry, vol. 1. Chicago: University of Chicago Press.

——— (1981). The prevalence of convictions. *British Journal of Criminology* 21:173–75.

——— (1983). Randomized experiments on crime and justice. In *Crime and justice,* ed. M. Tonry and N. Morris, vol. 4. Chicago: University of Chicago Press.

Farrington, D. P., and Morris, A. M. (1983). Sex, sentencing, and reconviction. *British Journal of Criminology* 23:229–248.

Farrington, D. P., and Nuttall, C. P. (1980). Prison size, overcrowding, prison violence, and recidivism. *Journal of Criminal Justice* 8:221–31.

Feldhusen, J. F.; Aversano, F. M.; and Thurston, J. R. (1976). Prediction of youth contacts with law enforcement agencies. *Criminal Justice and Behavior* 3:235–53.

Feldhusen, J. F.; Thurston, J. R.; and Benning, J. J. (1973). A longitudinal study of delinquency and other aspects of children's behavior. *International Journal of Criminology and Penology* 1:341–51.

Fergusson, D. M.; Fifield, J. K.; and Slater, S. W. (1977). Signal detectability theory and the evaluation of prediction tables. *Journal of Research in Crime and Delinquency* 14:237–46.

Floud, J. (1982). Dangerousness and criminal justice. *British Journal of Criminology* 22:213–28.

Floud, J., and Young, W. (1981). *Dangerousness and criminal justice.* London: Heinemann.

Fox, J. A. (1978). *Forecasting crime data.* Lexington: Heath.

Fuchs, C., and Flanagan, J. (1980). Stepwise fitting of logit models with categorical predictors in the analyses of parole outcomes. *Journal of Research in Crime and Delinquency* 17:273–79.

Gendreau, P.; Madden, P. G.; and Leipciger, J. (1980). Predicting recidivism with social history information and a comparison of their predictive power with psychometric variables. *Canadian Journal of Criminology* 22:328–36.

Gibbens, T. C. N. (1965). Prediction studies and psychiatric diagnosis. In *Criminology in transition,* ed. T. Grygier, H. Jones, and J. C. Spencer. London: Tavistock.

Glaser, D. (1962). Prediction tables as accounting devices for judges and parole boards. *Crime and Delinquency* 8:239–58.

Glueck, S., and Glueck, E. T. (1950). *Unraveling juvenile delinquency.* Cambridge, MA: Harvard University Press.

Goldkamp, J. S. (1978a). *Bail decision making and the role of pretrial detention.* Albany, NY: Criminal Justice Research Center, Working Paper 10.

——— (1978b). *Bail decision making in Philadelphia.* Albany, NY: Criminal Justice Research Center, Working Paper 11.

Goodman, L. A., and Kruskal, W. H. (1963). Measures of association for cross classifications. III. Approximate sampling theory. *Journal of the American Statistical Association* 58:310–64.

Gordon, R. A. (1977). A critique of the evaluation of the Patuxent institution, with particular attention to the issues of dangerousness and recidivism. *Bulletin of the American Academy of Psychiatry and the Law* 5:210–55.

——— (1982). Preventive sentencing and the dangerous offender. *British Journal of Criminology* 22:285–314.

Gottfredson, D. M., and Ballard, K. B. (1964). Association analysis, predictive attribute analysis, and parole behavior. Paper presented at Western Psychological Association meeting, Portland, Oregon.

——— (1965). *The validity of two parole prediction scales.* Vacaville, CA: Institute for the Study of Crime and Delinquency.

Gottfredson, D. M.; Gottfredson, M. R.; and Garofalo, J. (1977). Time served in prison and parole outcomes among parolee risk categories. *Journal of Criminal Justice* 5:1–12.

Gottfredson, D. M.; Hoffman, P. B.; Sigler, M. H.; and Wilkins, L. T. (1975). Making paroling policy explicit. *Crime and Delinquency* 21:34–44.

Gottfredson, D. M.; Wilkins, L. T.; and Hoffman, P. B. (1978). *Guidelines for parole and sentencing.* Lexington: Heath.

Gottfredson, M. R. (1974). An empirical analysis of pre-trial release decisions. *Journal of Criminal Justice* 2:287–304.

——— (1979). Parole guidelines and the reduction of sentencing disparity. *Journal of Research in Crime and Delinquency* 16:218–31.

Gottfredson, M. R., and Gottfredson, D. M. *Decisionmaking in criminal justice.* Cambridge, MA: Ballinger.

Gough, H. G.; Wenk, E. A.; and Rozynko, V. V. (1965). Parole outcome as predicted from the CPI, the MMPI, and a base expectancy table. *Journal of Abnormal Psychology* 70:432–41.

Graham, S. A. (1981). Predictive and concurrent validity of the Jesness Inventory asocial index. *Journal of Consulting and Clinical Psychology* 5:740–42.

Greenberg, D. F. (1979). *Mathematical criminology.* New Brunswick, NJ: Rutgers University Press.

Greenwood, P. W. (1980). Career criminal prosecution. *Journal of Criminal Law and Criminology* 71:85–88.

——— (1982). *Selective incapacitation.* Santa Monica, CA: Rand Corporation.

Harris, C. M.; Kaylan, A. R.; and Maltz, M. D. (1981). Recent advances in the statistics of recidivism measurement. In *Models in quantitative criminology* ed. J. A. Fox. New York: Academic Press.

Hathaway, S. R.; and Monachesi, E. D. (1957). The personalities of pre-delinquent boys. *Journal of Criminal Law, Criminology and Police Science* 48:149–63.

Hathaway, S. R.; Monachesi, E. D.; and Young, L. A. (1960). Delinquency rates and personality. *Journal of Criminal Law, Criminology and Police Science* 50:433–40.

Havighurst, R. J.; Bowman, P. H.; Liddle, G. P.; Matthews, C. V.; and Pierce, J. V. (1962). *Growing up in River City.* New York: Wiley.

Hewitt, J. D., and Little, B. (1981). Examining the research underlying the sentencing guidelines concept in Denver, Colorado. *Journal of Criminal Justice* 9:51–62.

Hinton, J. W.; ed. (1983). *Dangerousness.* London: Allen and Unwin.

Hodges, E. F.; and Tait, C. D. (1963). A follow-up study of potential delinquents. *American Journal of Psychiatry* 120:449–53.

Hoffman, P. B.; and Beck, J. L. (1976). Salient factor score validation. *Journal of Criminal Justice* 4:69–76.

Jesness, C. F. (1971). Comparative effectiveness of two institutional treatment programs for delinquents. *Child Care Quarterly* 1:119–30.

Kahn, A. J. (1965). The case of the premature claims. *Crime and Delinquency* 11:217–28.

Kantrowitz, N. (1977). How to shorten the follow-up period in parole studies. *Journal of Research in Crime and Delinquency* 14:222–36.

Kassebaum, G.; Ward, D; and Wilner, D. (1971). *Prison treatment and parole survival.* New York: Wiley.

Kirby, B. C. (1954). Parole prediction using multiple correlation. *American Journal of Sociology* 59:539–50.

Kleinman, P. H.; and Lukoff, I. F. (1981). Official crime data. *Criminology* 19:449–54.

La Brie, R. A. (1970). Verification of the Glueck prediction table by mathematical statistics following a computerized procedure of discriminant function analysis. *Journal of Criminal Law, Criminology, and Police Science* 61:229–34.

Lancucki, L., and Tarling, R. (1978). The relationship between mean cost rating and Kendall's rank correlation coefficient. In *Guidelines for parole and sentencing*, ed. D. M. Gottfredson, L. T. Wilkins, and P. B. Hoffman. Lexington: Heath.

Larntz, K. (1980). Linear logistic models for the parole decision making problem. In *Indictors of crime and criminal justice*, ed. S. E. Fienberg and A. J. Reiss. Washington, DC: Government Printing Office.

Lerman, P. (1975). *Community treatment and social control*. Chicago: University of Chicago Press.

Little, A. (1962). Borstal success and the "quality" of borstal inmates. *British Journal of Criminology* 2:266–72.

Loftus, A. P. T. (1974) Predicting recidivism using the Glueck Social Prediction Scale with male first offender delinquents. *Australian and New Zealand Journal of Criminology* 7:31–43.

Mannheim, H. and Wilkins, L. T. (1955). *Prediction methods in relation to borstal training*. London: Her Majesty's Stationery Office.

Martinson, R. M. (1974). What works? *The Public Interest* 35:22–54.

Meehl, P. E. (1954). *Clinical versus statistical prediction*. Minneapolis: University of Minnesota Press.

Miller, H. D. (1981). Projecting the impact of new sentencing laws on prison populations. *Policy Sciences* 13:51–73.

Monahan, J. (1978). The prediction of violent criminal behavior. In *Deterrence and incapacitation*, ed. A. Blumstein, J. Cohen, and D. Nagin. Washington, DC: National Academy of Sciences.

——— (1981). *Predicting violent behavior*. Beverly Hills: Sage.

Nuffield, J. (1982). *Parole decision-making in Canada*. Ottawa: Supply and Services Canada.

Nuttall, C. P., et al. (1977). *Parole in England and Wales*. London: Her Majesty's Stationery Office.

Ohlin, L. E. (1951). *Selection for parole*. New York: Russell Sage.

Ohlin, L. E., and Duncan, O. D. (1949). The efficiency of prediction in criminology. *American Journal of Sociology* 54:441–51.

Palmer, J., and Carlson, P. (1976). Problems with the use of regression analysis in prediction studies. *Journal of Research in Crime and Delinquency* 13:64–81.

Palmer, T. B. (1971). California's Community Treatment Program for delinquent adolescents. *Journal of Research in Crime and Delinquency* 8:74–92.

Payne, C.; McCabe, S.; and Walker, N. (1974). Predicting offender-patients' reconvictions. *British Journal of Psychiatry* 125:60–64.

Petersilia, J., and Greenwood, P. W. (1978). Mandatory prison sentences. *Journal of Criminal Law and Criminology* 69:604–15.

Peterson, M. A.; Braiker, H. B.; and Polich, S. M. (1980). *Doing crime*. Santa Monica, CA: Rand Corporation.

Potter, R. S. (1981). Prediction of the need to place children in secure accommodation. *British Journal of Criminology* 21:366–70.

Pritchard, D. A. (1979). Stable predictors of recidivism. *Criminology* 17:15–21.

Putnins, A. L. (1982). The Eysenck Personality Questionnaires and delinquency prediction. *Personality and Individual Differences* 3:339–40.

Sapsford, R. J. (1978). Further research applications of the "parole prediction index." *International Journal of Criminology and Penology* 6:247–54.

Sapsford, R. J., and Smith, D. D. (1979). Predicting sentence-length and time actually served in prison. *British Journal of Criminology* 19:164–67.

Sawyer, J. (1966). Measurement and prediction, clinical and statistical. *Psychological Bulletin* 66:178–200.

Schumacher, M. (1974). Predicting subsequent conviction for individual male prison inmates. *Australian and New Zealand Journal of Criminology* 7:22–30.

Sechrest, L.; White, S. O.; and Brown, E. D., eds. (1979). *The rehabilitation of criminal offenders.* Washington, DC: National Academy of Sciences.

Simon, F. H. (1971). *Prediction methods in criminology.* London: Her Majesty's Stationery Office.

Smith, J. Q. (1980). The prediction of prison riots. *British Journal of Mathematical and Statistical Psychology* 33:151–60.

Solomon, H. (1976). Parole outcome: A multidimensional contingency table analysis. *Journal of Research in Crime and Delinquency* 13:107–26.

Soothill, K. L.; Way, C. K.; and Gibbens, T. C. N. (1980). Subsequent dangerousness among compulsory hospital patients. *British Journal of Criminology* 20:289–95.

Steadman, H. J., and Morrissey, J. P. (1982). Predicting violent behavior. *Social Forces* 61:475–83.

Steer, D. (1973). The elusive conviction. *British Journal of Criminology* 13:373–83.

Stott, D. H. (1960). A new delinquency prediction instrument using behavioral indications. *International Journal of Social Psychiatry* 6:195–205.

——— (1964). Prediction of success or failure on probation. *International Journal of Social Psychiatry* 10:27–29.

Swets, J. A.; Tanner, W. P.; and Birdsall, T. G. (1961). Decision processes in perception. *Psychological Review* 68:301–40.

Tarling, R. (1982). Comparison of measures of predictive power. *Educational and Psychological Measurement* 42:479–87.

Thurston, J. R.; Benning, J. J.; and Feldhusen, J. F. (1971). Problems of prediction of delinquency and related conditions over a seven-year period. *Criminology* 9:154–65.

Trevvett, N. B. (1965). Identifying delinquency-prone children. *Crime and Delinquency* 11:186–91.

Uusitalo, P. (1972). Recidivism after release from closed and open penal institutions. *British Journal of Criminology* 12:211–29.

Van Alstyne, D. J., and Gottfredson, M. R. (1978). A multidimensional contingency table analysis of parole outcome. *Journal of Research in Crime and Delinquency* 15:172–93.

Van Dine, S.; Dinitz, S.; and Conrad, J. (1977). The incapacitation of the dangerous offender. *Journal of Research in Crime and Delinquency* 14:22–34.

Venezia, P. S. (1971). Delinquency prediction. *Journal of Research in Crime and Delinquency* 8:108–17.

Veverka, M. (1971). The Gluecks' social prediction table in a Czechoslovak research. *British Journal of Criminology* 11:187–89.

Vold, G. B. (1949). Comment on *The efficiency of prediction in criminology. American Journal of Sociology* 54:451–52.

Wadsworth, M. E. J. (1978). Delinquency prediction and its uses. *International Journal of Mental Health* 7:43–62.

Waldo, G. P., and Chiricos, T. G. (1977). Work release and recidivism. *Evaluation Quarterly* 1:87–108.

Waldo, G. P., and Griswold, D. (1979). Issues in the measurement of recidivism. In *The rehabilitation of criminal offenders*, ed. L. Sechrest, S. O. White, and E. D. Brown. Washington, DC: National Academy of Sciences.

Walker, N., and McCabe, S. (1973). *Crime and insanity in England*, vol. 2. Edinburgh: Edinburgh University Press.

Waller, I. (1974). *Men released from prison*. Toronto: University of Toronto Press.

Ward, P. G. (1968). The comparative efficiency of differing techniques of prediction scaling. *Australian and New Zealand Journal of Criminology* 1:109–12.

Weis, K. (1974). The Glueck Social Prediction Table—An unfulfilled promise. *Journal of Criminal Law and Criminology* 65:397–404.

Wenk, E. A.; Robison, J. O.; and Smith, G. W. (1972). Can violence be predicted? *Crime and Delinquency* 18:393–402.

West, D. J., and Farrington, D. P. (1973). *Who becomes delinquent?* London: Heinemann.

Wilkins, L. T. (1980). Problems with existing prediction studies and future research needs. *Journal of Criminal Law and Criminology* 71:98–101.

Wilkins, L. T.; Kress, J. M.; Gottfredson, D. M.; Calpin, J. C.; and Gelman, A. M. (1978). *Sentencing guidelines*. Washington, DC: Government Printing Office.

Wilkins, L. T., and MacNaughton-Smith, P. (1964). New prediction and classification methods in criminology. *Journal of Research in Crime and Delinquency* 1:19–32.

Zeeman, E. C.; Hall, C. S.; Harrison, P. J.; Marriage, G. H.; and Shapland, P. H. (1977). A model for prison disturbances. *British Journal of Criminology* 17:251–63.

CHAPTER 2

The Politics of Prediction

LESLIE T. WILKINS

SUMMARY

It has been claimed that the use of predictive inference is universal among humans and hence that it is difficult and probably also absurd to seek to inhibit its use in decisions concerning offenders. The moral questions that arise in this area are related to the ways in which information is processed into predictive statements, not to the moral legitimacy of making predictions. The major moral issues derive from concepts of freedom, democracy, and the balance between individual citizens' and states' rights and privileges.

These abstract ideas take shape in concerns as to the appropriate uses of information about persons who have been found guilty of crimes, as well as about those who are (at a particular time) merely accused of offenses. If, as is a current critical issue, "discrimination" (distinguishing?) between certain persons in terms of particular attributes (for example, such factors as ethnic origin) is forbidden, then it may be argued that the use of such information is morally unacceptable even if not also illegal. If an unacceptable type of information is included in equations, the use of it may be hidden among other data. This may present a problem, but the final use of the conglomerate of data should, perhaps, provide the criterion. For this reason it is argued that the most efficient prediction equations should be sought, but only in order to test for any loss of efficiency due to the exclusion of certain data, in order to estimate the probable cost of using the simpler methods.

In addition to the policy (and political) issues that arise in regard to kinds of information and kinds of uses, there are concerns relating to the legal status of the offender at the time of the decision. Persons who have been found guilty by due process of law are usually assumed to have lost some of the individual rights accorded to those who are awaiting trial, who in turn have fewer rights than have ordinary citizens. It is possible to relate categories of legal status to the probabilities attributed to evidence against the accused—"beyond reasonable doubt" or "probable cause to believe" being the verbal descriptions most frequently used to designate the first two categories. It is argued that one of the rights that becomes derogated by reason of the weight of the evidence is the right to withhold personal information. (The United States Bill of Rights acknowledges this right in a number of ways.) Thus, the moral issues concerning the use of predictive techniques for persons who have not been found guilty may be seen as differing from those raised by the use of techniques for the prediction of recidivism. The present author draws his personal moral line between these two points. I have conducted research into the prediction of recidivism and see no moral objection to this, but I have not, and would not, carry out research aimed at predicting probable delinquency. No individual citizen (and this includes juveniles) while that individual retains his full quota of individual rights, should be placed in a position of risk of becoming a "false positive" and no personal information should be used in the manner we have discussed.

The concepts of "due process" and "just deserts" are necessary and provide useful constraints on the uses of predictive instruments. This is because freedom must be defended at its frontiers. To defend freedom for saints and ordinary citizens it is necessary to defend the freedom of criminals and freaks.

IS PREDICTION ETHICAL?

For all practical purposes, it is the government that expresses the ethical concerns of citizens. Ethical issues arise in the development and potential uses of prediction methods in criminal justice. Such concerns are of academic interest, of course, but there are practical consequences attaching to the various moral choices that must be made; hence, political (or as some might prefer to say, policy) considerations are appropriate. I will examine some of these issues in this chapter.

It may seem absurd to ask whether human behavior should be predicted, because all persons predict the behavior of others all the time. Indeed, if human behavior were unpredictable all forms of social and economic life as we know them would cease. Almost always people do what they are expected to do. But is this a sufficient reason for seeking to apply more systematic methods to the task of predicting human actions? Is there something unnatural about the use of mathematical models to do something that we all do intuitively? Is there a qualitative difference between intuitive methods of prediction and methods based on a reproducible procedure of data analysis? Some persons clearly seem to think so. The reasons put forward in opposition to the development of prediction methods concerning the probable behavior of offenders (or the probability of criminal behaviors, which is not the same thing!) are not usually concerned with the methods but with the likely uses of the resulting systems. Strangely, these concerns are much less often expressed in regard to intuitive or clinical prediction.

The Freedom Problem

Some writers have attempted to separate the development of scientific methods from the purposes to which those methods might be applied. There may be occasions when this is a reasonable approach, but there are other situations in which it is possible to imagine only an inappropriate use of a new technique. Is the prediction of criminal behavior an example of the latter form of knowledge? Certainly if any society is to protect the freedom of its general populace, it must defend the freedom of those who are seen as the least entitled to it. Freedom must be defended at its frontiers: therefore, in order to defend the freedom of saints and citizens it is necessary to defend the freedom of criminals and freaks. It is also true that knowledge is power and that the ability to predict likely outcomes could be a powerful tool of control.

It is not possible in this paper to go into the moral problems raised by the fact that (within useful limits) prediction of criminal behavior is possible and that with a little more investment still more powerful techniques might be available. It is necessary to remind ourselves from time to time that essential moral questions surface in very close proximity to scientific issues. Moral questions cannot be answered by the application of either more or different scientific methods. The case for a moral position may be argued and the relationships of any premises or deductions considered in the light of ends and means and of other premises and deductions. At some point, however, an arbitrary stand must be taken; but, although arbitrary, such a stand need not be capricious. On moral issues I should know (believe) what is right for me, but I should not assume that what I believe for myself applies to others. It may make my position clear if I discuss the use of prediction methods in the field of criminal justice, and define, for me, the line between acceptable and unacceptable applications of predictive methods.

The Justice Question

My personal position is that I would be willing to work on prediction of recidivism but that I would not use my skills in the task of developing a predictive device for identification of likely first offenders. It would seem to me that until an individual has been found guilty of (at least one) crime by the appropriate method (in this country, the courts), that individual has an absolute entitlement to be protected from being treated as a "false positive." Furthermore, the *courts* are the usually accepted mechanism of our society for the imposition of any form of punishment or of compulsory treatment. We have set up a system that safeguards the freedom of individuals and we have developed considerable traditions for testing evidence. These procedures should not lightly be set aside. Interference in the personal autonomy of individuals requires social as well as scientific safeguards. If it is not possible to have both scientific and social safeguards, then it seems desirable to opt for the social ones. This is mainly because these tend to be more open to comment by a wider section of the society.

Objections to the identification of persons who may commit crimes in future, based upon ideas of due process, may be agreed, but how, it may be asked, is it possible to take a different view when the prediction concerns further (not initial) criminality? The individual who has been found guilty by due process of law (that is, who has passed through all the ceremonial as well as the functional aspects of court determinations) has, in the course of this process, yielded information about himself that would not normally be expected to be provided by those who have not been through the courts. Thus, to obtain the necessary information for effective prediction of the future behavior of those who have passed through due process requires no further intrusive activity by authority. Such intrusiveness, if extended to others, could threaten the freedom of all citizens.

The Information Question

The right to protect personal information is a right we might consider to be derogated upon a finding of guilt of a criminal act. Punishment for criminal acts involves action that, for the offender, is intrusive. Indeed, punishment may almost be defined and quantified in terms of its degree of intrusiveness upon the normal life of the punished. By this argument, the requirement of an individual that he provide information that may be used to his disadvantage is a form of punishment. This is, of course, an absurd generalization, but it helps to separate information that is provided voluntarily, (for example, by a patient to a medical practitioner) from information that is "demanded." At the extreme, of course, is the extraction of information by "third degree," and few would disagree that this is of the same form (from the viewpoint of the subject) as any punishement. Hence, the information gathering process requires a similar quality of justification as do acts that are directly recognized as punishments.

Some means for obtaining from individuals information they would not normally provide willingly is an essential requirement of the application of predictive techniques. If only information that is easy to obtain and that is freely provided is to be used, the power of the predictions is likely to be low and, for that reason, scientifically unsatisfactory. The issue, then, resolves into whether the fact of a finding of guilt by means of due process of law provides the necessary justification for obtaining and using information to make predictions of recidivism. There is some merit in the claim that it is reasonable (intuitively) to believe that persons will continue to act in the manner that has characterized their past. That is, there is a *prima facie* case for assuming that a person who has been found to have committed a crime in the past will continue to commit crimes. If the only item of information available to us were that the individual did ("in fact"!) commit the crime, then we are perhaps entitled to assume further criminality. If further crime is not to be assumed, our belief must be modified by other information than the simple fact of the act. Thus, frequently, further information supplied by (or required of) those found guilty of a crime may be of advantage to them. For example, it is common practice for offenders to be dealt with more or less severely according to their prior record.

The justification for punishing an offender, and if so to what degree, relies upon our concept of guilt—not merely whether the person did or did not commit (that is, was guilty of) the crime. Accordingly, the strategy adopted by offenders will follow two main lines. First will be an attempt to deny the act or the qualities of the act of which they are accused, by a plea of not guilty or by pleading guilty to a lesser offense than that originally charged. Once no further gain is likely from this line, it will be useful if the accused can persuade the court that the act was not typical, that it was out of character. The purpose in this line of approach is to suggest that the offense or similar offenses are not likely to be repeated.

It is interesting to note that the first strategy—the plea of not guilty or not guilty as charged—is tested thoroughly by all known methods, with scientific rules of evidence and procedures of applied democracy. The finding of fact in such questions is highly developed in our society and the methods which safeguard against incorrect decisions are jealously watched. However, regarding the second strategy (to diminish the punishment perceived as likely), there is no rigorous testing of the evidence.

Take a simple hypothetical case. Suppose that the ordinary citizen were to be asked to assess the culpability of two offenders who had committed precisely the same crime and in the same circumstances. One has stated that he will repeat the act in future, no matter what the court may do, while the other states that he has learned his lesson and will not do this kind of thing again. It is almost certain that most persons would rate the culpability of the former as greater than that of the latter. But on precisely what grounds? Is it that we consider the former statement to show lack of respect for the court and is it this "contempt" which is to receive extra punishment? This seems unlikely to be the reason. More likely the statement is seen as predictive—as some indication of future behavior. We shall return to this example, but at this time we may note that we have arrived at a concept of "degree of belief" regarding likely recidivism and that the average person would be expected to take this kind of information into account in setting the level of punishment.

Many more arguments could be made, some appealing to one reader and others appealing to another. However, the point of this digression is not to seek to persuade anyone about a different opinion, but to serve to illustrate the difficulties of making decisions at the interface between science and morality, and particularly where decisions involve the so-called prediction techniques of criminology.

IS CRIMINOLOGICAL PREDICTION REALLY PREDICTION?

It is unfortunate that the term *prediction* has come to be used in the criminal justice field to describe the application of certain methods that, when practiced in other fields, are given more modest titles. A prediction is a predictive act or declaration made by a decisionmaker. The methods we are discussing produce estimates of probabilities but, clearly, only when it is reasonable to accept certain assumptions. Often the necessary assumptions are not tested in the design and hence the reliability of the results is most uncertain.

The key to the appropriate use of prediction instruments lies in the methods employed to produce them. At one time attempts were made to rename the resulting analyses as "experience tables" because they were tabulations summarizing the experience or the outcome for persons who possessed sets of characteristics or background qualities. Another attempt to rename proposed the label "base expectancy tables" because the resulting tables set down the levels of recidivism that might be expected. This phrase related the idea of life-expectancy tabulations to estimates of the likelihood of further convictions. Insurance companies set their premiums in accord with their experience of accidents or the frequency of the conditions against which they offer indemnity. If in the field of criminal justice there are decisions that are essentially similar to those of insurance

companies in fixing their premiums, then the experience or base
expectancy tables prepared by similar means are similarly useful. But
are the decisions similar? Are the methods used to derive the tables
sufficiently similar? Are the data upon which the methods rely of
sufficient quality to withstand the detailed analysis? Are the samples
available of sufficient size for the assumption of similar validity to
hold?

Perhaps the answers to the preceding questions and others of a
like kind must be a qualified yes and no. It is certain that the major
problems with the use of the prediction methods lie not in the
techniques of analysis but rather in the appropriate choice of
application. That is to say, the issues of efficiency and ethics in the
use of prediction tables relate to the matching of the techniques to
questions and to a willingness to accept the inherent uncertainty as
an ethical concern as well as a matter of cost-effectiveness.

IS HISTORY MORE RESPECTABLE?

It is often argued that there is a difference between, on the one
hand, decisions based on information regarding the past and, on the
other hand, decisions that rely on projections as to probable future
conditions. This view received official approval in the reports of the
Law Reform Commission of Canada:

> Perception of the need for protective measures may be based on
> an inference from past actions, an assessment of present
> intention . . . or a prediction of probable future action based on
> general predisposition. Proposals that restraint be imposed in
> reliance on predictive judgments, however they are based, raise
> serious liberty issues . . . [I]mposition of restraint on the ground
> of . . . probable predisposition [is] harder to justify because the
> accuracy of assessments . . . [is] subject to merely statistical proof
> [Vandervort, 1981].

This kind of argument is absurd on more than one count. In the
first instance it is based on a false logic. The issue is not whether we
may know the past with more precision than we may estimate the
future; the issue is the quality of the decisions that we can make. We
may elect different conditions for our inference, but the criteria
relate to qualities of those decisions, not to the qualities of any
method. The argument put forward in the report would seem to be
based on the assumption that decisions must be more appropriate if
the information available is restricted to that derived from the past,
and that is, hence, more accurate *in its own right*. But it is not the rights
of the data that are relevant, but the rights of the persons who will

suffer the determinations made on the basis of the inference drawn from the data. Of course, we cannot predict the future at all well, but it is also true that we do not know the past data precisely. Indeed, it may well be that errors in the recording of past events reduce the power of predictive statements. Data with respect to both past and future are equally probabilistic—the difference is quantitative, not qualitative, in this respect. Predictions of the future can be based only on data available from the past. Thus *prediction is one of the methods of utilizing data from the past;* it does not use a different form of data.

Those who reject predictive analyses for projection are stating that better decisions would be made if the qualities of the available data were *not* fully exploited or that more appropriate decisions can be made with regard to offenders if a restriction is set upon the uses of information. For those persons who make this claim, any information would only be embarrassing if it led them to make any inferences with regard to the probable future conduct of the offender. This seems to be a very odd way to regard information. Is it not more likely that better decisions will be possible if we exploit to the full the limited information available?

ONE HAND TIED BEHIND?

Some decisionmakers may prefer a restriction on the inferences that may be made from the available data because this restriction can lead to more satisfaction with their role in making dispositions. Some judges, it seems, believe that it is possible for them to go through the whole of their career without making a single mistake in sentencing (Young, 1981). Such a claim was, indeed, made by no less an authority than Sir Fred Lawson of the Court of Appeal. Asked by a reporter whether, in twenty years of imposing and reviewing sentences, he had ever made a mistake, he replied: "It's very conceited of me to say so, but the answer is No." A rather more modest claim was made by an American judge with whom I worked. He claimed that he had not made a wrong decision in sentencing at the time he made it. He was willing to accept that in the light of later events he might have come to consider that the disposition was not appropriate. This is like a claim often put forward in mitigation that, at the time, the actor did not "know better"! Thus if it is regarded as "right" to reject all qualities of available information indicative of future conditions, then, when the future overtakes us, we can claim that the decision was still "right." Since there is no duty *at the time* to seek to know more nor to exploit the information further, *at the time* the decision was made it was not in error. There can be no stirring of conscience at any later time, because later time would have involved prediction *at the time,* and that was ruled out of question on principle. If the information search and use is restricted, and this restriction can be defended on moral grounds, then the defense of the decisionmaker is satisfactory and complete.

The issue confounded in the Canadian Law Reform Commission document has nothing to do with the quality or the quantity of available information, in regard to the past, present, or future; the issue is whether it is morally correct for decisionmakers to ignore the qualities of data that are indicators of the future. Convenient it may be, but the question of its morality stands. If it is the claim that such rejection of data is morally acceptable (or, some would seem to claim, required), then on what grounds is this claim made? As has been noted earlier, one of the functions of people in all other aspects of their existence is to make predictions. Without the ability to anticipate (predict), people would hardly qualify as human. All business relies upon anticipation. Is it the claim that in any moral decisions people should behave in a more primitive manner than they do in making any other kinds of decisions? Or is this constraint intended to apply only to sentencing and like determinations in the criminal justice system? Does the idea of justice require the approach of a primitive intuition?

MERELY STATISTICS?

The absurdity of the argument in the Canadian Law Reform Commission document reaches a peak in the phrase *subject to merely statistical proof.* "Merely," indeed: "proof?" *Statistics* is the term applied to that discipline devoted to the study of the nature of inference. Statistical evidence is, perhaps, the highest form of evidence in that, if an estimate of probability can be made, it can be stated simply and the probable error of the estimation can be known. Statistics acknowledges error and uncertainty and works with them; it does not deny either. The quality of the estimates derived from statistical analysis cannot be achieved by any methods other than "merely statistical" inference. Others can only hope that they are right; statistical estimation can give a good estimate as to how likely it is to be wrong. But the confusion is both an old and a common one. It comes from a partial understanding of statistical thinking.

It is realized in statistical analysis that information must at least be categorized, ordered or, if possible, quantified. It is not so frequently realized that a statement of preference is an ordering. Thus it is seen that statistical methods do not deal with persons, but only with information regarding persons: it is the information that is processed by the methods that provides the inference. It is then argued that the statistical analysis gives estimates only for classes of persons—those persons who have the characteristics used in the analysis. Thus, although it may be possible to put an individual in a class of individuals who have a probability of, say 90 percent recidivism within three years, this probability does not apply to any single individual in the group. Alternatively, or simultaneously, it is claimed that the statistical prediction (for the 90 percent class) will, when applied to individuals, be found to be wrong on average in 10 percent of the cases. Clearly, the fact that an average 10 percent of persons will be incorrectly classified as recidivists validates the estimate of 90 percent. If it were possible to say which 10 percent would not recidivate, we could form two groups and be right every time. But statisticians do not think that is humanly possible, nor should humanitarians believe that it could be. If statistical methods are used, decisionmakers must take into account the uncertainty. When such methods are rejected it becomes possible to believe that all one's decisions are right.

Perhaps our decisionmakers should believe that they are always right? If this is the view we wish to take, then statistical methods should be rejected. All equations are written to include an error term. That represents a view of the world shared by most, if not all scientists.

ERRORS, FALSE POSITIVES, AND FALSE NEGATIVES

If errors are admitted, then there will be errors of two different kinds. It does not matter by what means decisions are made; if there are statistical estimates there are two kinds of error, and if there are clinical estimates there are two kinds of error. Only if we can deny error can we deny that there are two kinds of it. There will be those cases (1) where all the indications are that people will recidivate, but in fact they do not do so, and (2) where all the indications are for success, but further crimes are committed. These kinds of errors are well recognized in industrial quality control, where they are named (1) "consumer risk" and (2) "producer risk." In criminal justice we may see these as (1) risks to the individual and (2) risks to the community. If we overinsure against recidivism it is possible that the community will be saved some crime, but this can be only at the price of increased risk of individual suffering. It has become conventional in the legal area to call the excess of individual risk "false positives," although what is false and what is positive remains in doubt! The power of any prediction device can be tested by asking how many persons are identified as, say, dangerous but at what cost. The cost is that of classifying a percentage of others who have the same profiles as those classified as dangerous where in fact their behavior will not justify this conclusion. There is also the converse risk, and this too may be seen as part of the cost of using these kinds of classifications. In statistical prediction these probabilities can be stated and estimates of their error can also be given. (This is the performance characteristic of the predictive equation.) In clinical prediction, as we noted, no similar estimates can be given. Where follow-up studies have been made to test statistical against clinical predictions, the statistical has shown itself to be superior, even in cases where the statistical analyses left much to be desired.

What can be done about false positives? This is a question in the field of morality, not of statistics. Clearly there should be every attempt to make the proportions of false positives and false negatives as small as possible. But no matter how small the percentage of risk of incorrect classification, there will always remain a problem of trade-off of false positives against false negatives. Indeed, some may even consider this trade-off at such a level that the term *false positive* comes to be reversed—that is to say, it is the risk to society that is seen as of greater weight than the risk to the individual. It is usually thought that it is better that a large number of guilty persons should be found not guilty than that one innocent person be convicted. But how many to one? It is likely that, in the finding of guilt by due process of the courts, few incorrect determinations are made, but we know that, even in the case of murder, there have been errors in the finding of guilt. There is a risk. It may be useful to deny it, or to ignore it, and certainly to seek to avoid obtaining any measure of it. Such avoidance may be convenient, but there is a serious question as to whether it is ethical. Is there not a moral duty for intelligent beings to seek information, even where it may be inconvenient? Is there not a moral duty for us to seek to know the proportion of false positives in the decisions made in the criminal justice system? Perhaps this question may be transformed into a proposition: It is a moral requirement of government that it invest some proportion of its national product in social research.

It is obvious that not all decisions can be investigated by the scientific means now available to us. We must balance the cost of data collection and analysis against the probable outcomes, and much of this balancing must be subjective, informed guessing. However, although we may have to employ inferences that do not derive from scientific analysis, we should not claim superiority for those methods which rely only on the status of the decisionmaker. There are, of course, advantages to the latter approach. Such decisions reinforce the authority of the decisionmaker and offer a means to preserve his power, because it is then possible to avoid challenge and public accountability. Reasons are not given because it is said to be impossible to give reasons: the decisions must, it is then argued, rest upon the authority of the assigned role, but decisions do not rest only upon two independent bases. Even subjective guessing can be made at a variety of levels of rationality and morality. There are procedures for testing as well as for monitoring decisions.

It is when such controls on the decisionmakers become replaced by ceremonial and other kinds of support for assertions of authority that we meet again the interface between ethics and science. No public decisionmaker should defend his determinations only in terms of a request for personal trust. If a decision can be made, it can be explained to the public and some measure of accountability can be devised. Or, to put this general position into one specific, illustrative claim: there is a moral objection to the refusal of parole boards to give reasons for their determinations, particularly in the cases where parole is not granted. But perhaps parole boards are always right, at the time they make the decisions, and in that case all the decisions are beyond improvement. Is this really to be believed?

RETRIBUTIVE RATIONALE VS. PREDICTIVE ASSESSMENTS

The viewpoint associated with the term *just deserts* provides the main support for the idea that predictions of recidivism should not be permitted to have weight in sentencing decisions. It emphasizes that it is what the offender *did*, not what he is likely to do, that should be the concern of the sentencer (for example, Von Hirsch, 1976). However, most advocates of this rationale take the view that previous convictions should receive consideration in fixing the instant penalty. It is difficult to justify this (reasonable) view in terms of strict retributive theory as set forth in Kant and Hegel. By permitting weight to be given to prior convictions, the advocates of just deserts are using the most powerful predictive item in any statistical test of likely recidivism. Thus, although they deny that they take note of likely future events, they take cognizance of the same items of information as they would if they were doing so! Of course, the weight given to prior convictions in a just deserts approach is not determined in accord with any probabilistic measure, but seems to be set in accord with the subjective feelings of the · decisionmaker.

It is possible that it is because we know that prior convictions are prognostic of future criminality that the strict retributive model is, to most persons, unacceptable. It is difficult to make any other argument in support of this obviously reasonable concern, although several tortuous arguments have been attempted to fit prior criminality into a retributive approach. Returning to the hypothetical case of the offender who stated that he would continue in crime, it is difficult to believe either (a) that the penalty would be the same if he had not made that statement or (b) that if his punishment were increased it was due only to the demonstration of his lack of respect for the court in making such a claim and not in any way due to the nature of that claim. It is far easier to believe that most persons would consider that the statement indicated that, in fact, there was a greater chance of recidivism and that this represented a greater degree of culpability and hence justified an increased level of punishment. If, then, we can accept the predictive statements of offenders (a somewhat unreliable source), why can we not accept probabilities of the same event when worked out by statistics?

STARTING TO USE PREDICTIVE METHODS

If it is accepted that the prediction of human behavior is, to a lesser or greater degree, a possibility and that the general moral questions can be satisfied, we must ask about the practical uses of the technique. It is, of course, not so much a question of how to predict but what to predict. What, precisely, is meant by "success" or "failure"?; what are the "consumer" risks and the "producer" risks? And, assuming that these can be measured, how is the scientific work to be presented to the decisionmaking authority concerned?

Predictive work cannot be carried out by social-research workers on their own. For the basic data they need the assistance of those who collect and store it—not merely in terms of making it available, but in providing background on its quality and interpretation. The criteria to be worked with can come only from those who have the right or duty to decide on matters of social policy. But while it is clear that social research cannot function alone, it is also true that the social administrator cannot go it alone. A team approach is essential. It is not possible to do prediction research *for*, *to*, or *on* social policymakers, but only *with* them (see Wilkins, 1981). The social administrator needs also to recognize that he cannot call upon the social scientist to produce an instrument to his specification. There is much more to cooperation than that of master and slave or employer and employee.

The team should quickly develop to a point where an outsider would find it impossible to distinguish scientists from administrators, judges from sociologists, or statisticians from anybody else. The focus upon the task should be such that the individual interests become submerged in the common cause. This requires an openness and honesty in all communications within the operational team of potential user and producer interests. There must be a positive honesty; that is to say, members must be willing to communicate with each member as they would with their personal psychiatrist. Any lesser degree of frankness cannot result in a useful product. Within the bounds of the task (and these must be strictly adhered to) the level of intensity is certainly likely to be as great as in any therapeutic association. It does not matter, of course, at what level the association begins, provided that it can develop into a powerful association of minds.

It is obvious that it is no use seeking a solution to a problem until it is specified in appropriate terms. The first task is, then, the transformation of the problems into researchable questions. Questions posed initially in administrative language will need to be translated into postulates and tentative models. All questions are to be treated as tentative. It has been this writer's experience that successful research has almost always started with the wrong questions. If these questions could not be modified as the research progressed (because of research contract specifications, for example), the project was on a course towards disaster. Perhaps the value of research can be measured by the degree of surprise occasioned by its results. Research workers enjoy the element of surprise in their work; the unexpected is a challenge and can be fun. Administrators are not conditioned to regard as a source of enjoyment any surprises in their work; rather, good administration is seen as needing a quiet, smooth continuance of management procedures.

There will be a tendency for administrators to press research workers to say what the outcomes of the investigations are likely to be. If these outcomes have any probability of being regarded as undesirable, cooperation will become very difficult. In research inquiry, however, priority must be given to the question and to the rigor of the investigation. If the question is important and the methods of investigation rigorous, there should be only secondary attention paid to the likely outcomes. To take any other view may lead to the suggestion that to know more about the problem could be undesirable. This may be true, but to fail to continue to seek information on these grounds poses a moral issue. The moral issue, however, relates to the probable *uses of the results* and not to the nature of the results themselves, nor to the form or style of the inquiry. Here the scientist has to be cautious that the more powerful group in society does not say, "Give me the formula; I will decide what to do with it." The scientist has a responsibility, as does every other person who possesses the information, to use the power of that information in accord with moral principles. The research worker who becomes involved in a team investigation of predictive methods cannot avoid making value judgments. At this interface values and scientific methods grind together. Social science cannot be value-free.

It is obvious that an estimate of the probability that an offender will recidivate does not of itself point to any specific decision.* It does not follow that punishment should be increased in proportion to risk. It is more reasonable to use prediction tables to restrict the use of the just-deserts concept. It does not seem reasonable to use an item of information as an excuse to increase punishment over and above that appropriately assessed as "desert" for the instant crime, unless two conditions are satisfied: (1) the item of information relates to behavior that is in itself reprehensible (for example, prior convictions); and (2) the item of information is predictive of further criminality.

If, for example, ethnic group were found to be predictive, it would be rejected as an item to be used to increase the penalty. That is, it is an item that should not be used in prediction tables for assisting the determinations of courts, parole boards, or similar bodies. On the other hand, the input of information on race and other sensitive data should not be inhibited, because such censorship would represent again the "I do not wish to know" syndrome, the morality of which has been previously called into question. There would seem to be good reason for us to know whether age, sex, race, social background, educational level, and the like, are related to decisions in sentencing and also whether these items are related to subsequent criminality. But we should reject the idea that punishment is to be differentiated in accord with these variables.

At this point, that which it is ethical *to study* diverges from that which it is ethical *to use* in determinations regarding individuals. In the former case the information is sought without any regard to potential use. We merely wish to know, and the options for action remain open. Thus, at that time, appropriate moral issues of utilization cannot be asked. (We must, of course, distinguish between an unanswerable question and an unaskable question.) In the latter case the use is stated in advance, and ethical issues of use can be posed prior to undertaking the research, because the necessary information to frame the questions already exists.

It may be useful to state a tentative rule for the censorship of data that should be used to test for inclusion in prediction studies. It seems that any feature the accused does not have within his

---

*The United States Parole Commissioners use a set of rules that includes a specific prediction instrument that is tested and revised periodically. See, for example, annual reports, The Parole Commission Act, and several class-action cases in Federal Appeals Court.

individual control should not be used to bias the selection of punishments and hence should be excluded from equations that will inform such selection. Although age is not within a person's control, it might be admitted on these grounds because all persons pass through a particular age, unless the expectation of life is less than the age category used.

SAFEGUARDS AND OBJECTIVES

In the development of prediction instruments it is necessary, but not sufficient, to seek the most efficient set of equations. Clearly, we should know how much of the variance of the criteria can be explained by the most efficient predictive system; but if that efficiency is obtained at the cost of including information relating to certain details about the accused, the use of the instrument should be constrained. The most efficient prediction instrument can be used to suggest and compare simplified instruments that may be easier to use in practice. For example, two-dimensional expectancy tables are easier to read than three-dimensional tables. It is likely that the additional power obtained by the third dimension is within error limits and considerable simplification may be possible without loss of a significant degree of efficiency. It must also be remembered that nonstatistical errors (errors of calculation, interpretation, definition, and the like) can diminish the efficiency of an instrument. The more complex the instrument in use, the more errors of application may be anticipated. It is, however, necessary to know the cost of the simplification, and for this the full and most efficient form of the equation is required. For the purposes of testing equations, information that would be inhibited on moral grounds may well be included. The moral issue lies in the use of these unacceptable items in decisions that will have an impact upon persons, not in their impact upon equations or on the thinking of the research scientist.

The level of current practice in the use of prediction tools in criminal justice decisionmaking is far below the prescriptive level proposed here. To quote only one example, the VERA bail decision rules (see, for example, Carter and Wilkins, 1979, pp. 143–44) consist in the main of items of information which would fail on the first part of the test proposed above and whose relationship to the second test is unknown.* Most of the items relate to the social position of the accused—items not normally within his control. The level of efficiency is certainly unknown and there are no available

---

*One example almost universally included in the VERA scale relates to the length of residence in the area.

comparisons with alternative methods. Perhaps, again, this case illustrates the need for administrators to recognize a moral requirement to seek to test their beliefs by means of scientific analysis.

The ultimate test of predictive methods is, of course, neither the scientific nor the statistical nature of the exercises, but their honesty, rigor and moral underpinnings. Whether information is coded into numerical form or expressed in technical jargon or in common language makes no difference to the form of logical analysis that must be applied. There is not one kind of logic for working with numbers and another for working with words, nor for that matter with any other symbols. Words are as much a code form as are numbers. Those who use words to describe offenders are placing them into categories in much the same way as are those who use other systems of categories. Words are not necessarily a better or more morally acceptable medium for all processes than are numbers.

One thing is certain. All persons who make decisions that affect offenders make those decisions in terms of *information*. Although it may be claimed that there is an awareness of the person, the only aspects of the person that can be included in any decision must reduce to information and be handled as such. It is how the individual accused *is seen*, not how the individual *is*, that enters the decision processes. Can we do better by placing persons in categories determined by words alone or by a more extended code? That is the issue which underlies claims and counterclaims about prediction. There is clear evidence that we do better by the use of the more extended code—words and numbers.

For many purposes it is preferable to use simple language; for other purposes it is possible to justify the use of jargon, and very often (more than is usually thought) the methods of statistical analysis are the most powerful and honest ways of dealing with issues, including those relating to moral values.

CONCLUDING REMARKS

It must be recognized that the problem of crime cannot be simplified to the problem of the offender. Two quite distinct policies are needed to deal with two almost independent social problems: (a) what to do about crime, and (b) what to do about those who are found guilty of committing a criminal act. We do neither society nor scientific thought a service if we assume that by working on the latter problem we contribute solutions to the former. Like fundamentalist Christians who believe that the only way to save the world is by saving individual sinners, social-policy criminologists seem to have assumed that the way to save the world from crime is to save (or destroy!) the individual offender. Religious fundamentalism and the idea of individual salvation is not highly regarded as a specification of social policy for the world's political and economic ills. "Fundamentalist criminology," with its idea that crime can be dealt with by action taken against individual offenders, is an interesting but outdated and arrogant faith in our abilities to modify the behavior of others.

Decisions have to be made about offenders. Predictive techniques can provide evidence which it is reasonable to take into account in making such decisions. In the disposal of offenders, we must accommodate, both morally and scientifically, the idea of uncertainty. Uncertainty need not be disabling if it is transformed into probabilities. This, then, is the interface between politics, science, and morality—the interface where prediction techniques provide the medium of operational-level discussion and action. Because this is an interface, it is unreasonable for any sector of authority to arrogate to itself the task of making the determinations, and it is equally unreasonable to delegate that responsibility. The moral necessity is for a shared responsibility. Critical policy (moral) problems are not divided up as are government departments, nor are they located in sectors corresponding to university disciplines. Those who believe that they know most certainly what to do about either crime or criminals are those who have never studied the subject. Thus the best thing that social scientists should seek to do is to destroy myths. Perhaps the critical public message that we must propagate at this time is that, whatever is done to offenders, the expected impact upon the incidence and prevalence of crime will be trivial.

REFERENCES

Carter, R., and Wilkins, L. T. (1979). *Probation and parole.* 2d ed. New York: Wiley.

Vandervort, L. (1981). *Changing persons.* Working Paper on Behavior Modification and Human Subject Research. Ottawa: Law Reform Commission of Canada.

Von Hirsch, A. (1976). *Doing justice: The choice of punishments.* New York: Hill and Wang.

Wilkins, L. T. (1981). *Principles of guidelines for sentencing.* Washington, DC: National Institute of Justice.

Young, H. (1981). How will the judges defeat Mr. Whitelaw? *Sunday Times* (London), 17 May, p. 32.

II
Parole Prediction

CHAPTER 3

Screening for Risk among Parolees: Policy, Practice, and Method

STEPHEN D. GOTTFREDSON AND DON M. GOTTFREDSON

SUMMARY

For the past half-century, much effort has been expended in the development of statistical devices intended to aid criminal justice decisionmakers, and such devices are increasingly being used. Although the methods used have become very sophisticated, little increase in predictive utility has been noticed. This study compares the statistical efficiency of five prediction methods (two linear additive models, two clustering models, and a multivariate contingency table model) within the context of parole risk assessment. Although no differences in predictive efficiency are noted, it is stressed that practical efficiency is important as well. Finally, we consider issues of values, ethics, and fairness in the construction of parole risk instruments and demonstrate that consideration of policy and practice, as well as of method, can result in devices that are parsimonious and that can be defended on statistical, ethical and practical grounds.

INTRODUCTION

Prediction is central to most general concerns of the criminal justice system. Deterrence, treatment or rehabilitation, and incapacitation are all forward-looking, crime-preventive goals that require prediction in some sense. The concept of *deterrence* involves the "prediction" that punishment of known offenders will discourage others from crime. (In the case of *specific deterrence*, the prediction made is that the punishment of a known offender will deter him from future criminal involvement.) The concept of *treatment* involves the "prediction" that offenders may be changed to reduce the likelihood of repeated offending; and that of *incapacitation* requires the "prediction" that new offenses will occur if offenders are not restrained from committing them. The aims of desert (the application of deserved punishment) or of retribution or retaliation of course do not involve prediction—nor, for that matter, a utilitarian attitude. Rather, they look backward only, to the gravity of the harm done or the culpability of the offender; see, for example, O'Leary, Gottfredson, and Gelman (1975).

In view of the centrality of prediction to many policy issues in criminal justice, it is important that we consider (a) the relevance of statistical prediction methods to criminal justice goals, (b) questions of policy and practice in the use of such methods in criminal justice, and (c) some general advantages and limitations of statistical prediction methods that may have particular importance for policy decisions about their use.

In the application of statistical prediction methods, controversies surrounding their use may arise from scientific, empirical evidence, from ethical value perspectives, or from both; but these are concerns that should not be confused. Rather, issues of value and of evidence should be uniquely identified in order to add clarity to arguments concerning policy formulation. In this paper, we seek not only to point out the important distinctions between the scientific and the value questions, but to show how they often can be related. Thus, in addition to comparing statistical prediction models, we will note illustrative ethical issues that may be of fundamental importance to policy decisions concerning the applications of prediction methods.

Relevance of Statistical Prediction to Criminal Justice Goals
The relevance and potential utility of statistical prediction methods to criminal justice decisionmaking depend obviously on the objectives of the decisions involved. If the decision problem is one that requires prediction information for the selection of alternative actions, then statistical prediction is likely to be a relevant issue.

It generally has been found that statistical prediction devices can be developed that are both more reliable and more valid than unguided or intuitive clinical predictions. Such devices are more dependable, and they work better (Meehl, 1954; Gough, 1962; Dawes and Corrigan, 1974; Dawes, 1971; Mosteller, 1977). However, as we have noted elsewhere (Gottfredson and Gottfredson, 1979; see also Underwood, 1979), statistical and clinical prediction methods may be used together in mutually supportive ways. In most practical situations, decisions based on predictions will be made, and help toward more rational decisions can come from either the clinical or the actuarial sector (or from some combination of the two).

In general, behavioral scientists are not—and have no interest in becoming—decisionmakers. We do, however, have great interest in the prediction of behavior and in the decisionmaking process itself. For us, the real question is not "Which approach is better, the clinical or the actuarial?" but "Can behavioral scientists using actuarial methods be of practical help to the decisionmakers?" Our focus, then, is on issues of the development and use of actuarial methods and not on comparisons of such devices with clinical judgments.

The usefulness of statistical prediction methods depends on the objectives of the decisions that are to be based on the methods. The objectives, however, are rarely completely agreed upon; and rarely are they stated with the clarity needed for any careful analysis. Nevertheless, we would claim that when the aims include those of incapacitation, deterrence, or treatment (more generally, any attempted reduction in the probability of future crimes by the offenders concerned), statistical prediction methods may be expected to be relevant and potentially useful.

The explication of an agency's or decisionmaker's objectives is an obvious requisite to deciding whether statistical prediction methods are to be regarded as possibly useful. If the aim is limited to the provision of deserved punishment, then it is difficult to see how prediction methods (of any type) can be helpful. If, on the other hand, the objectives include crime reduction among the population of offenders being considered, then it is difficult to see how statistical prediction is *not* a relevant issue.

Screening for Parole Risk

One of the most common applications of statistical prediction devices in criminology is in the assessment of parole risk. Indeed, it is here that the implicit predictive intent of many of the classification decisions made in the criminal justice process is most apparent. Almost all inmates are eligible for some form of early release from a period of incarceration, and most eventually do achieve this. In making these early-release decisions, members of paroling agencies routinely attempt to "predict" the future behavior of eligible inmates.

Historically—and, in general, still—these decisions are made subjectively rather than statistically. Since the 1920s, however, behavioral scientists have attempted to aid these decisionmakers through the construction of actuarially based instruments (compare Burgess, 1928; Glaser, 1955, 1964; Gottfredson and Ballard, 1965; Ohlin, 1951; Mannheim and Wilkins, 1955). Although even the crudest such devices have proven of value, the sophistication of the methods used to develop predictive devices for parole risk assessment has increased rapidly (see Simon, 1971; Gottfredson and Gott-fredson, 1979).

Further, the operational use of such devices is accelerating. This is spurred by governmental agencies such as the National Institute of Corrections and by court requirements that decisionmakers must be able to demonstrate the rationality of the decisionmaking process.

Since so much of this work has involved parole prediction, that is the issue we treat here.

When to Predict What

That which is to be predicted depends on prior judgments concerning goals and objectives. Specific subobjectives may be perceived as steps toward the attainment of more general aims. Thus, the specific objectives of an intended use of prediction methods, as well as the general aims, must be identified and considered.

Choices—often rather arbitrary ones—must be made in defining a criterion of "success" or "failure" or other classification of outcomes to be predicted. Whether arrests, as well as convictions, should be counted as indicators of failure is an issue providing an obvious example of a definitional choice that may be influenced heavily by value questions in relation to the specific intended operational use of the instrument.

One guide in some such choices is an understanding of the procedures underlying the development and validation of statistical prediction devices. A specific criterion *must* be used; and any generalizations of predictive validity to *different* criteria must be suspect until such validity has been demonstrated. Classifications relevant to one purpose may have no relevance to another. For example, classifications relevant to the risk of repeated offending may have no relevance or utility for the problem of assignment to different treatment programs. Thus, the decisionmaker is well advised that, although a particular prediction instrument may provide helpful information about one objective, it may give *no* —or indeed, *faulty*—information about other outcomes that may be related to other decision objectives.

To return to our example, it is quite plausible that for some purposes the inclusion of arrests as an unfavorable criterion element may be appropriate, and for other purposes it may not. Only careful consideration of goals will allow a determination.

Why Prediction?

The "why" question is related to questions of "when" and "with what." Generally, four categories of purposes for developing prediction tools may be discussed. These involve research aims and applications for program planning, selection, or decision policy.

The process of developing prediction instruments inherently

involves the testing of hypotheses and thus may provide an aim in itself. Further, however, the purpose may be the provision of a research tool. In many program-evaluation studies, for example, such measures are used to provide an indication of the "prior probabilities" of an outcome—that is, of the likelihood of that outcome without treatment or before treatment. This may be useful in making comparisons of outcomes for groups treated differently.

Alternatively, the objective may be to provide a tool for the general screening of a population for some program-planning purpose. An example might be the screening of all offenders received in prison with an escape risk scale in order to identify a pool to be considered for immediate placement in a minimum security setting.

Again, the intention might be the development of an instrument to be used as an aid in selection, such as for probation or parole. A similar application is the use of a prediction device in the allocation of probationers or parolees to differing levels of intensity of supervision—for example, providing only minimal supervision of those in the most favorable expected-outcome groups. Finally, a somewhat different (but related) use of prediction methods is found in their inclusion in policy or guidelines such as those now sometimes used in sentencing or parole decisionmaking (Gottfredson, 1975; Gottfredson, Wilkins, and Hoffman, 1978).

Evidence, Values, and Fairness

In any selection application, value questions arise particularly in relation to three sets of concerns: issues surrounding what items may justifiably be included in the instrument, issues of errors in prediction, and issues of policy and intended use.

The first question is one of values and of fairness—and more recently, of law (see Underwood, 1979, for a review). For example, suppose that the purpose of an instrument under development is to provide an aid to selection for parole. (The paroling authority has determined already that the risk of new crimes is an appropriate issue for inclusion in paroling policy.) Suppose further that income level is found uniquely and rather powerfully predictive of new crimes, such that offenders who have been poor are worse risks. In this wholly hypothetical example, the paroling authority obviously must resolve the policy issue of whether it is *fair* to include the item.

The second problem, of errors in prediction, must be confronted as well. Whether clinical or statistical predictions of failure are made, there will be errors of two kinds: predicted successes who fail ("false negatives") and predicted failures who succeed ("false positives"). This problem also raises complex questions of both evidence and values, for it may well prove the case that the costs to society are not equivalent for the two types of errors.

Third, at different states in the criminal justice process, decision-makers may have markedly different amounts and types of information available to them. Accordingly, an important issue in the development of actuarial aids involves decisions about the information to be included in the model. For example, a parole board might wish to use such a device at the intake stage of the parole hearing; however, the board may find the necessary data unavailable. Again, the selection of items to be included in the device must be guided by its intended use.

Finally, these issues are made more complex because neither organizations nor persons have single goals. Rather, they have multiple, sometimes conflicting, aims. Suffice it to say that prediction models useful for one purpose may have little utility for another.

The greatest limitation of statistical prediction methods is obvious when it is remembered that devices of the type discussed are developed and validated with respect to specific criteria, using available data, in a specific jurisdiction, during a specific time period. Thus, any generalizations made to other outcomes of interest, or after modifications of the item definitions used, or to other jurisdictions or populations, or to other time periods, are to be questioned.

WHICH ACTUARIAL APPROACH?

There are a large number of statistical methods available and useful for the development of prediction models. Both Meehl (1954) and Gough (1962) have provided good reviews of specific actuarial methods that have been used widely in the behavioral sciences, often with particular reference to problems of criminal justice. Mannheim and Wilkins (1955) and Simon (1971) have provided reviews of specific methods used in criminology, and the latter includes comparisons of predictive efficiency resulting from the use of different methods of combining predictor variables.

Despite considerable experience in the development of such methods, there has been a great deal of theoretical and practical debate about the most efficient—most valid, least costly, and most operationally useful—methods for selecting and combining information with some predictive utility. Later reports (Simon, 1971; Gottfredson et al., 1974) have suggested that, in practice, statistical techniques that are theoretically less powerful and that are computationally and procedurally relatively simple may demonstrate equal or superior predictive validity to that obtained by more complex and theoretically superior methods. In general, however, the comparative studies which have been done have suffered from one or more of several limitations:

1. lack of attention to the base-rate problem;
2. failure to cross-validate;
3. lack of application of methods to the same set(s) of data; or
4. consideration of few methods.

In a recent study (Gottfredson and Gottfredson, 1979, 1980), we were able to overcome each of these limitations. Since our study had the comparison of efficiency as its primary goal, all analyses were carried out on the same data base (advantages of which are outlined later). All comparisons were made with full attention to the base rate and validation issues, and we included a wide variety of markedly different methods. In particular, we studied (a) two general additive linear models, (b) two clustering models, and (c) a recent multi-dimensional contingency table (log-linear) approach.

Linear Additive Models

Perhaps the most widely used actuarial predictive method has been the linear additive model.

Least Squares (Multiple) Regression. The best-known and most widely used additive linear model is that of least-squares regression. As previously discussed, it has been known for some time that least-squares models improve substantially over intuitive clinical approaches to prediction. Moreover, Dawes and Corrigan (1974) have shown that even linear regression models that use *random* regression weights do substantially better than do humans in predictive situations. More recently, Wainer (1976) demonstrated that a simple unweighted (or, more accurately, equally weighted) linear additive model is essentially as good as, and in some important respects may be better than, a weighted least-squares model.

The Burgess Method. In the criminal justice field, the unweighted additive model in use has been patterned after the work of Burgess (1928). In brief, the procedure involves the use of attribute data (or the dichotomization of predictor variables). Resulting attributes then are used in an unweighted, linear additive fashion to predict the criterion classifications.

Clustering Models

Many clustering algorithms are available (Johnson, 1967; Lance and Williams, 1966; Cormack, 1971). Hierarchial clustering schemes are of two types: *divisive* methods proceed by successively partitioning or subdividing the sample into increasingly homogeneous groups, and *agglomerative* methods reverse this process. (The latter start with the individual and successively group or cluster.) Further differences among methods lie in the specific rules for division or clustering, for termination of the process, or for item inclusion.

Predictive attribute analysis and *association analysis* are the two methods used in the present study. Both proceed by classifying a heterogeneous population into relatively homogeneous subgroups, thereby minimizing (or reducing) individual variation *within* subgroups while maximizing (or increasing) variation *between* subgroups. Predictive attribute analysis and association analysis can be distinguished with respect to the criteria by which the sample is partitioned successively. Predictive attribute analysis goes directly to the purpose: the aim is to maximize predictive efficiency by classifying individuals in terms of those predictive attributes that are most strongly associated with the criterion classification. Association analysis, on the other hand, classifies individuals by those attributes that most effectively summarize shared variance on those same attributes *without* respect to any particular criterion (see Williams and Lambert, 1959, 1961; Ballard and Gottfredson, 1963; Gottfredson, Ballard, and Lane, 1965).

Multidimentional Contingency Table Analysis

Multidimensional contingency table analysis, developed by Goodman (1970, 1971) and others, requires few assumptions about the nature of the variables under consideration (or about the nature of relations among them). The technique is complex, although the rationale underlying it is relatively straightforward. Rather than utilizing a multiplicative model in order to account for potential interactions among predictor variables, it uses logarithms of the odds ratios, resulting in an additive model. For an example of the application of the method to the assessment of risk, see Solomon (1976) and Van Alstyne and Gottfredson (1978).

The model (1) inherently allows for nominal-level measures, (2) can estimate different "weights" for different predictors, (3) can conveniently be used to estimate interaction terms, (4) does not require the assumption of a particular multivariate distribution for significance testing (as does regression analysis), and (5) provides a means of estimating an "optimal" model. These advantages, plus the potential for identifying a parsimonious set of predictors, make this model worth a close examination.

COMPARING METHODS

The specific predictive methods we compared are summarized in table 3.1 with respect to the several characteristics discussed earlier. Specifically considered are (a) the extent to which a given method accounts for predictor variable intercorrelation, whether the method assumes (b) linearity and/or (c) additivity of relations, and (d) the expected tendency of the model to overfit construction-sample data (capitalize on chance variation), with concomitant shrinkage on validation. The methods selected for use in our comparative study were intended to provide variation in these characteristics, as can be seen in table 3.1.

The Data Base

The data used in this study were collected for an earlier project on parole decisionmaking (Gottfredson et al., 1974) and concern about 4,500 persons released from federal prisons in the years 1970-1972. Of these, 2,400 were released in the calendar year 1970. The sample is not representative of all who were released, and different proportions were sampled in different years. Samples were drawn, however, in a manner assumed to approximate random selection. A systematic "track down" was accomplished for releasees for whom no disposition was indicated in FBI rap sheets. A large number of data items are available for each subject, and the intercoder reliabilities of the data items are known to be fairly high (Gottfredson and Gottfredson, 1979).

Table 3.1. Characteristics of Five Prediction Methods

Method	Account for Predictor Intercorrelation?	Linear Relations Assumed?	Additive Relations Assumed?	Expected Tendency for Overfitting
Burgess	No	Yes*	Yes	Low
Multiple Regression	Yes	Yes	Yes	Moderate/High
Association Analysis	Yes	No*	No	Low/Moderate
Predictive Attribute Analysis	Yes	No*	No	High
Multidimensional Contingency Table Analysis	Yes	No	Yes	Moderate/High

*Since all variables are dichotomized, the issue of linearity is essentially ignored. Assumptions of linearity *are* needed in the Burgess technique; they are less important in the hierarchical clustering techniques.

SOURCE: A version of this table first appeared in an unpublished report prepared by K. Andreason, W. Brown, G. Dodsley, M. Neithercutt, G. Pasella, D. Pfoutz, and S. Springer, of the National Council on Crime and Delinquency Research Center.

Construction and Validation Samples

The 1970-release sample was selected to serve as the construction subsample, and the 1972-release sample was designated the validation subsample. The entire 1970 and 1972 samples were used, including any females (*N* = 120) released during those years, since preliminary analyses suggested that substantive conclusions would not be affected by including females (Gottfredson and Gottfredson, 1979).

With failure defined as (a) any return to prison, or (b) any conviction for any new offense, or (c) death during the commission of a criminal act, or (d) absconding from parole supervision, the base rate for successful performance during two years after release for the 2,382 cases in the 1970 sample was 64 percent. For those 1,124 who were in fact released under parole supervision, the success rate was 70 percent. The 689 subjects who were mandatorily released under supervision had a success rate of 57 percent. Finally, 61 percent of the 569 subjects who were released at the expiration of their sentence and without supervision were successful.

Table 3.2. Variable Descriptions, by Group

Variables	Coding
Relating to Present Offense	
How committed	Probation, parole, or mandatory release violation vs. all other commitments
Type of admission	New court commitment vs. all other types of admissions.
Commitment offense	a) Burglary, larceny, theft (any type) vs. all other offenses
	b) Homicide, manslaughter, all robbery, all theft, larceny, fraud, forgery, counterfeiting, kidnapping vs. all other offenses (person and property vs. other)
	c) Vehicle theft, forgery, fraud, larceny by check, heroin vs. all other offenses
	d) Vehicle theft, forgery, fraud, larceny by check vs. all other offenses
Dollar value of offense	a) Dollar value
	b) Unknown or less than or equal to $499 vs. $500 or more
Relating to Criminal History	
Age at first arrest	a) $\leq$ 14; 15–17; 18–21; $\geq$ 22
	b) $\leq$ 18; > 18
Age at first conviction	a) $\leq$ 15; 16–18; 19–22; $\geq$ 23
	b) $\leq$ 18; > 18
Age at first commitment	a) $\leq$ 17; 18–20; 21–25; $\geq$ 26
	b) $\leq$ 18; > 18
Longest time free since first commitment	a) $\leq$ 6 mo.; 7–18 mo.; 19–36 mo.; 37–60 mo.; >60 mos. (includes code of "0")
	b) Code "0" and > 60 mo. vs. $\leq$ 60 mos.

Number of prior convictions	a) None; 1; 2–3; 4 or more b) None vs. any
Number of prior sentences	a) None; 1; 2 or more b) None vs. any
Number of prior sentences with probation	a) None, 1; 2 or more b) None vs. any
Number of prior incarcerations	a) None; 1; 2 or more b) None vs. any
Number of prior parole or probation revocations	None vs. any
Number of prior convictions for burglary	a) Number of prior convictions for burglary b) None vs. any
Number of prior convictions for larceny	a) Number of prior convictions for larceny b) None vs. any
Number of prior convictions for auto theft	a) Number of prior convictions for auto theft b) None vs. any
Number of prior convictions for forgery, fraud, or larceny by check	a) Number of prior convictions for forgery, fraud, or larceny by check b) None vs. any
Total number of prior convictions for property offenses	a) 0–1; 2; 3; 4 or more b) 0–1; 2 or more
Longest time served on any commitment	0–6 mo. vs. more than 6 mo.
Reason for first arrest	Burglary, check offenses, forgery, theft, delinquent child vs. all others

Relating to Social History

Highest grade completed	a) None through Ph.D. b) 0–11; 12 or greater
Marital status at admission	Married or common-law vs. any other status
Living arrangement before commitment	Wife and/or children vs. any other arrangement
Use of synthetic and/or natural opiates	Known use vs. no known use
Employment during last two years of civilian life	Employed more than 25% of the time; or student; or unemployable 75% of the time vs. unemployed
Longest job in free community	a) Unknown or less than one year; 1–4 years; more than 4 years b) Unknown or 4 or fewer years vs. more than 4 years

Relating to Institutional Adjustment

Escape history	No escapes or attempted escapes from any custody vs. one or more escapes or attempted escapes
Latest custody classifications	a) Maximum or close; medium; minimum; work-release or unknown b) Unknown, minimum, or work-release vs. maximum, close, or medium
Prison punishment	None vs. any

Additional Variable

Planned living arrangement	Wife and/or children vs. any other arrangement

ANALYSES

Based on a series of preliminary analyses, the original data set was reduced to a subset of 29 items that appeared to have both predictive and practical utility for the development of risk-screening devices. Table 3.2 gives summary descriptions of these variables and the various codings or transformations we used. Each of these variables correlated at least $|0.10|$ with the outcome criterion described earlier, and the highest such correlation was 0.27 (see Gottfredson and Gottfredson, 1979, for a detailed description).

Most of the variables under consideration fall into one of four general categories: (a) variables relating to the instant offense, (b) variables relating to a subject's history of criminal or delinquent involvement, such as age at first arrest or conviction and number of prior convictions, (c) "social history" variables, such as the highest completed grade claimed or living arrangements prior to commitment, and (d) variables relating to institutional adjustment during either the present or some past incarceration. (One variable, having to do with planned living arrangement, although used in some analyses, did not seem to fall easily into any one of these four categories.)

The various statistical methods employed in this study require different characteristics of predictor variables. Some, like the Burgess technique, demand that variables consist (typically) of dichotomies. Others, like multiple regression, usually require that variables possess characteristics of interval scales. Still others, like the log-linear techniques, allow for the inclusion of multicategory, nominal-level data. Although such data may be analyzed using the log-linear techniques, very large numbers of categories are problematic for two reasons: (a) the size, in terms of numbers of cells, of the n-dimensional table can quickly become too large to handle, and (b) zero-frequency cells are problematic given this approach. Hence, a balance between too many categories (resulting in problems (a) and (b) noted above) and too few categories (to allow for the adequate consideration of interaction) was sought.

These variables (in appropriate transformation, if required) were used in all analyses performed. For each of the five methods discussed above, a number of analyses were performed. This chapter reports findings of only a few selected analyses and concentrates primarily on the issue of comparative utility.*

*Issues treated in Gottfredson and Gottfredson (1979), but not reported in this chapter, include: (a) descriptions of the analyses, (b) methods used to create operationally useful decisionmaking aids from the analytic equations or models tested, (c) comparisons and discussions of different analyses of the same type (for example, the potential advantages of one clustering solution over another), (d) verbal descriptions of final or "preferred" solutions for each analytic model, and (e) a variety of methodological concerns.

Using the 1970 data set as described above (N = 2,382), decision-making aids felt to be potentially operationally useful were developed using each analytic method. These devices were then cross-validated using the 1972 data set (N = 1,004).

Table 3.3 summarizes our findings with respect to the predictive utility of the five methods considered. This evidence suggests no clear advantage of any given method. Given all methods of instrument development, prediction is at best modest, although (a) prediction is better than that which would result from simple use of the base rate alone, regardless of the method of construction employed, and (b) the estimates derived here are well within the ranges typically found in "state of the art" studies of recidivism prediction.

With the possible exception of the association analyses (the results of which are depressed relative to those of the other analyses), all techniques result in virtually the same degree of prediction. Therefore, those who would develop risk-screening devices for operational use on the basis of these analyses would be advised to base their decisions as to the method(s) to employ on factors other than the statistical power inherent in the technique.

Typically, researchers involved in the development of statistical risk-screening devices are confronted with data of unknown (but generally suspect) reliability. Chance or random variation can have quite different consequences given different methods of instrument development. Although little or no differential shrinkage is evident in table 3.3, it may be of interest to compare the relative power of the various devices given data of known degrees of *un*reliability.

Since the construction-sample data are known to have high reliability (of one sort, at any rate), this sample was chosen for study. In the first phase, 10 percent random error was introduced into the predictor item pool. That is, any given data element had a probability of 0.10 of being changed to some other—but still legitimate—coding category. Each prediction device was then "validated" on the resulting data set. This process was then repeated, except that the probability of change was increased to 0.30.

Table 3.4 displays these results (along with the original construction-sample findings). Not until we reach the highest "level" of perturbation (30 percent) do substantive conclusions change to any degree. Indeed, the striking result is the remarkable stability all devices demonstrate (again, with the exception of the association analyses). Although differences are small, the Burgess device performs better given the severely perturbed data set.

Whereas all devices discussed thus far may indeed result in the same degree of predictive utility, it may still be the case that the

Table 3.3. A Comparison of the Predictive Validity of Five Methods

Device (Method Used)†	Measure of Association*		Proportion of Outcome Variance Explained		Mean Cost Rating (MCR)	
	Construction Sample (N = 2,382)	Validation Sample (N = 1,004)	Construction Sample (N = 2,382)	Validation Sample (N = 1,004)	Construction Sample (N = 2,382)	Validation Sample (N = 1,004)
Burgess: 19 items	.345	.335	.119	.112	.408	.404
Multiple regression: Hierarchical inclusion: present offense variables, criminal history variables, institutional adjustment variables	.370	.362	.137	.131	.440	.436
Association Analysis: Eight terminal groups	.299	.279	.089	.078	.338	.328
Predictive Attribute Analysis: Eleven terminal groups	.364	.330	.132	.109	.429	.389
Multidimensional Contingency Table Analysis	.355	.339	.126	.115	.419	.394

*The measure of association used differed in accordance with characteristics of the method employed. The point-biserial correlation coefficient was used for the burgess analyses; R, the multiple correlation coefficient, was used for the regression analyses; and η, the coefficient of nonlinear correlation, was used for the remainder.
†All assessments are based on operationally collapsed instruments. See Gottfredson and Gottfredson (1979) for details.

Table 3.4. A Comparison of Five Prediction Methods Under Varifying Degrees of Known Reliability

Device (Method Used)†	Original Construction Sample (N = 2,382)		Construction Sample with 10% Random Error (N = 2,382)		Construction Sample with 30% Random Error (N = 2,382)	
	Association with Outcome (r or η)	MCR	Association with Outcome (r or η)	MCR	Association with Outcome (r or η)	MCR
Burgess: 19 items	.345	.408	.334	.395	.249	.295
Multiple Regression: Stepwise procedure	.370	.440	.339	.402	.222	.264
Association Analysis: Eight terminal groups	.299	.338	.247	.285	.145	.167
Predictive Attribute Analysis	.364	.429	.338	.399	.233	.273
Multidimensional Contingency Table Analysis	.335	.419	.338	.399	.224	.252

Note: See notes to table 3.3

different devices tend to classify the same individual differently. To investigate this issue, we examined the interrelations among the various devices themselves. Since some methods (the clustering and the log-linear methods) result in "predictions" that are typological only, we based these comparisons on the probability level associated with membership in a given strata (terminal cluster or cell for the clustering and log-linear models; grouped or collapsed probability levels for the Burgess and regression models) for each operational instrument (as opposed to the original equation or model developed).*

Table 3.5 presents the results of this investigation. With the exception of the association analysis (which performed substantially less powerfully in all analyses), interrelations of devices were quite high. In no case (again, with the exception of the association analysis) was less than 50 percent of the variance in one instrument accounted for by another, and the more typical proportion of the variance explained was of the order of 70–75 percent. Indeed, instruments developed using any of the three methods most commonly employed for such purposes (Burgess, multiple regression, and predictive attribute analysis) were all very highly intercorrelated. This could, of course, provide a very real practical and policy-relevant benefit, since it suggests that, by and large, each device would recommend a similar decision for the same person. Should this not prove the case, one could well imagine legal action alleging discriminatory treatment based on the properties of different statistical decisionmaking aids.

Conclusions, Limitations, and Recommendations

The conclusion to which all analyses lead is that given the types, level, and sophistication of available data and outcome criteria, no

*Analyses were repeated using odds ratios and log-odds ratios instead of the simple probabilities. All results were substantively identical.

Table 3.5. Intercorrelations of Five Prediction Instruments

	Burgess	Multiple Regression	Association Analysis	Predictive Attribute Analysis	Multidimensional Contingency Table Analysis
Burgess	—	.864 (.877)	.782 (.777)	.833 (.830)	.824 (.830)
Multiple Regression		—	.717 (.717)	.818 (.813)	.848 (.838)
Association Analysis			—	.736 (.745)	.640 (.645)
Predictive Attribute Analysis				—	.866 (.867)

Note: Values in parentheses are based on the 1972 validation sample.

one method for developing operationally useful statistical decision-making aids appears to provide a statistical advantage over the others considered. As mentioned earlier, with the exception of the association analysis, the analyses we report suggest that those who develop risk-screening devices for operational use would be advised to base their decisions as to which method(s) to employ on factors other than the statistical power inherent in the method.

Having made this proclamation, a few caveats are in order. First, it is the case that in some respects, the data used—while the best known to be available—may not be optimal for purposes of comparing the utility of different predictive methods. For example, with respect to the regression model, the data base includes few items having the requisite level of measurement (that is, interval or ratio), thus partially robbing the technique of power. With respect to the log-linear model, we were forced to limit the number of categories for any given variable to two, given the sizes of the samples available. This too could restrict the power (and hence potential benefits) of the method.

Second, the clustering methods employed are both divisive; one might well suspect that an agglomerative algorithm (which typically would make use of a substantially larger number of data items) could perform better.

Finally, as stressed early in this chapter, the criterion variable chosen for examination is critical. Studies of this type quite typically employ a criterion such as that decided upon here—that is, a simple dichotomous good/bad, success/failure measure. Such a decision has serious statistical implications. Restriction of range constrains coefficients of relation (Guilford, 1965). Further, one might well suggest that this particular range restriction is artificial—as it presumes that there are no degrees of success or failure. Given a more sophisticated outcome measure, our results could well have been different.

However, the points made earlier still obtain. If our purpose is the development of an operationally viable aid to practical decision-making, then the criteria that decisionmakers are willing to accept (and employ) may be those which should be employed.

Although improved methods of data collection and outcome measurement are needed, it nonetheless is important periodically to assess our progress given the current state of the art. One might well ask, then, "Does it matter which method is used?" Given the available evidence—from this study as well as from others cited earlier—the answer seems to be no. No clear statistical advantage is given by one method over another.

EVIDENCE AND VALUES RECONSIDERED

In interpreting the findings of the previous section, it is important that two points be remembered. First, all analyses performed were constrained to a greater or lesser degree by the available data. We therefore make no claim other than that, given the nature of the data and of the criteria typically available for parole prediction studies, the choice of prediction methods would seem to make little difference.

Second, empirical advantages may not be the only—nor even the primary—advantages that may accrue given use of different methods. For example, some methods may be easier to implement and operationalize simply because their procedures may be more readily understood by decisionmakers.

Finally, it should be remembered that the analyses presented focus only on the comparative power of prediction devices constructed using different statistical methods. As we have discussed, this is but one—and perhaps not even the most important—index of utility which could be considered. Indeed, it is in the assessment of practical, operational utility that issues of evidence and of values become paramount.

Consider table 3.6, which gives the multiple regression equation derived from the 18 variables (of the available set of 29) that contributed statistically significant increments to R when variables were free to enter in any order. The equation resulted in an R of .385, which shrank on validation to .356.

A common finding in multiple regression research is that little predictive power is provided by the inclusion of more than the first few variables in the equation. That is, the first few variables to enter the equation explain the bulk of the variance that the equation eventually will explain, and little additional predictive efficiency is gained by the inclusion of subsequent variables. Clearly, the first five or six variables account for the bulk of the explained variance in release outcome (table 3.6), and little useful information is gained from the use of the rest.

Note that the equation developed in table 3.6 includes variables only with respect to their statistical contribution to the prediction of recidivism. However, and as we argued earlier, the items one may wish to include in a risk-screening device may depend not only on the contribution to explained variance, but also on issues of data availability, law, and policy. Thus, for example, items reflecting institutional adjustment will not be available at the time of reception in prison; and (depending on the intended use of the device) issues of fairness and law may arise with respect to the justifiable use of information other than that concerning the offense and perhaps the prior criminal record (see Underwood, 1979). It is potentially of interest, therefore, to assess the viability of equations developed with regard to variable classifications.

Most of the variables included in this equation can be classified into four categories relating to the present offense, criminal history, social history, and institutional adjustment (see table 3.2). Of these four sets of variables, it seems unlikely that many would argue against the inclusion of variables pertaining to the present offense (that is, the offense for which the subject is presently incarcerated).

Table 3.6. Multiple Regression of Eighteen Predictor Variables on Release Outcome

Variable	Standardized Weight	R
Longest time free	−.1049	.269
Crime group	.0710	.318
Prison punishment	.0902	.336
Living arrangement	.0507	.349
Age at first arrest	−.0632	.356
Known use of synthetic and/or natural opiates	.0852	.362
Type of admission	.0352	.367
Prior commitments for auto theft	.0648	.370
Employment	.0364	.373
Escape	.0344	.375
Highest grade claimed	−.0375	.376
Commitment offense	−.0478	.378
Reason for first arrest	.0461	.380
Planned living arrangement	.0434	.381
Prior commitments for forgery	.0437	.382
Custody classification	.0295	.384
Prior commitments for burglary	.0281	.384
Prior parole/probation revocations	.0317	.385

Note: Outcome was defined as follows:

Favorable category
a) Continued on parole (no difficulty or sentences < 60 days) (N = 1,068),
b) No F.B.I. entry during follow-up period (N = 301),
c) Arrests, but no convictions or returns to prison noted (N = 146),
d) Parole or mandatory release violation, no return to prison (N = 15).

Unfavorable category
a) Any return to prison, or
b) Any conviction for any new offense, or
c) Death during the commission of a criminal act, or
d) Absconding from supervision.

An argument could be made, however, that consideration of criminal history variables may be inappropriate. Such an argument would likely invoke the concept of double jeopardy.

A still more powerful argument could arise over the inclusion of social history variables. Is it just, or legal, to consider variables such as a subject's sex or race in a paroling decision? Without much effort, the argument can readily be extended to variables such as marital status, educational level, or living arrangments. Other arguments can be made as well; Underwood (1979), for example, argues convincingly for a consideration of privacy of the information to be considered for inclusion in prediction devices.

Tables 3.7 and 3.8 summarize regression equations that attend to variable classifications in their development. Since few would argue that consideration of the present offense would be inappropriate, both variables concerning the present offense have been entered (simultaneously) as the first step in calculating both equations, resulting in a multiple R of .196.

Subsequent variable groups were included in the following manner (using table 3.7 as an example). A series of hierarchical stepwise regressions for each variable set was computed. In the first step, all *present offense* variables were entered. Steps 2 through *n* (where *n* exhausts the list of criminal history variables) allowed criminal history variables to enter, one at a time, until all variables in the *criminal history* group were exhausted. Variables that did not, through this inclusion, add significantly to the proportion of variance explained (R^2) were then excluded from the list of the criminal history variables.

In the next step (step *n* + 1), all present offense variables and the criminal history variables selected via the preceding process were

Table 3.7. Stepwise Multiple Regression: Present Offense, Criminal History, Social History, and Institutional Adjustment

Variable	Standardized Weight	R
Present Offense		
Type of admission	.0589	.196
Present offense	−.0468	
Criminal History		
Longest time free	−.1307	.335
Crime group	.1458	
Age at first arrest	−.0667	
Social History		
Opiate use	.0757	.356
Living arrangement	.0846	
Institutional Adjustment		
Prison punishment	.0988	.369
Validation Sample		.358

allowed to enter simultaneously. The analysis then proceeded to select from the subset of social history variables, and then from the institutional adjustment variables. Table 3.7 displays the final result of this process, and table 3.8 shows results from the same process with a different ordering of variable groups (present offense, followed by social history, followed by criminal history, followed by institutional adjustment).

Both equations result in the same degree of predictive efficiency, although they clearly use different variables (and use the different groups of variables differently). Further, both equations result in roughly the same degree of predictive power as that given in table 3.6, which uses many more items.

Comparison of tables 3.7 and 3.8 demonstrates that: (a) including criminal history variables before social history ones increases the multiple correlation coefficient R from 0.20 to 0.34, whereas (b) including social history before criminal history variables increases R from 0.20 to 0.30; and (c) including only five variables, two of which are related to the present offense and three of which are related to the criminal history, allows us to predict as well as does any other scheme. Thus, this technique allows, within limits, consideration of both the appropriateness of including variables of different types and their relative impacts on the resulting device.

Table 3.8.   Stepwise Multiple Regression: Present Offense, Social History, Criminal History, and Institutional Adjustment

Variable	Standardized Weight	R
Present Offense		
Type of admission	.0575	.196
Present offense	−.0528	
Social History		
Opiate use	.0764	.300
Planned living arrangement	.0765	
Employment	.0375	
Highest grade claimed	−.1213	
Longest job in free community	−.0414	
Criminal History		
Longest time free	−.1213	.362
Crime group	.1320	
Age at first arrest	−.0577	
Institutional Adjustment		
Prison punishment	.0950	.373
Validation Sample		.357

CONCLUSIONS

To what conclusions, then, are we led? We have observed that simpler and more easily understood and implemented statistical prediction devices may work as well as those based on more complex techniques. This may be expected to appeal to decisionmakers, who often are not well versed in the methods themselves. Further, devices constructed using a variety of statistical methods appear to be remarkably robust even when used on data sets of highly suspect reliability. We have also seen that, by and large, devices constructed using any of the most commonly used statistical methods tend to be highly intercorrelated. Again, this may be expected to provide a practical advantage, since it suggests that devices constructed using various methods would tend to provide a similar recommendation for a given individual.

Further, we have seen that predictor variables that may be most vulnerable to legal and ethical attack may actually add little to the statistical efficiency of devices designed to predict recidivism. Indeed, using only information relative to the instant and previous offenses, we were able to construct a recidivism prediction instrument that appeared (in our samples, at least) to be just as powerful as any others we were able to construct.

Social scientists involved in practical prediction problems have increasingly become aware of the ethical implications of their work (Monahan, 1980, provides an expanded discussion), and increasingly are called upon to demonstrate the sufficiency of their devices on other than simply statistical grounds. As we have seen, the consideration of policy and practice, as well as of method, can result in a device that not only is parsimonious, but also may be defended on statistical, ethical, and practical grounds.

ACKNOWLEDGMENTS

Portions of this research were conducted under a grant (AM-1) from the National Institute of Corrections, United States Department of Justice. Points of view or opinions stated in this paper are those of the authors and do not necessarily represent the official position or policies of the United States Department of Justice. Some portions of this discussion have appeared elsewhere (see Gottfredson and Gottfredson, 1979, 1980). We thank Paul J. Hofer for his valuable suggestions on our presentation.

REFERENCES

Ballard, K. B., Jr., and Gottfredson, D. M. (1963). *Predictive attribute analysis and prediction of parole performance.* Vacaville, CA: Institute for the Study of Crime and Delinquency.

Burgess, E. W. (1928). Factors determining success or failure on parole. In *The workings of the indeterminate sentence law and the parole system in Illinois*, ed. A. A. Bruce et al. Springfield, IL: Illinois State Board of Parole.

Cormack, R. M. (1971). A review of classification. *Journal of the Royal Statistical Society Series* A 134: 321-53.

Dawes, R. (1971). A case study of graduate admissions: Application of three principles of human decision making. *American Psychologist* 26: 180-88.

Dawes, R. M., and Corrigan, B. (1974). Linear models in decision making. *Psychological Bulletin* 81: 95-106.

Glaser, D. (1955). The efficacy of alternative aproaches to parole prediction. *American Sociological Review*, 20: 283-87.

――― (1964). *The effectiveness of a prison and parole system*. New York: Bobbs-Merrill.

Goodman, L. A. (1970). The multivariate analysis of qualitative data: Interactions among multiple classifications. *Journal of the American Statistical Association* 65: 226-65.

――― (1971). The analysis of multi-dimensional contingency tables: Stepwise procedures and direct estimation methods for building models for multiple classifications. *Technometrics* 13: 33-61.

Gottfredson, D. M. (1975). *Decision-making in the criminal justice system: Reviews and essays*. Washington, DC: U. S. Government Printing Office.

Gottfredson, D. M., and Ballard, K. B., Jr. (1965). *The validity of two parole prediction scales: An eight year follow-up study*. Vacaville, CA: Institute for the Study of Crime and Delinquency.

Gottfredson, D. M.; Ballard, K. B., Jr.; and Lane, L. (1965). *Association analysis in a prison sample and prediction of parole performance*. Vacaville, CA: Institute for the Study of Crime and Delinquency.

Gottfredson, D. M.; Wilkins, L. T.; and Hoffman, P. B. (1978). *Guidelines for parole and sentencing*. Lexington, MA: Lexington Books.

Gottfredson, D. M.; Wilkins, L. T.; Hoffman, P. B.; and Singer, S. M. (1974). *The utilization of experience in parole decision making: Summary report*. Washington, DC: U. S. Government Printing Office.

Gottfredson, S. D., and Gottfredson, D. M. (1979). *Screening for risk: A comparison of methods*. Washington, DC: U. S. Government Printing Office.

――― (1980). Screening for risk. *Criminal Justice and Behavior* 7:315-30.

Gough, H. G. (1962). Clinical versus statistical prediction in psychology. In *Psychology in the making*, ed. L. Postman. New York: Knopf.

Guilford, J. P. (1965). *Fundamental statistics in psychology and education*. New York: McGraw-Hill.

Johnson, S. C. (1967). Hierarchical clustering schemes. *Psychometrika* 32: 241-54.

Lance, G. N. and Williams, W. T. (1966). Computer programs for nomothetic classification. *Computer Journal*, 9: 246-49.

Mannheim, H., and Wilkins, L. T. (1955). *Prediction methods in relation to borstal training*. London: Her Majesty's Stationery Office.

Meehl, P. E. (1954). *Clinical versus statistical prediction*. Minneapolis: University of Minnesota Press.

Monahan, J., ed. (1980). *Who is the client? The ethics of psychological intervention in the criminal justice system.* Washington, DC: American Psychological Association.

Mosteller, F. (1977). Assessing unknown numbers. In *Statistics and public policy,* ed. W. Fairley and F. Mosteller. Reading, MA: Addison-Wesley.

Ohlin, L. (1951). *Selection for parole.* New York: Russell Sage Foundation.

O'Leary, V.; Gottfredson, M.; and Gelman, A. (1975). Contemporary sentencing proposals. *Criminal Law Bulletin* 11: 555–86.

Simon, F. (1971). *Prediction methods in criminology.* London: Her Majesty's Stationery Office.

Solomon, H. (1976). Parole outcome: A multidimensional contingency table analysis. *Journal of Research in Crime and Delinquency* 13: 107–26.

Underwood, B. D. (1979). Law and the crystal ball: Predicting behavior with statistical inference and individualized judgment. *Yale Law Journal* 88: 1408–48.

Van Alstyne, J., and Gottfredson, M. (1978). A multidimensional contingency table analysis of parole outcome: New methods and old problems in criminological prediction. *Journal of Research in Crime and Delinquency* 15: 172–93.

Wainer, H. (1976). Estimating coefficients in linear models: It don't make no nevermind. *Psychological Bulletin* 83: 213–17.

Williams, W. T., and Lambert, J. M. (1959). Multivariate methods in plant ecology I: Association analysis in plant communities. *Journal of Plant Ecology* 47: 83–101.

——— (1961). Multivariate methods in plant ecology, II: The use of an electronic digital computer for association analysis. *Journal of Plant Ecology* 49: 717–29.

CHAPTER 4

Predicting Failure on Parole

WILLIAM L. WILBANKS

SUMMARY

The aim of this chapter is to compare the predictive efficiency of five parole prediction methods (Burgess, Glueck, multiple regression, association analysis, and predictive attribute analysis). In order to form construction and validation samples, 854 men released on parole from the Texas Department of Corrections were randomly divided into two groups of 427. Since 142 parolees in the construction sample were successful on parole, each technique was designed to predict about 142 successes. According to the criterion of the number of correct predictions, multiple regression and predictive attribute analysis were the best techniques in the construction sample. However, the Glueck method was the best in the validation sample. The Burgess and Glueck methods did not experience any shrinkage, and they were also least affected by the introduction of random error ("noise") into the data.

INTRODUCTION

For more than five decades (since Burgess, 1928), social scientists have been involved in efforts to predict parole performance. Their general procedure has been very much like that of a life insurance statistician who estimates the risk of death for persons with varying demographic profiles. Analogously, the parole actuary calculates the relative frequency of parole failure for selected categories of parolees and projects these rates into the future (Schuessler, 1954). In other words, parole prediction studies attempt to record human experiences in some systematic form so as to utilize them for predicting future conduct. The results of this procedure are usually presented in simple expectancy tables. Hakeem (1945, p. 36) defines parole prediction as "an organization and scoring of social data in such a way as to determine the parole risk of subjects on the basis of experience with similar subjects and in terms of the same social data. Essentially it is an actuarial method."

The half-century covered by this research movement has been devoted largely to a search for factors that accurately predict success or failure on parole and to the discovery of techniques that best organize and score those factors for maximum predictive efficiency. Although this chapter will be concerned primarily with the development of the techniques with which certain factors are organized and scored, some attention will necessarily be given to the nature of the items included as predictive factors. The following types of items, in addition to the more common background data such as offense, number of arrests, age, and race, are suggested as important by researchers:

1. changing attitudes while in prison (Laune, 1936);
2. sociological classifications such as "conventional," "respected citizen," "socially maladjusted," and the like (Glaser, 1955);
3. psychological traits (Glaser, 1955); and
4. release plan, employment record, and whether the person completed high school (Solomon, 1976).

The main aim of this chapter is to investigate the relative predictive efficiency of five prediction techniques. In the past, most predictive efforts have been limited to one or two techniques, and thus the relative predictive power of different techniques utilizing the same data has rarely been tested. Much of the prior literature denigrates the use of simple weighting scales such as those developed by Burgess and the Gluecks and advocates the use of multivariate techniques such as multiple regression, association analysis, predictive attribute analysis, and multidimensional contingency table analysis, since these more sophisticated mathematical techniques are thought to be more efficient predictors. However, the assumption of greater predictive power of the multivariate techniques over the simpler weighting schemes is largely unproved.

Some studies (for example, Ohlin and Lawrence, 1952) have demonstrated that there is considerable shrinkage in predictive power from the construction to the validation sample, whereas others (Hakeem, 1945; Hoffman and Beck, 1976; Robuck, 1976) have found little or no shrinkage. Several studies have found that the simpler techniques maintain their predictive power from the construction to the validation sample, while others (for example, Gottfredson and Ballard, 1964; Grygier, Blum, and Porebski, 1971) found that the shrinkage was greater for the more sophisticated techniques. Van Alstyne and Gottfredson (1978) found that their multidimensional contingency table analysis was no more efficient than the more parsimonious Burgess method in either the construction or the validation sample.

The recent literature in parole prediction does not pay much attention to the relative efficiency of different prediction techniques. Although some studies have attempted to develop more sophisticated methods (for example, Solomon, 1976; Van Alstyne and Gottfredson, 1978; Fuchs and Flanagan, 1980), there has been little effort to compare the predictive power of various techniques in both the construction and validation samples. One alleged overview of the problems inherent in using prediction tables in parole decisions (Underwood, 1979) completely ignores the choice of predictive technique and concentrates on the type of predictors chosen.

THE PRESENT STUDY

As already stated, the major aim of the present study was to compare the predictive efficiency of five parole prediction methods in both construction and validation samples. The techniques of Burgess (1928) and the Gluecks (1930, 1960) were chosen for their historical importance and because there is some evidence that they are as efficient in prediction as more sophisticated techniques. Also, the Burgess technique is essentially that utilized by the United States Board of Parole (Hoffman and Beck, 1976). Multiple regression was chosen since it is a commonly used predictive device (Grygier, 1970). Predictive attribute analysis (Wilkins and MacNaughton-Smith, 1970) and association analysis (Wilkins and MacNaughton-Smith, 1970; Gottfredson and Ballard, 1964) were chosen since they were considered superior by critics of the other three techniques.

In order to compare the five techniques on predictive efficiency for construction and validation samples, it was necessary to develop a uniform method of counting errors so that the techniques would have the same basis of comparison. After considering various alternatives, it was decided that each technique would predict every subject as either a success or a failure in both the construction and the validation samples. Parolees who were mispredicted by a technique (predicted failures who actually succeeded on parole and predicted successes who actually failed on parole) would be counted as errors. No judgment was made as to whether it was worse to mispredict failures as successes or successes as failures. The total of both types of errors was taken for each technique.

The Sample

The data used in this study consisted of information on 854 parolees released on parole from the Texas Department of

Corrections. The information on each parolee consisted of 84 variables dealing with his social, educational, and criminal history. In addition, the parole performance of each parolee was available. Successes were those parolees who were not rearrested for felonies or reincarcerated as technical violators of parole within five years. In order to reduce the 84 variables to a more manageable number of predictors, a subset of variables was selected. To be included in this subset, a variable had to show some correlation with the criterion or to have been a useful predictor of parole outcome in prior research. This procedure resulted in 20 variables being selected for inclusion (see table 4.1). The variables eliminated were only trivially related to the dependent variable and not found to be significant predictors in past research.

In order to create construction and validation samples, the 854 parolees were randomly split into two groups of 427, and one group

Table 4.1. The Subset of Twenty Predictor Variables

Variable*	r†	Mean	S.D.	Range
1. Age	−.301	29.6	10.5	17–75
2. Counts for current offense	−.090	2.0	2.2	1–40
3. Maximum sentence in years	−.325	15.4	25.3	2–99
4. Times in prison	−.053	.4	.9	0–13
5. Age at first offense	−.229	17.6	5.8	8–59
6. Felony convictions	.026	2.5	2.1	0–21
7. Misdemeanor convictions	.157	4.1	6.1	0–55
8. Sex offenses	−.136	.1	.3	0–5
9. Narcotic offenses	−.111	.1	.5	0–6
10. Times on probation	.314	.7	.6	0–5
11. Violated probation or parole	.187	.5	.6	0–4
12. Codefendants	−.108	.9	1.2	0–7
13. Use of narcotics	.047	—	—	No = 85% Yes = 15%
14. Employment history	.155	—	—	Regular = 37% Irregular or Unknown = 63%
15. Marital failures	−.140	.7	.9	0–5
16. Prison punishments	−.098	.9	1.9	0–18
17. Points In Progress score, or PIP (prison merit system)	−.256	126.9	40.0	0–800
18. Education Achievement score (EA)	.098	65.3	28.2	0–120
19. I.Q. Score	.297	73.4	32.0	0–127
20. Academic achievement in prison	.045			Yes = 29% No = 71%

*The dependent variable is parole outcome: successes = 33.3%; failures = 66.7% (technical violators = 34.2%, felony violators = 32.5%).
†This is the Pearson product-moment correlation coefficient. A positive sign indicates that the likelihood of failure on parole increases as the value of the predictor variable increases.

was randomly designated the construction sample. Since 142 parolees in the construction sample were successful on parole, one constraint was placed on each technique with respect to the counting of errors. Each technique was constructed so as to predict 142 successes (or as close to that figure as the technique would allow). This constraint was imposed due to the greater difficulty of predicting successes (being less common than failures) and since in predicting the performance of parolees in the validation sample the best guess as to the success rate would be that of parolees in the construction sample.

Table 4.1 suggests (on the basis of the magnitude of the Pearson r values) that the best overall predictor of parole success/failure was variable 3, maximum sentence in years, with an $r = -0.325$. Since parole success was coded as 1 and failure as 2 the $r = -0.325$ indicates that longer sentences were associated with success. Likewise, the second-best predictor (number of times on probation) suggests that the more times an offender had been on probation, the more likely he was to fail on parole.

The Burgess Technique

The 20 factors described in table 4.1 were used in developing a Burgess score for each subject in the construction and validation samples. Each of the 20 predictors was divided as nearly as possible at the median into two categories. For each variable, if the parolee in question fell into the category associated with parole success, he was given a score of +1, and if he fell into the category associated with parole failure, he was given a score of 0.

The Burgess scores for all subjects were then cross-tabulated with the parole outcomes for the same subjects. Thus, 21 (0 to 20) Burgess scores were cross-tabulated with parole outcome (success or failure). Associated with each possible Burgess score in the construction sample was a certain proportion of successes and failures.

Since a requirement for all of the techniques in the present study was that 142 predictions of success were to be made in both samples, it was necessary to decide which individuals should be so predicted. The Burgess scale is shown for both construction and validation samples in table 4.2. Since the individuals with the highest success rates are at the upper end of the scale, the persons to be predicted as successes should come from that end of the scale. Since 142 successes are needed, I simply counted down the column indicating the number of persons in each score interval (the "N" column) until at least 142 cases were found. Table 4.2 indicates that 150 cases were found in the intervals between 10 and 20.

Table 4.2   Burgess Scores in the Two Samples

Construction Sample				Validation Sample			
Score	N	S	Success Rate	Score	N	S	Success Rate
20	0			20	0		
19	0			19	0		
18	0			18	0		
17	0			17	0		
16	0			16	2	1	50.0%
15	2	2	100.0%	15	4	3	75.0%
14	7	5	71.4%	14	2	2	100.0%
13	25	20	80.0%	13	24	19	79.2%
12	34	24	70.6%	12	36	23	63.9%
11	30	18	60.0%	11	39	26	66.7%
10	52	23	44.2%	10	37	19	51.4%
Total	150	92		Total	144	93	
9	56	19	34.5%	9	49	15	30.6%
8	50	14	28.0%	8	68	12	17.6%
7	55	9	16.4%	7	56	9	16.1%
6	48	2	4.2%	6	54	6	11.1%
5	30	2	6.7%	5	30	4	13.3%
4	26	3	11.5%	4	21	2	9.5%
3	11	1	9.1%	3	5	1	20.0%
2	1	0	0.0%	2	0	0	0.0%
1	0			1	0		
Total	277	50		Total	283	49	

Note: S = number of successes.

Thus a line, or cut-off point, was drawn between intervals 9 and 10. Everyone above that cut-off point was predicted to be a success and everyone below it a failure. This cut-off point was also used for the validation sample, since the purpose of the "experience table" is to predict success or failure in a validation sample.

The number of errors in prediction made by this technique can easily be obtained from table 4.2. This table indicates that 92 successes (the "S" column above the cut-off line) and 227 failures (the 277 subjects below the cut-off line minus the 50 successes below it) were correctly predicted in the construction sample. Thus 319 correct predictions were made in the construction sample while 108 errors (427 - 319) were made. Table 4.2 indicates that 58 persons (150 - 92) were predicted as successes when in fact they were failures while 50 were predicted to be failures and were in fact successful.

When the procedure described above was followed in counting errors in the validation sample, 100 were found; 51 persons were incorrectly predicted as successes and 49 as failures.

The Glueck Method

The Glueck technique is similar to that of Burgess except that the Glueck technique allows for more precise weighting, in that each attribute or dichotomized variable is given a weight equal to the percentage of offenders who failed on parole with that attribute. The total score for each parolee is the sum of these percentages (depending on which category of each attribute he falls in) across the 20 predictors. The lowest total Glueck score obtained for an individual parolee was 1,144.2, while the highest was 1,457.7. Following the Glueck procedure, total scores were divided into intervals. Information is given in table 4.3 regarding the number of persons whose scores lie within each of the intervals (column "N"), the number of successes in the interval (column "S"), and the success rate for the interval.

Since the highest success rates are at the upper end of the scale and since 142 successes are needed, again I counted down the "N" column until at least 142 successes were found. Table 4.3 indicates that 146 cases were found in the construction sample in the top three intervals. Thus a cut-off line was drawn below the third interval. Again, everyone above that cut-off point was predicted to be a success and everyone below it a failure.

The number of prediction errors obtained in the two samples can be easily obtained from table 4.3. This table indicates that 94 successes and 233 failures (281 - 48) were correctly predicted in the construction sample while 48 successes and 52 failures were incorrectly predicted. Thus a total of 100 errors in prediction (48 + 52) were made in the construction sample. A similar procedure showed 97 errors in prediction in the validation sample.

Multiple Regression

The multiple regression technique weights each variable in the predictive battery according to its relative contribution to the

Table 4.3 Glueck Scores in the Two Samples

Construction Sample				Validation Sample			
Interval	N	S	Success Rate	Interval	N	S	Success Rate
1	45	37	82.2%	1	47	37	78.7%
2	52	36	69.2%	2	50	31	60.8%
3	49	21	42.9%	3	50	28	56.0%
Total	146	94		Total	147	96	
4	23	9	39.1%	4	17	4	23.5%
5	76	21	27.6%	5	86	22	25.6%
6	57	5	8.8%	6	49	5	10.2%
7	62	9	14.5%	7	55	5	9.1%
8	37	2	5.4%	8	62	9	14.5%
9	26	2	7.7%	9	11	1	9.1%
Total	281	48		Total	280	46	

Note: S = number of successes.

explained variance in parole outcome when the effects of other predictors in the equation are statistically controlled. The weighting by this technique is more precise than that of the Burgess and Glueck techniques and takes into account the correlations among predictors (which the latter techniques fail to do). The calculation of the multiple regression score for each subject involves multiplying the multiple regression weight by the individual's score on each variable (for example, age) and summing these products across all predictors.

The 427 cases in the construction sample were ranked according to their total multiple regression scores. Since 142 successes were needed, a cut-off line was drawn between cases 142 and 143 on the list of ranked scores. Then, just as for the previous techniques, all subjects falling above that line were predicted as successes and all falling below it as failures. Table 4.4 summarizes the relation between parole outcome and scores falling above and below the cut-off line. For the construction sample, 48 successes and 48 failures were incorrectly predicted by the multiple regression technique, for a total of 96 errors. In the validation sample, 50 successes and 50 failures were incorrectly predicted, for a total of 100 errors.

Association Analysis

Association analysis is a technique that generates an empirical typology of offenders based on the possession (or not) of groups of attributes. Though this classification process is basically descriptive rather than predictive, it can be utilized in prediction if the

Table 4.4   Results of Multiple Regression Analysis

Variable	Regression Coefficient	Variable	Regression Coefficient
1	−.00273	11	.04660
2	−.04600	12	−.04779
3	−.00277	13	.05327
4	−.01030	14	.10723
5	−.00894	15	−.02797
6	.03818	16	.00660
7	.00848	17	−.00249
8	−.09499	18	−.00098
9	−.10845	19	.00238
10	.06791	20	−.03653
		Constant	.19414

Construction Sample			Validation Sample		
	P.S.*	P.F.†		P.S.*	P.F.†
Ranked Scores	1–142	143–427	Ranked Scores	1–142	143–427
Success	94	48	Success	92	50
Failure	48	237	Failure	50	235
Total of 96 errors			Total of 100 errors		

*P.S. indicates predicted successes.
†P.F. indicates predicted failures.

contrasting homogeneous groups of individuals isolated by the method have significantly different outcome probabilities.

The technique involves a hierarchical design. At each stage one or more groups are divided into subgroups on the basis of the possession (or not) of a particular attribute. The attribute chosen as the "divider" is that which maximizes the homogeneity within the resulting subgroups. The underlying idea behind this method is to classify a large population of subjects into subgroups so that the "end groups" of the hierarchical process are homogeneous. Furthermore, the intent is to maximize the similarities *within* the end groups and the contrasts *between* them.

This dividing or branching process is continued until predetermined rules indicate that no further divisions should be made. For this study each of the 20 variables was dichotomized as near the median as possible, so that any division would result in approximately equal subgroups.

First, a matrix of Pearson product-moment correlation coefficients was obtained, which indicated the correlation between each of the 20 variables and each of the other 19. In the next step of association analysis, the 19 coefficients of each variable with every other variable were then summed and divided by 19 to obtain an average correlation coefficient for that particular variable.

Second, the entire construction sample was then divided on the basis of the variable (age) with the largest average coefficient. Thus, splitting the initial group on age maximized the homogeneity within the two resulting subgroups. Third, each of the two subgroups produced by the splitting process was in turn split again in the same way. This splitting process continued until either of two rules indicated that the process should cease in a particular branch. One rule required the dividing process to cease when a subgroup to be split had less than 30 cases, since smaller end groups would be less stable with respect to success rates. The other rule required the process to cease if the subgroup had a success rate of either 0 or 100 percent, since further division would not produce subgroups with differing success rates.

When the final end groups ($N = 25$) had been determined, the success rates of each were calculated. The success rates ranged from 0 (for the 9 inmates who were over 26 years old, had two or more felony convictions, had been on probation, had not been disciplined in prison, and had a history of drug use) to 83 percent (for the 24 inmates who were over 26 years old, had less than one felony conviction, had not violated probation, had no narcotic history, had been over 18 at first offense, and had an educational achievement score of 50 or more). The 25 end groups were ranked in terms of their success rates to develop the scale for the construction sample. Once the association analysis end groups were in the form of a scale it became possible simply to count down the scale (the ranked end groups) until a number as near as possible to 142 was reached. Table 4.5 indicates that the cut-off line was drawn for both samples between groups 20 and 12.

The procedure for counting errors that was followed for the first three techniques was then employed. In the construction sample, 57 successes and 53 failures were incorrectly predicted, for a total of 110 errors. In the validation sample, 50 successes and 68 failures were incorrectly predicted, for a total of 118 errors.

Predictive Attribute Analysis

Predictive attribute analysis is very similar to association analysis in procedure and final appearance (the "tree" design). The central difference between the two is that in predictive attribute

Table 4.5 Results of Association Analysis

Construction Sample				Validation Sample			
Group	N	S	Success Rate	Group	N	S	Success Rate
22	24	20	83.3%	22	16	11	68.8%
23	11	8	72.7%	23	21	14	66.7%
13	10	7	70.0%	13	5	1	20.0%
21	9	6	66.7%	21	15	13	86.7%
24	3	2	66.7%	24	2	2	100.0%
14	10	6	60.0%	14	19	9	47.4%
15	23	13	56.5%	15	21	13	61.9%
10	15	8	53.3%	10	11	8	72.7%
16	8	4	50.0%	16	12	6	50.0%
20	25	11	44.0%	20	38	15	39.5%
Total	138	85		Total	160	92	
12	20	8	40.0%	12	16	7	43.8%
2	10	4	40.0%	2	7	1	14.3%
11	25	9	36.0%	11	31	10	32.3%
17	23	6	26.1%	17	9	3	33.3%
25	28	7	25.0%	25	27	6	22.2%
18	25	5	20.0%	18	25	4	16.0%
6	17	3	17.7%	6	21	5	23.8%
8	12	2	16.7%	8	16	0	0.0%
1	25	4	16.0%	1	16	5	31.5%
5	14	2	14.3%	5	14	0	0.0%
3	18	2	11.1%	3	10	0	0.0%
7	20	2	10.0%	7	18	2	11.1%
4	27	2	7.4%	4	32	6	18.8%
9	16	1	6.3%	9	18	0	0.0%
19	9	0	0.0%	19	7	1	14.3%
Total	289	57		Total	267	50	

Note: S = number of successes.

analysis the groups are split on the basis of which variable has the strongest association to the *dependent* variable.

The predictive attribute analysis procedure is relatively simple. Cross-tabulations of each of the 20 independent variables with the dependent variable were obtained. The independent variables were dichotomized at the same points used in the association analysis. Thus, 20 two-by-two tables were obtained.

The next step involved computing a measure of association between the independent variables and the dependent variables. Goodman and Kruskal's τ^* was used because it measured the relative decrease in the number of mistakes in predicting a dependent variable when the categories of an independent variable are known. Thus, the independent variable (maximum sentence) that resulted in the greatest decrease in the number of prediction errors in the dependent variable was chosen as that on which all the subjects in the construction sample were split.

As in association analysis, the two resulting subgroups from the original split were then split again on the same basis. This splitting process continued until certain predetermined rules indicated that it should stop. As before, the rules adopted were that the procedure would cease in a particular branch when the number of cases in a subgroup was less than 30 or when the success rate of the subgroup was either 0 or 100 percent.

When the final end groups (*N* = 25) were determined, the success rate of each was calculated. The success rates ranged from 0 percent for 4 groups to 100 percent (for the 15 inmates who were over 26 years old and had a sentence greater than 6 years, less than 2 felony convictions, an IQ of 75 or less, and no punishment record while in prison). The 25 end groups were ranked in terms of their success rates to develop the scale (see table 4.6) for the construction sample. A cutoff line was drawn at the point on the scale where about 142 cases were above the line (and thus were predicted as successes). This line was also applied to the validation sample, since the scale of the construction sample is intended as a prediction scale for the validation sample.

Table 4.6 indicates that 141 cases were predicted to be successes in the construction sample and 157 in the validation sample. In the construction sample, 43 successes and 42 failures were incorrectly predicted, for a total of 85 errors. In the validation sample, 49 successes and 64 failures were incorrectly predicted, for a total of 113 errors.

---

*τ here is not the same as Kendall's τ referred to in Chapter 1. See Table 4.7 for the definition of Goodman and Kruskal's τ used here.

Table 4.6   Results of Predictive Attribute Analysis

Construction Sample				Validation Sample			
Group	N	S	Success Rate	Group	N	S	Success Rate
3	15	15	100.0%	3	12	12	100.0%
9	14	13	92.9%	9	21	12	51.1%
2	15	12	80.0%	2	13	11	84.6%
12	13	10	76.9%	12	19	10	52.6%
14	16	11	68.8%	14	17	9	52.9%
4	9	6	66.7%	4	18	12	66.7%
5	16	9	56.3%	5	12	5	41.7%
8	16	9	56.3%	8	16	11	68.8%
1	15	8	53.5%	1	10	7	70.0%
20	12	6	50.0%	20	19	4	21.1%
Total	141	99		Total	157	93	
11	26	11	42.3%	11	24	11	45.8%
16	12	5	41.7%	16	15	1	6.7%
6	22	8	36.4%	6	20	7	35.0%
13	14	3	21.4%	13	10	4	40.0%
17	17	3	17.6%	17	11	4	36.4%
25	25	4	16.0%	25	28	4	14.3%
21	27	4	14.8%	21	28	4	14.3%
19	9	1	11.1%	19	11	3	27.3%
15	28	2	7.1%	15	24	3	12.5%
7	16	1	6.3%	7	12	3	25.0%
22	16	1	6.3%	22	11	0	0.0%
10	4	0	0.0%	10	6	0	0.0%
24	13	0	0.0%	24	17	3	17.6%
18	21	0	0.0%	18	21	1	4.8%
23	36	0	0.0%	23	32	1	3.1%
Total	286	43		Total	270	49	

Note: S = number of successes.

COMPARING THE RESULTS

Evidence of the efficiency of a predictive technique does not lie in an examination of its theoretical and statistical underpinnings but in its ability to predict accurately. Table 4.7 summarizes the errors made in the construction and validation samples with each of the five methods. Note that in the construction sample the more sophisticated predictive methods—predictive attribute analysis and multiple regression analysis—were the most efficient. However, in the validation sample the efficiency ranking (in terms of τ) was very different from that found in the construction sample. In the closest approximation to "true" prediction (in the validation sample), the much criticized method of the Gluecks was the most efficient, followed by the Burgess method and multiple regression. Predictive attribute analysis dropped from first in the construction sample to fourth in the validation sample.

Table 4.7   Relative Predictive Efficiency of Five Prediction Techniques

	Construction Sample			Validation Sample		
	Predicted		Number	Predicted		Number
	Success	Failure	of Errors	Success	Failure	of Errors
Burgess Method						
Actual success	92	50		93	49	
Actual failure	58	227		51	234	
τ_i		.24	108		.30	100
Glueck Method						
Actual success	94	48		96	46	
Actual failure	52	233		51	234	
τ		.30	100		.32	97
Multiple Regression						
Actual success	94	48		92	50	
Actual failure	48	237		50	235	
τ		.32	96		.30	100
Association Analysis						
Actual success	85	57		92	50	
Actual failure	53	232		68	217	
τ		.23	110		.17	118
Predictive Attribute Analysis						
Actual success	99	43		93	49	
Actual failure	42	243		64	221	
τ		.40	85		.20	113

Note: τ = proportional reduction in error using the predictive technique. For example, the Burgess method made 108 errors in the construction sample, compared with 142 errors that would be made if all parolees were predicted as failures. Thus,
$$\tau = \frac{142 - 108}{142} = .24.$$

In short, it appears that the more sophisticated statistical methods make worse predictors of parole outcome than do the less complex methods. It also appears that, although "shrinkage" from the construction to the validation sample would be expected in all methods, such shrinkage was greater with the more sophisticated techniques. It seems that the more "information" is extracted from the construction sample, the less powerful it is when used to make statements about a follow-up sample. As Wilkins (1971) says:

In general the less efficient the methods of prediction table construction the less powerful in regard to the "construction" sample, but there is little or no loss when these are used for the validation sample. On the other hand, the more efficient methods show better results with the construction sample, but they lose so much in shrinkage that they end up worse as guides to predictive or classificatory statements than do the inefficient methods.

Table 4.7 also indicates that two of the techniques, those of Burgess and the Gluecks, did not experience any shrinkage from the construction to the validation sample. If anything, fewer errors in prediction were made by both methods in the validation sample than in the construction sample. This is unlikely to be found as a general rule.

An attempt was made to determine which method, if any, was significantly better in eliminating certain types of errors. There was little difference among the techniques in respect to the two types of errors: failures predicted as successes and successes predicted as failures. All five techniques divided their errors about equally between the two types, although in the validation sample predictive attribute analysis and association analysis were more prone to predict failures as successes than the reverse. However, this tendency was not significant in either case at the 0.05 level (using the χ^2 test of independence with one degree of freedom). Therefore, it cannot be concluded that there is an association between type of error and predictive technique. Any tendency for a particular type of error is partly a function of the percentage of parolees who are successes. If the success rate of the general prison population were more extreme than 33 percent (for example, 5 or 95 percent), differences in type-I or type-II errors might occur. It is more difficult to predict a rare event, and one or more of the five techniques might be more efficient at this task.

An analysis was also carried out to determine which of the five predictive techniques were most similar. The Glueck and Burgess methods agreed in their predictions as successes or failures in 394 of the 427 cases (92.3 percent) and were more similar than any other two methods. The fewest agreements between any two methods were the 313 (73.3 percent) between association analysis and multiple regression. It should be noted that this range of percentage agreement among the methods was greater than the relatively small range of agreement (72.5–77.3 percent) between each of the five techniques and the actual parole outcome for the validation sample. Thus, although there was a range of 97–118 in the number of errors in prediction for the five techniques, the difference in the percentage agreement with parole outcome between the best and worst methods was only 4.9 percent.

Overall there was a great deal of agreement among the five methods. In the validation sample 234 subjects were correctly predicted as failures by at least four of the five methods. Likewise, 80 subjects were correctly predicted as successes by at least four of the methods. On the other hand, 33 subjects who failed on parole and 30 who succeeded were incorrectly predicted by at least four of the five methods. Thus, 88 percent of the subjects in the validation sample were similarly predicted (either correctly or incorrectly) by at least four of the five predictive techniques.

An effort was also made in this study to go beyond summary

statements of the relative efficiency of each of the five techniques. A stepwise regression was employed with actual parole outcome as the dependent variable and the five predictions (from each of the techniques) as the independent variables. The Glueck method alone accounted for 24 percent of the variance in parole performance, while the five methods together accounted for 33 percent of this variance. The variance explained by the five methods together was almost exactly equal to the 33 percent of the variance explained when the 20 variables were used as independent variables and parole outcome was used as the dependent variable. Thus it would seem that all five methods combined used all of the information contained in the 20 variables that accounted for variance in parole outcome (further evidence for this conclusion is given in the following paragraphs). The remaining 67 percent of the variance cannot be accounted for by the 20 predictors used in this study.

One possible test to determine if the predictive techniques were making full use of the predictive potential of the 20 variables involves the computation of a t-test between the means of similarly predicted cases whose actual outcomes were different. In other words, if all the information having predictive utility and contained in the 20 variables is used, there should be no significant differences between the means of failures correctly predicted and of successes incorrectly predicted (since both were predicted to be failures). Likewise, there should be no significant differences between the means of successes correctly predicted and failures incorrectly predicted. Of 40 t-tests, four were found to be significant at the 0.05 level. If these t-tests were independent—and, of course, they are not—two would be expected to be significant by chance alone. Thus it appears that the techniques in combination use virtually all the information in the data.

Finally, at the suggestion of Leslie Wilkins, the effect of introducing "noise" (random error) into the data set was investigated. This was accomplished by generating "dummy subjects" for whom scores on all variables were randomly and independently created. Such dummy subjects were then used as replacements for a 10 percent random selection of subjects of our total sample of 854. When the predictive techniques of Burgess, the Gluecks, and multiple regression were applied to the data with noise, all three methods (as expected) produced more errors than when used with the original (no-noise) subjects. Further, whereas multiple regression showed substantial shrinkage from the construction to the validation samples (10 percent more errors) and the Glueck method showed a little shrinkage (3 percent), the Burgess method once again showed *fewer* errors (9 percent) in the validation than in the construction sample. These results suggest that errors contributing to noise in actual parole prediction studies—clerical errors, poor records, errors in interpreting information in files, keypunching errors, and the like—would be expected to have the greatest effect on the methods that make the most demands on the data.

CONCLUSIONS

The present study used construction and validation samples that, taken together, originally comprised a single cohort. It seems likely that, in parole prediction studies where there is temporal separation between the construction and validation samples, more errors in prediction will be made. How this will affect the relative efficiency of the predictive methods examined herein is unknown. It should also be noted that, if the success rate were different from that in the present study (33 percent), the relative predictive efficiency of the methods studied in this research may also be different. Thus, future research should examine the predictive efficiency of such techniques both when the distribution of the dependent variable is more skewed (say, 5 percent versus 95 percent) and when it is less skewed (50 percent versus 50 percent).

The relative predictive efficiency of the various techniques are likely, in a very general sense, to depend on the data. For example, when the data are more reliable, those methods which make most demands on the data might be expected to fare better. Several factors make it imprudent to generalize our results to data sets with very different characteristics. Also, it should be noted that, in order to compare the methods, some compromises had to be made. For example, exactly the same number of successes could not be predicted by each method and errors were counted in terms of a simple dichotomy.

With these limitations in mind, the results indicate that in our data the simpler techniques of Burgess and the Gluecks are just as efficient as—or even more efficient than—the more complex methods of multiple regression, predictive attribute analysis, and association analysis. The Burgess technique was also found to be superior to multiple regression when the data contained noise. Because data in criminal justice are notoriously noisy, researchers should be cautious about using techniques that make heavy demands on the quality of the data.

REFERENCES

Burgess, E. W. (1928). Factors determining success or failure on parole. In *The workings of the interminate sentence law and the parole system in Illinois*, ed. A.

A. Bruce, A. J. Harno, E. W. Burgess, and J. Landesco. Springfield, IL: Illinois State Board of Parole.

Fuchs, C., and Flanagan, J. (1980). Stepwise fitting of logit models with categorical predictors in the analysis of parole outcomes: On the Van Alstyne and Gottfredson study. *Journal of Research in Crime and Delinquency* 17:273–79.

Glaser, D. (1955). A reconsideration of some parole prediction factors. *American Sociological Review* 20:340–41.

Glueck, S., and Glueck, E. T. (1930). *500 criminal careers.* New York: Alfred A. Knopf.

———. (1960). *Predicting delinquency and crime.* Cambridge, MA: Harvard University Press.

Gottfredson, D. M., and Ballard, K. B. (1964). *Association analysis, predictive attribute analysis and parole behavior.* Vacaville, CA: Institute for the Study of Crime and Delinquency.

Grygier, T. (1970). Treatment variables in non-linear prediction. In *The sociology of punishment and correction,* ed. N. Johnston, L. Savitz, and M. E. Wolfgang. New York: Wiley.

Grygier, T., Blum, F., and Porebski, O. R. (1971). Decision and outcome: Studies in parole prediction. *Canadian Journal of Criminology and Corrections* 13:133–46.

Hakeem, M. (1945). Prediction of criminality. *Federal Probation* 3:31–38.

Hoffman, P. B., and Beck, J. L. (1976). Salient factor score validation—A 1972 release cohort. *Journal of Criminal Justice* 4:69–76.

Laune, F. F. (1936). The application of attitude tests in the field of parole prediction. *American Sociological Review* 1:781–96.

Ohlin, L. E., and Lawrence, R. A. (1952). A comparison of alternative methods of parole prediction. *American Sociological Review* 17:268–74.

Robuck, B. E. (1976). *A study of inmate outcome in Kentucky.* Ann Arbor, MI: University Microfilms.

Schuessler, K. F. (1954). Parole prediction: Its history and status. *Journal of Criminal Law and Criminology* 45:425–31.

Solomon, H. (1976). Parole outcome: A multidimensional contingency table analysis. *Journal of Research in Crime and Delinquency* 13:107–26.

Underwood, B. D. (1979). Law and the crystal ball: Predicting behavior with statistical inference and individualized judgment. *Yale Law Jurnal* 88:1408–48.

Van Alstyne, D. J., and Gottfredson, M. R. (1978). A multidimensional contingency table analysis of parole outcome: New methods and old problems in criminological predictions. *Journal of Research in Crime and Delinquency* 15:172–93.

Wilkins, L. T. (1971). *Why are inefficient statistics best for parole research?* School of Criminal Justice, Albany, NY. Photocopy.

Wilkins, L. T., and MacNaughton-Smith, P. (1970). Predictive attribute analysis. In *The sociology of punishment and correction,* ed. N. Johnston, L. Savitz, and M. E. Wolfgang. New York: Wiley.

III
Custodial Prediction

CHAPTER 5

Predicting Recidivism Using Institutional Measures

GILLIAN HILL

SUMMARY

This chapter reviews literature that investigates the extent to which measures of personality or behavior in institutions after sentencing add to the efficiency of predictions of recidivism that could be made at the time of sentencing. The main institutional variables that have been studied are parole prognosis, institutional misconduct, personality, participation in work or education, and frequency of family contacts. Institutional misconduct was the most reliable predictor of recidivism, but the extent to which it adds to known predictors, such as previous criminal record, is unclear.

INTRODUCTION

The aim of this chapter is to establish the extent to which recidivism can be predicted using measures of personality or behavior in custodial institutions. Parole boards often take into account factors that were not known (in principle or in practice) at the time of sentencing. It is important to establish the extent to which measures of personality or behavior in institutions after sentencing add to the accuracy of predictions of recidivism that could be made at the time of sentencing. This review is limited to studies carried out in the English-speaking world.

Many of the research projects reviewed were concerned with parole success. It may be difficult to compare studies from different jurisdictions or from the same jurisdictions at different times. There may be different sentencing policies leading to different prison populations and different parole schemes releasing different proportions of prisoners and using different criteria to decide eligibility for release. In particular, results obtained in American states, where a high percentage of prisoners were often released on parole, cannot necessarily be applied in the United Kingdom or Canada, where paroling rates are lower.

There are other difficulties in drawing conclusions from the research. Predictors of recidivism may be different for different subgroups of inmates (for example, parolees versus nonparolees). Different criterion variables may give different results. For example, Waller (1974) found that arrest and parole violation were not equivalent. Methods of measurement may differ (for example, dichotomized or continuous criterion variables: see Simon, 1971). Furthermore, predictor variables that are not related to the criterion may not be reported.

JUVENILE RECIDIVISM

Table 5.1 lists studies relating institutional measures to post-release recidivism of juvenile offenders. All the studies listed in this table are American. In general, parole prognosis and institutional adjustment tended to predict recidivism. Parole prognosis was based on staff assessments of the likelihood of reoffending. In some cases, this assessment was made on clinical grounds (Cowden, 1966) and in others it was based on behavior in the institution (Friedman and Mann, 1976). Friedman and Mann found that different methods of assessment did not affect the predictive accuracy of this variable. Institutional adjustment was measured by the extent of institutional infractions. Unfortunately, many of the studies did not include validation samples.

Cowden's (1966) study of first releasees from training school also investigated age, seriousness of offense, and home environment as predictors, but found that institutional adjustment and personality prognosis (in that order) were the best predictors. Furthermore, the combination of institutional adjustment and personality prognosis was slightly better in predicting recidivism than either of these variables individually. Similarly, for female first releasees studied in Wisconsin (1965), only the location of release was a better predictor than institutional adjustment, despite the wide range of family background and institutionally based variables studied.

In general, when psychological tests were used in predicting recidivism, they were administered soon after the person was incarcerated. An exception to this is seen in Joplin's (1972) research, which suggests that changes in personality during institutionalization may be a better predictor of future recidivism than initial assessments of personality.

Gough, Wenk, and Rozynko (1965) investigated 16 MMPI (Minnesota Multiphasic Personality Inventory) scales, but found only

Table 5.1   Prediction of Recidivism for Juvenile Offenders

Study	Sample	Criterion of Failure	Predictor Variables (*indicates variables related to success)
Arbuckle and Litwack (1960)	200 boys released from training school as construction sample, 100 boys in validation sample.	Returned to an institution for parole violation or as a sentence for a new offense.	Number of times in discipline cottage.*
Black and Glick (1952)	100 parolees from a special training school.	Conviction or admitted delinquency within 5 years.	Parole prognosis as assessed by clinical means.*
Cowden (1966)	270 boys admitted to training school for the first time.	Recommitment to a penal institution within 5 years.	Institutional adjustment,* personality prognosis,* both rated from official records.
Friedman and Mann (1976)	236 inmates of 3 correctional institutions.	Eight different measures of extent and seriousness of recidivism within 2 years.	Staff predictions of delinquency,* related to 6 of the 8 measures of recidivism.
Ganzer and Sarason (1973)	50 parole violators and 50 nonviolators (male), plus similar samples of females.	Return as parole violator or on a new sentence within 20 months.	*Males*: diagnosed as neurotic, diagnosed as aggressive personality,* diagnosed as sociopath,* short-term prognosis,* long-term prognosis. *Females*: diagnosed as neurotic,* diagnosed as aggressive personality, diagnosed as sociopath,* short-term prognosis,* long-term prognosis.
Glaser (1964)	322 dischargees.	Parole violation, belated success—paroled, returned but successful second parole.	Level of institutional schooling,* increase in academic achievement during confinement,* family contact,* having a job promise for parole,* prison punishment,* custody level reduced in confinement.*
Gough, Wenk, and Rozynko (1965)	444 parolees in construction sample, 295 in validation sample.	Parole violation or commitment of new offense within 2½ years.	CPI socialization scale,* CPI self-control scale,* MMPI K-corrected Ma scale.*
Jenkins et al. (1942)	119 successful and 107 unsuccessful parolees.	Success is discharge on good adjustment. Failure is recommitment to an institution.	Defiance of authority,* homicidal tendencies,* obscenity,* impudence,* compulsive stealing,* 24 other personality traits of less importance also identified as potential predictors.
Johns (1967)	7,186 parolees.	Revocation or violation of parole within 15 months	Major infractions,* parole prognosis.*

Study	Sample	Criterion	Variables
Johnson (1962)	97 cases released to an experimental project of the California Youth Authority.	Parole revoked or unfavorably discharged within 18 months.	Researcher rating of supports and stresses in the environment the delinquent is to be released to.* (Similar rating by parole officer was related to outcome at 10 months but not at 18 months.)
Joplin (1972)	28 dischargees from a special residential project.	Recommitment to another institution within 2 years.	Initial scores on Tennessee self-concept scale,* change in scores during program,* scores on scale just before discharge.*
Lunday (1950)	262 juveniles who completed parole successfully, 263 who did not.	Conduct resulting in an official disposition.	Rating on dependability,* obedience,* sociability,* institutional conduct,* improvement in the institution,* home contacts.*
Mack (1969)	159 parolees.	Defined as failure by supervisor during parole period.	MMPI mean scores, MMPI personality profiles.
Wisconsin (1965)	354 releasees (girls). Partially validated on a sample of 188 releasees and a sample of 221 releasees.	Return to custody within a year.	Social worker's prognosis,* cottage counselor's prognosis,* institutional adjustment,* educational progress in the institution, vocational progress in the institution,* change in institutional adjustment,* living arrangements prior to release.

one (Hypomania) that showed a significant difference between recidivists and nonrecidivists at the 0.05 level of significance. This result could be due to chance. In contrast, their work on the socialization scale of the CPI (California Personality Inventory) shows that, when measured after incarceration, it predicts parole outcome. It may be that this scale measured at the time of sentence would also be predictive.

Gough, Wenk, and Rozynko (1965) used base expectancy scores, CPI scores, and MMPI scores alone and in combination to form different risk scores for recidivism. Predicted recidivism based on these risk scores was compared with actual recidivism in the validation sample. The prediction table based on the CPI alone gave slightly better predictions than that derived from the base expectancy alone. The best predictions came from a combination of base expectancy and CPI scores. All these predictions were better than an undifferentiated prediction based on the recidivism rate.

YOUNG ADULT RECIDIVISM

Table 5.2 lists (British) studies relating institutional measures to postrelease recidivism of young adult offenders. Mannheim and Wilkins (1955) and Rose (1954) had behavioral as well as personality-prognosis measures. Both used official records as their data source and included in their analysis all the variables that they thought had been adequately recorded. The difference between their results is a reflection of the difference in their attitudes toward adequacy of variables (Rose taking a wider view than Mannheim and Wilkins in defining what was adequate). Rose included, for example, subjective factors such as borstal work habits, which Mannheim and Wilkins did not. The small number of predictors identified by Mannheim and Wilkins is a direct result of the paucity of adequate information in the files.

Mannheim and Wilkins (1955) found that the number of previous convictions was the best individual predictor of reconviction. Of the ten best predictors, eight could be measured at the time of the sentence. The only institutional predictor that was included in the best ten was the number of institutional misdemeanors (fifth best). Mannheim and Wilkins also studied prognoses by the institutional staff, but found them to be less efficient predictors than the number of institutional misdemeanors. Rose (1954) found that the best predictors were the housemasters' assessments of progress, personality type, the housemasters' prognosis, preborstal work habits, general conduct, and the number of previous convictions. None of the more objective institutional

Table 5.2. Prediction of Recidivism for Young Adult Offenders

Study	Sample	Criterion of Failure	Predictor Variables (*indicates variables related to success)
Eysenck and Eysenck (1974)	178 borstal releasees.	Reconviction within 3 years and 9 months of testing.	EPI P scores, EPI N scores, EPI E scores.*
McGurk, Bolton, and Smith (1978)	315 inmates at a detention center.	Reconviction within 2 years.	HDHQ,* PSI (social nonconformity scale*), 16 personality factor questionnaire form E (factor G,* factor L*).
Mannheim and Wilkins (1955)	700 borstal entrants in 1946–47.	Reconviction by 31 August 1951.	Absconding from borstal,* number of borstal misdemeanors,* housemaster's prognosis,* governor's prognosis* (low correlations on last two variables).
Ogden (1954)	250 borstal trainees.	Reconviction within 4 years of release.	Typology of offenders based on past history, physical and mental assessment and reaction to borstal training. Different groups had significantly different rates of failure.*
Rose (1954)	472 boys released from borstal in 1941–44.	Three levels of offending within 5-year follow-up; nonoffender, occasional offender, and habitual offender.	Major institutional offenses,* abscondings,* general conduct in borstal,* home contacts,* work habits,* housemaster's reports on progress,* housemaster's prognosis of success,* personality type.*
Sealy and Banks (1971)	200 borstal boys.	Reconviction within 1 year.	Social maturity* (as rated by researchers following interviews by psychologists).
Taylor (1967)	33 borstal girls.	Reconviction within 6 months.	Pooled predictions by borstal inmates of parole success,* pooled predictions by borstal parole board of parole success,* MMPI, 16 personality factor test, IPAT humor test, Eysenck TR scale, criminal attitude scale, 2 behavior rating scales.

variables was as good. Unfortunately, the ratings of progress, prognosis, and conduct made by Rose were based on the trainees' files, after the outcome of success or failure was known. Therefore, these ratings may have been biased.

Ogden (1954), Rose (1954), and Sealy and Banks (1971) all developed personality typologies that were related to recidivism. Sealy and Banks's (1971) typology was based on a theory of interpersonal maturity. They found that the high- and low-maturity groups differed considerably in reconviction, but that it was difficult to distinguish between intermediate groups. There was also a complex interaction between the type of borstal (as measured by the average Mannheim-Wilkins risk scores of the intake), the level of social maturity, and postrelease recidivism. However, the nature of these interaction effects was not specified in sufficient detail to be used in prediction. It might be misleading to use the general findings about social maturity for prediction in any particular borstal.

Studies using personality tests do not usually specify at what stage during incarceration the tests were given. Furthermore, it is not possible to determine whether personality tests administered at the time of sentencing would have any less (or greater) predictive power. Only McGurk, Bolton, and Smith (1978) compared the predictive power of personality-test data with that of other variables that could be measured at the time of the sentence. They found that the best predictors of recidivism were the number of previous convictions, age at the second conviction, reading attainment, and the PSI social nonconformity scale (in that order).

PERSONALITY TESTS AS PREDICTORS OF ADULT RECIDIVISM

Table 5.3 lists studies that have used tests such as the MMPI and the CPI with adult institutionalized offenders. The results were generally disappointing. The only study using a follow-up period of a year or more and finding MMPI or CPI scores predictive of future recidivism in a nonspecialized sample of prisoners was carried out by Panton (1962). However, Panton's research involved small numbers and no validation sample. Mandel and Barron (1966) found that some MMPI test items distinguished between recidivists and nonrecidivists in a construction sample, but that no logical combination of these items could distinguish between violators and nonviolators in a validation sample.

Tennenbaum (1977), in his review of the use of personality tests with offenders, concluded that the MMPI and CPI distinguished between criminal and noncriminal samples only because of the item content. Presumably most prisoners are not going to answer such

Table 5.3. Personality Tests and Recidivism for Adult Offenders

Study	Sample	Criterion of Failure	Predictor Variables (*indicates variables related to success)
Andry (1963) [U.K.]	114 dischargees from prison, all serving sentences less than 6 months.	Return to prison for a further offense (varying follow-up periods not exceeding 10½ months).	Emotional immaturity,* neuroticism,* extra-punitiveness.*
Blum and Chagnon (1967a, 1967b) [Canada]	339 property offenders (releasees and parolees).	Conviction for an indictable offense resulting in a custodial sentence of more than 1 year. No follow-up time specified.	Factor R (restraint) of the Guilford-Zimmerman temperament survey, factor E (extraversion) on same survey.
Gottfredson and Ballard (1966)	721 parolees in study sample, 701 in validation sample.	Return to prison, 90 days or more in jail, or parole violator at large in 2-year follow-up period.	CPI, your opinion (attitude scale), self-esteem scale, anomie scale, inmate cohesion and criminal self-conception, 4 MMPI scales, fake good and fake bad scales, interpersonal personality inventory, Gough's maturity score.
Gunn et al. (1978) [U.K.]	Grendon prisoners: 61 discharged by May 1973, 61 other prisoners matched on 8 variables. Plus 18 prisoners receiving psychiatric treatment at Wormwood Scrubs, and 18 matched but untreated prisoners.	Reconviction in average follow-up time of about 22 months.	Psychiatric data, MMPI, attitudes to crime and to psychiatry, motivation for treatment, attitudes to authority figures and to self. *Grendon prisoners only:* changes in attitude in prison, personality-test results, attitude to psychiatry,* attitude to police,* staff assessment of motivation.*
Mandel and Barron (1966)	372 men released from a reformatory not less than 5 years previously.	One or more serious offenses or several minor offenses.	Parole prognosis based on MMPI scores, MMPI items, MMPI item scores (test taken on admission and just prior to release).
Mueller and Coon (1964)	268 construction sample, 236 validation sample: parolees released from prison to a drug-control program.	A major disposition (that is, one resulting in more than 89 days in jail or a prison sentence).	MMPI scale scores on L,* F, K, Hs, D, Hy, Pd,* Mf,* Pa,* Pt, Sc, Ma.
Panton (1962)	41 parole violators, 41 nonviolators.	Parole violation.	26 MMPI items distinguished significantly between violators and nonviolators.*
Waller (1974) [Canada]	210 parolees, 213 men released unconditionally at the end of their sentence.	Rearrest at 6, 12, and 24 months.	Jesness combination score,* self-image measured on CPI and Jesness Inventory,* prerelease views on effectiveness of prison* (at 6 months only).

Note: Studies conducted in U.S. unless otherwise specified.

items as "I have never been in trouble with the law" in the affirmative; yet these are the very items that produce the discriminatory power of the tests in relation to offending in a normal population. It is not surprising if the tests fail to predict recidivism in institutional samples.

Gottfredson and Ballard (1966), Mueller and Coon (1964), and Waller (1974) examined whether personality variables might add to the discriminatory power of predictions based on other variables. They did this by using regression techniques with both construction and validation samples. However, in no case did the personality-test variables add to predictions that could have been made at the time of the sentence. Waller (1974) concluded that personality-test results were more likely to identify those who failed quickly (within the first six months) than those who failed in the long run (in a follow-up period of a year or more).

Personality-test variables might have different effects in different subgroups. Gottfredson and Ballard (1966) used association analysis to group individuals into categories that were relatively homogeneous with respect to certain known predictors of recidivism. Prediction equations were developed for each subgroup and tested in a validation sample. For the subgroup called "check offenders" the validation prediction equation included the CPI femininity score and the "your opinion" score. For the subgroup called "persistent offenders property II" the prediction equation included the "fake bad" score (Kase, 1956). The other subgroups either did not have validated prediction equations or had prediction equations that did not include personality-test variables.

Gottfredson and Ballard compared predictions using the above method with predictions from base expectancy scores. They found that the above method gave more efficient predictions and reduced the size of the average risk group from 39 percent to 18 percent of the total sample. However, it is not clear to what extent these results could be generalized to other prison populations, especially as there is no theoretical basis for the identified personality characteristics to be considered predictors of recidivism for these particular subgroups.

PAROLE PROGNOSIS AND ADULT RECIDIVISM

The most common forms of parole prognosis consist of staff assessments of the likelihood of reoffending, the most detailed studies of which were completed in the same institutions in Illinois and are thus comparable (Bruce et al., 1928; Tibbitts, 1931; Hakeem, 1945; Ohlin, 1951; Glaser, 1955). These institutions had an explicit system of recording parole prognosis. Table 5.4 shows that parole prognosis usually predicted future recidivism. A number of the studies, however, had large samples and a weak relationship between prognosis and recidivism. The significance of this relationship may be more a function of sample size than of the strength of the relationship (Borden, 1928; Tibbitts, 1931; Bruce et al., 1928). Only Hakeem (1945) found a reasonably strong relationship between parole prognosis and future recidivism, but his sample related to a specialized subgroup of offenders (non-Negro burglars).

Lack of adequate information may reduce the usefulness of parole prognosis as a predictor. Even in Illinois, where parole prognosis was supposed to be recorded as a matter of course, there was a considerable amount of missing data. Burgess (1928) found information missing on parole prognosis in about half the files in two of the prisons studied and in about a third of the files in the third prison. Individual skill in predicting may also be important in determining whether parole prognosis is an efficient predictor. Glaser (1962) found that individuals used prognostic categories differently and differed in their ability to make accurate prognoses. None of the studies examined in any detail the skills that were related to the ability to make accurate predictions of future criminality.

The key issue is on what information parole prognosis is based and whether it adds to the predictive power of other variables. Borden (1928) found that the prognosis was highly correlated with the number of prior commitments, which was a better predictor of future recidivism. Gottfredson (1962) reported that parole prognosis did not add to the power of a prediction table which had been developed by multiple regression from variables known at the time of sentencing.

Parole prognoses may be based on subjective assessments of personality. Table 5.4 shows that these assessments were not always predictive of future recidivism. Vold (1931), Borden (1928), and Hakeem (1945) all made an *a priori* choice of personality types and found some relationship between personality and future recidivism. However, in all cases the relationship was quite weak. Personality was not among the most efficient individual predictors of recidivism. Laune (1936) attempted to identify the attitudinal and personality factors that prison inmates thought were predictive of parole success. Ohlin and Lawrence (1952) then tested whether this approach to personality assessment produced useful predictors of recidivism. They found that a number of Laune's factors were predictive in the construction sample (see table 5.4), but they did not specify which factors, if any, maintained their predictive power in the validation sample.

Table 5.4. Parole Prognosis and Recidivism for Adult Offenders

Study	Sample	Criterion of Failure	Predictor Variables (*indicates variables related to success)
Allen (1947)	100 discharged from parole; 100 returned for parole violation.	Parole violation.	Physical health at release,* psychiatric diagnosis.
Arkoff (1957)	165 men released from prison.	Return to prison for breach of parole or new offense within 4 years.	Institutional adjustment measured by staff assessments.
Borden (1928)	263 consecutive parolees.	Five categories of parole success relating to criminal behavior within 1 year.	Temperamental traits (amenable*), psychologists' prognosis.*
Bruce et al. (1928)	3,000 consecutive parolees.	Parole violation within at least 2½ years.	Personality type, psychiatric prognosis.*
Challinger (1974) [Australia]	593 adult male parolees (297 in construction sample, 296 in validation sample).	Cancellation of parole or reimprisonment within 2 years.	Sociological type, psychological type.
Glaser (1954, 1955)	2,693 inmates released on parole.	Parole violation.	Personality type, prognosis. (Found that sociologists were better than psychiatrists in assessments of parole prognosis but still not very good.)
Glaser (1962)	1,015 federal prisoners with sentences of more than 1 year.	Return to prison for parole violation or a new offense or convicted of a felony.	Satisfactory adjustment assessed by staff.*
Glueck and Glueck (1937)	510 men whose parole had expired.	Known commission of serious offenses or number of minor offenses between 5 and 10 years after expiry of parole.	Mental abnormality.*
Gottfredson (1962)	283 parolees.	Parole revocation.	Superintendent's rating of parole prognosis,* rating of parole prognosis based on psychiatric reports.*
Hakeem (1945)	1,861 non-Negro burglars paroled between 1925 and 1935, inclusive.	Major violation, minor (technical) violation.	Personality classification,* psychiatric prognosis.*
Miles (1957)	200 males aged 17–30 paroled between March and August 1940.	Parole violation by August 1941.	Parole prognosis based on interviews, tests, and knowledge of previous history* (but such prognosis could be made in only 59% of cases).

Study	Sample	Outcome measure	Predictors
Ohlin (1951)	4,941 parolees.	Parole violation.	Personality as assessed in prison,* psychiatric prognosis,* mental rating.
Ohlin and Lawrence (1952)	110 inmates.	Parole violation.	Hunches of other inmates on whether a man might succeed on parole or not* (the 2 best inmate hunches were as effective as the Burgess table).
Ohlin and Lawrence (1952)	405 in construction sample, 418 in validation sample.	Parole violation.	Absence of desire for clothes,* absence of foolhardiness,* timidity,* lack of conceit,* religiosity,* absence of love of comfort,* absence of laziness,* absence of weak character, shrewdness, selfishness, absence of tendency to agitate, absence of failure to learn lesson, absence of sharp practices, trade in prison, absence of lack of working ability, absence of wanderlust (listed in order of relationship).
Takagi (1965)	161 male felons.	Reconviction. Follow-up periods of 8 to 20 months.	Measures of hostility toward institutional authority and inmate cohesion, combined to give a typology of prisoners.
Tibbitts (1931)	3,000 parolees.	Parole violation within 1 year.	Personality type,* psychiatric prognosis.*
Vold (1931)	1,192 parolees.	Parole violation.	Laziness,* dishonesty,* prison officer's estimate of mentality,* prison officer's judgment of conduct.*

Note: Studies conducted in U.S. unless otherwise specified.

BEHAVIORAL MEASURES AND ADULT RECIDIVISM

The remaining predictors of adult recidivism include breaches of institutional discipline, participation in work and education in prison, and frequency of family contacts while in prison (see table 5.5). Breaches of institutional discipline have usually been measured according to recorded misconduct reports or loss of good time (remission). Generally, institutional misbehavior has been shown to predict reoffending, although of course there are differences between prisons in their disciplinary structures (see O'Leary and Glaser, 1972).

Glueck and Glueck (1930) reported that the strength of the relationship between disciplinary infractions and recidivism depended on how infractions were measured. The frequency of prison offenses was more closely related to recidivism than seriousness or a dichotomous measure (whether or not the inmate had offended). A number of studies (Carlson, 1973; Glueck and Glueck, 1930; Hakeem, 1945; Schnur, 1949; Tibbitts, 1931; Vold, 1931) make it possible to compare the predictability of prison misbehavior with that of presentence variables. In all cases, and no matter how prison misbehavior was measured, presentence variables had high correlations with the criterion variable.

Institutional misconduct was correlated with other known predictors of recidivism, including variables that were more strongly related to the criterion. Glueck and Glueck (1934), Jaman (1972), and Schnur (1949) all found that institutional behavior was related to age, previous penal experience, and offense type. Jaman (1972) further showed that the number of disciplinary infractions could be predicted from age, previous record, and base expectancy scores. The key question is whether institutional misbehavior predicts recidivism independently of presentence variables. Glueck and Glueck (1930) found that adding institutional misconduct to a prediction table based on variables that could be measured at the time of sentencing did not increase the predictive efficiency. Similarly, Ohlin (1951) reported that the institutional-punishment rating did not make a useful contribution to his prediction table. Also, Carney (1967), Mac-Naughton-Smith (1976), Metzner and Weil (1963), and Vichert and Zahnd (1965) all reported that prison misconduct made no contribution to prediction tables derived from predictive attribute analysis or configural analysis.

Attempts to study the extent to which participation in prison work or education predicts recidivism have been hindered by deficiencies in records of these topics (Glaser, 1964; Jaman, 1968; Warner, 1923) and by variability in the organization of work or

Study	Sample	Criterion of Failure	Predictor Variables (*indicates variables related to success)
Attorney General (1939)	53,033 parolees from 29 institutions.	Parole violation.	Violation of prison rules* (significant relationship in 25 institutions).
Borden (1928)	263 consecutive parolees.	Five categories of parole success relating to criminal behavior within 1 year.	Days lost for discipline infractions, nature of institutional offenses, industrial rating,* job held in institution, literacy.
Bruce et al. (1928)	3,000 consecutive parolees.	Parole violation within at least 2½ years.	Punishment record.*
Carlson (1973) [Canada]	1,070 releasees from a correctional center.	Recidivism (follow-up period not specified but by implication 5 years).	EEG reading,* number of institutional misconduct reports,* educational achievement in prison,* type of release.
Carney (1967)	363 consecutive releasees from an institution where the inmates were selected for their rehabilitative potential.	Return to prison or jail for more than 30 days, within 4 years.	Type of release, home contacts during commitment, good time withheld.*
Challinger (1974) [Australia]	297 male parolees in construction sample, 296 in validation sample.	Cancellation of parole or reimprisonment within 2 years.	Discharge postponed due to misconduct in prison,* family conduct in prison term, industry in prison term, no effort to secure job for parole period.*
Gearhart et al. (1967)	102 inmates who successfully completed vocational training and who were released on parole in 1963, 102 inmates who never participated in vocational training, who were released in 1963, and who were matched on preinstitutional variables with the first group.	Parole violation.	Participation in vocational training.
Gillin (1943)	Three groups of parolees released from supervision in 1932–33, 1933–34, and 1935.	Not clear.	Institutional behavior.*
Glaser (1955)	2,693 inmates released on parole between 1940 and 1949 to non-Army positions.	Parole violation.	Use of prison time.*

Table 5.5. Behavioral Measures and Recidivism in Adult Offenders (Continued)

Study	Sample	Criterion of Failure	Predictor Variables (*indicates variables related to success)
Glaser (1964)	1,015 federal prisoners with sentences of more than 1 year released in 1956.	Return to prison for parole revocation or a new offense or convicted of a felony.	Prison job,* evaluation of prison work, enrollment in academic education, family interest,* having job promise in prison.
Glueck and Glueck (1930)	510 men whose sentence expired in 1921 or 1922.	Conviction for felony, known commission of serious offenses or a number of minor offenses, or fugitive from justice, within 5 years after expiry of parole.	Type of reformatory worker, number of reformatory jobs,* institutional offender,* frequency of institutional offenses.*
Glueck and Glueck (1937)	510 men whose sentence expired in 1921 to 1922.	As above, during period from 5–10 years after expiry of parole.	Number of occupational experiences in reformatory, quality of reformatory work,* number of institutional offenses,* number of serious institutional offenses,* frequency of institutional offenses.*
Glueck and Glueck (1934)	500 women parolees.	Reoffending within 5-year period following expiry of sentence.	Quality of institutional work,* behavior in the reformatory.*
Gottfredson, Wilkins, and Hoffman (1978)	902 parolees in construction sample, 1,581 in validation sample.	No new conviction resulting in a sentence of 60 days or more, and no parole violation, within 2 years.	Prison adjustment, custody classification, custody level reduced during imprisonment, assaulting infractions, prison punishments, on-the-job training, participation in prison education, contact with family, number of parole hearings.
Hakeem (1945)	1,861 non-Negro burglars paroled between 1925 and 1935.	Three categories: major parole violation, minor parole violation, or success.	Disciplinary record,* family interest.*
Hakeem (1948)	1,108 parolees.	Parole violation within 6 years (at least).	Family interest,* job held in prison at time of parole hearing,* punishment record in prison.*
Hart (1923)	300 parole violators, 300 nonviolators, 80 discharged prisoners not on parole.	Parole violation.	Guilty of misconduct 6 times or more in the reformatory,* willingness to work, quality of work in reformatory.
Jaman (1971)	330 men paroled between May 1965 and May 1969.	Return to prison or to jail for 90 days or more, felony warrant. Follow-up at 6 months, 1 year, and 2 years.	Work assignment rating, vocational training rating, academic education rating, voluntary group participation, number of disciplinary actions, violence in prison, overall rating (all assessed in first year in prison).

Study	Sample	Criterion	Findings
Kassebaum, Ward, and Wilner (1971)	965 men released to parole between July 1962 and December 1963.	Felony conviction, return to prison either as parole violator or for new offense. Follow-up at 6, 12, 24, and 36 months.	Voluntary participation in group counseling, attitudes to staff, attitudes to counseling, CPI (one-third of men completed a questionnaire on inmate values and those who were most alienated did significantly better on parole). Attendance at prison school added to base expectancy predictive power, as did high attendance at group counseling and nonviolation of prison rules.*
Kirby (1954)	455 men released on parole between March 1944 and December 1949.	Parole violation.	Institutional behavior explained less than 1% of total variation in parole failure, and family interest even less.
MacNaughton-Smith (1976) [Canada]	143 men who were granted parole between 1962 and 1964 from penitentiaries. Validation sample: 147 parolees.	Arrest or return to custody within 3 years (maximum).	Drug problem anticipated on parole,* no personality problem anticipated on parole, legibility of the parole application, record of discipline reports, extent of trade training during imprisonment, prison record of steady work, custodial recommendation for parole, expected living conditions on release.
MacSpeiden (1966)	2,288 first felony offenders released 1961–1963.	Imprisonment for parole violation by 1966.	Amount of prison training.
Metzner and Weil (1963)	311 parolees.	Imprisonment for parole violation or new offense within 2½ years.	Home contacts, good time withheld.
Nuttall et al. (1977) [U.K.]	2,276 male prisoners serving at least 18 months released in 1965.	Reconviction within 2 years.	Escaped during sentence.*
Ohlin (1951)	4,941 parolees (validated).	Parole violation.	Family interest,* punishment rating, mental rating, last institutional assignment.
Ohlin and Lawrence (1952)	405 parolees in construction sample, 418 in validation sample.	Parole violation.	Family ties,* trade in prison, absence of good job in prison.
Saden (1962)	1,000 parolees.	Not clear.	Participation in prison education,* time spent in prison education.
Schnur (1949, 1951)	1,742 men released on parole.	Parole violation within 2 years.	Number of misconduct citations exclusive of periods of solitary confinement,* number of commitments to solitary confinement.*

Table 5.5. Behavioral Measures and Recidivism in Adult Offenders (Continued)

Study	Sample	Criterion of Failure	Predictor Variables (*indicates variables related to success)
Seashore et al. (1976)	995 individuals in all, participants in 8 college education programs in prison plus 2 control groups and a comparison group.	Return to prison or conviction leading to a jail sentence of more than 60 days (variable follow-up periods.)	Completion of prison education program.
Tibbitts (1931)	3,000 parolees.	Parole violation.	Punishment record in institution,* last work assignment in institution.*
Vichert and Zahnd (1965) [Canada]	100 parole successes and 100 parole failures from federal penitentiaries.	Suspension, revocation, or forfeiture of parole.	Prison conduct, prison work record, escapes* (none of these variables appeared in the predictive attribute analysis).
Vold (1931)	1,192 parolees.	Parole violation.	Prison punishment record,* aid given to dependents while in institution, prison officer's judgment of conduct.*
Waller (1974) [Canada]	210 parolees, 213 men released unconditionally at the end of their sentences.	Rearrest at 6, 12, and 24 months.	Offenses against prison staff,* skills involved in prison job, time in prison job, victimless offenses in prison, individual applied for parole.*
Ward (1968) [Australia]	1,637 prisoners, 17-22 years of age, serving first prison sentence.	Recidivism (not operationalized).	Received no replies to standard circulars sent to parents and employers.*
Wisconsin (1964)	Approximately 7,000 releasees.	Parole violation within 2 years.	Institutional work record, loss of institutional privileges,* educational progress.

Note: Studies conducted in U.S. unless otherwise specified.

educational schemes. In general, only a weak relationship exists between work or educational variables and recidivism (Borden, 1928; Carlson, 1973; Glaser, 1964; Glueck and Glueck, 1930; Tibbitts, 1931). Furthermore, after controlling for known predictors of recidivism (especially age and intelligence), participation in prison work and education had little predictive power (Gearhart, et al., 1967; Gottfredson, Wilkins, and Hoffman, 1978; Kassebaum, Ward, and Wilner, 1971; MacNaughton-Smith, 1976; MacSpeiden, 1966; Ohlin, 1951).

It appears from the scanty evidence available that having a job promise on release is not necessarily predictive of success on parole. Both Glaser (1964) and Waller (1974) included extended discussions on prisoners' employment history on release and its relation to both recidivism and prison work experience. However, Glaser (1964) pointed out that having a job promise on leaving prison was not necessarily indicative of future employment.

A number of the studies report a significant negative relationship between the frequency of a person's contacts with his or her family while in prison and recidivism. However, this relationship was often relatively weak (Hakeem, 1945; Ohlin and Lawrence, 1952). Ohlin (1951) found that family ties could add to the efficiency of a prediction table. The subgroups "very active family interest" and "no family interest" had violation rates significantly different from that of the sample as a whole. However, home contacts did not appear in Glaser's (1964) configuration table or in Carney's (1967) predictive attribute analysis.

CONCLUSIONS

The studies examined in this chapter have rarely produced prediction instruments that predict more than 15 percent of the variation in recidivism, whether they contain institutional variables or not. In fact, actuarial predictions are often little better than chance. This may be because predictor variables are chosen according to their availability in records rather than on any theoretical basis. Prediction instruments seem to be able to identify extreme-risk groups fairly easily, but there is always an intermediate group for whom prediction is difficult. This is true both for individual predictors (Sealy and Banks, 1971) and for prediction tables (Mannheim and Wilkins, 1955; Ohlin, 1951). More efforts should be made to develop prediction instruments for this intermediate-risk group.

The main institutional variables that have been investigated are parole prognosis (predicted reoffending by staff), institutional misconduct, personality, participation in work or education, and frequency of family contacts. Unfortunately, the studies do not usually consider whether institutional variables add to the efficiency of predictions that could be made at the time of sentencing. This has to be inferred from the evidence available in the research reports, and this inference is often difficult, partly because of the lack of validation samples in many studies. Summarizing all this research is also difficult because of problems of comparability, in definitions of predictor or criterion variables, or in institutional populations.

Institutional misconduct seems to be the most reliable institutional predictor of recidivism, and there is usually adequate information on this in prison files. Parole prognosis is often predictive, but this is rather subjective and it is difficult to know on what basis it is made. Personality measures can add to base expectancy scores for juvenile offenders (Gough, Wenk, and Rozynko, 1965), but scales such as Socialization on the CPI may not reflect "personality" so much as "previous misconduct," and in any case these could be assessed at the sentencing stage. The predictive utility of participation in work or education in prison, or of the frequency of family contact in prison, is less clear.

More research is clearly needed to establish the extent to which institutional variables, such as disciplinary infractions, add to known predictors of recidivism, such as previous criminal record. Until this question has been answered satisfactorily, the need to take such institutional variables into account in parole decisions will be unclear.

REFERENCES

Allen, R. M. (1947). Problems of parole. *Journal of Criminal Law, Criminology and Police Science* 38:7–13 and 636–38.

Andry, R. G. (1963). *The short-term prisoner.* London: Stevens.

Arbuckle, D. S., and Litwack, L. (1960). A study of recidivism among juvenile delinquents. *Federal Probation* 24:45–48.

Arkoff, A. (1957). Prison adjustment as an index of ability to adjust on the outside. *Journal of Correctional Education* 9(1):1–2.

Attorney General (1939). *Survey of release procedures.* Vol. 4, *Parole.* Washington, DC: Government Printing Office.

Black, B. J., and Glick, S. J. (1952). *Recidivism at the Hawthorne-Cedar Knolls School.* New York: Jewish Board of Guardians.

Blum, F., and Chagnon, J. (1967a). Extraversion and subsequent recidivism for a selected group of young adult offenders. *Canadian Journal of Corrections* 9:94–98.

———. (1967b). Some parameters of persistent criminal behavior. *Journal of Clinical Psychology* 23:168–70.

Borden, H. G. (1928). Factors for predicting parole success. *Journal of Criminal Law and Criminology* 19:328–36.

Bruce, A. A.; Harno, A. J.; Burgess, E. W.; and Landesco, J. (1928). *The workings of the indeterminate sentence law and the parole system in Illinois*. Springfield, IL: Illinois State Board of Parole.

Burgess, E. W. (1928). Factors determining success or failure on parole. In Bruce et al. (1928).

Carlson, K. (1973). Some characteristics of recidivists in an Ontario institution for adult male first incarcerates. *Canadian Journal of Criminology and Corrections* 15:397–409.

Carney, F. (1967). Predicting recidivism in a medium security correctional institution. *Journal of Criminal Law, Criminology and Police Science* 58:338–48.

Challinger, D. (1974). A predictive device for parolees in Victoria. *Australian and New Zealand Journal of Criminology* 7:44–54.

Cowden, J. E. (1966). Predicting institutional adjustment and recidivism in delinquent boys. *Journal of Criminal Law, Criminology and Police Science* 57: 39–44.

Eysenck, S. B. G., and Eysenck, H. J. (1974). Personality and recidivism in borstal boys. *British Journal of Criminology* 14:385–87.

Friedman, J., and Mann, F. (1976). Recidivism: The fallacy of prediction. *International Journal of Offender Therapy* 20:153–64.

Ganzer, V., and Sarason, I. (1973). Variables associated with recidivism among juvenile delinquents. *Journal of Consulting and Clinical Psychology* 40:1–5.

Gearhart, J., et al. (1967). *An analysis of the vocational training program in the Washington State correctional institutions*. Olympia, WA: State of Washington, Department of Institutions, Research Review 23.

Gillin, J. L. (1943). Prediction of parole success in Wisconsin. *Journal of Criminal Law and Criminology* 34:236–39.

Glaser, D. (1954). A reconsideration of some parole prediction factors. *American Sociological Review* 19:335–41.

——— (1955). The efficacy of alternative approaches to parole prediction. *American Sociological Review* 20:283–87.

——— (1962). Prediction tables as accounting devices for judges and parole boards. *Crime and Delinquency* 8:239–58.

——— (1964). *The effectiveness of a prison and parole system*. Indianapolis: Bobbs-Merrill.

Glueck, S., and Glueck, E. T. (1930). *Five hundred criminal careers*. New York: Knopf.

——— (1934). *Five hundred delinquent women*. New York: Knopf.

——— (1937). *Later criminal careers*. New York: Commonwealth Fund.

Gottfredson, D. (1962). Comparing and combining subjective and objective parole predictions. Reported in *Development and operational use of prediction methods in correctional work*, by D. Gottfredson and R. Beverly. Paper presented at the Social Statistics Section, American Statistical Association, Minneapolis, September.

Gottfredson, D., and Ballard, K. (1966). *Offender classification and parole prediction*. Vacaville, CA: Institute for the Study of Crime and Delinquency.

Gottfredson, D.; Wilkins, L. T.; and Hoffman, P. B. (1978). *Guidelines for parole and sentencing*. Lexington: Heath.

Gough, H. G.; Wenk, E. A.; and Rozynko, V. V. (1965). Parole outcome as predicted from the CPI, the MMPI, and a base expectancy table. *Journal of Abnormal Psychology* 70:432–41.

Gunn, J.; Robertson, G.; Dell, S.; and Way, C. (1978). *Psychiatric aspects of imprisonment.* London: Academic Press.

Hakeem, M. (1945). Glueck method of parole prediction applied to 1861 cases of burglars. *Journal of Criminal Law, Criminology and Police Science* 36:87–97.

——— (1948). The validity of the Burgess method of parole prediction. *American Journal of Sociology* 53:376–86.

Hart, H. (1923). Predicting parole success. *Journal of Criminal Law and Criminology* 14:405–13.

Jaman, D. (1968). *Behavior during the first year in prison.* Report 1, *Description.* Sacramento: Department of Corrections, Research Report 32.

——— (1971). *Behavior during the first year in prison.* Report 4, *As related to parole outcome.* Sacramento: Department of Corrections, Research Report 44.

——— (1972). *Behavior during the first year in prison.* Report 3, *Background characteristics as predictors of behavior and misbehavior.* Sacramento: Department of Corrections, Research Report 43.

Jenkins, R. L.; Hart, H. H.; Sperling, P. I.; and Axelrad, S. (1942). Prediction of parole success. *Journal of Criminal Law, Criminology and Police Science* 33:38–46.

Johns, D. (1967). *Institutional program patterns, parole prognosis and outcome.* Sacramento: Department of Youth Authority, Research Report 52.

Johnson, B. M. (1962). *An analysis of predictions of parole performance and judgments of supervision in the parole research project.* Sacramento: Department of Youth Authority, Research Report 32.

Joplin, G. (1972). Self-concept and the Highfields program. *Criminology* 9:491–95.

Kase, D. N. (1956). *The effects of faking on the D-scale of the Camp Elliott Inventory of Personal Opinion.* San Diego: Naval Re-Training Command.

Kassebaum, G.; Ward, D. A.; and Wilner, D. (1971). *Prison treatment and parole survival.* New York: Wiley.

Kirby, B. (1954). Parole prediction using multiple correlation. *American Journal of Sociology* 59:539–50.

Laune, F. F. (1936). *Predicting criminality.* Evanston, IL: Northwestern University.

Lunday, G. (1950). Vulnerable parolees. *Journal of Criminal Law, Criminology and Police Science* 40:620–21.

McGurk, B. J.; Bolton, N.; and Smith, M. (1978). Some psychological, educational and criminological variables related to recidivism in delinquent boys. *British Journal of Social and Clinical Psychology* 17:251–54.

Mack. J. (1969). The MMPI and recidivism. *Journal of Abnormal Psychology* 74:612–14.

MacNaughton-Smith, P. (1976). *Permission to be slightly free.* Ottawa: Law Reform Commission of Canada.

MacSpeiden, T. R. (1966). *The influence of scholastic and vocational training programs on the rate of parole violation.* Ph.D. diss., Purdue University, Lafayette, Indiana.

Mandel, N., and Barron, A. (1966). The MMPI and criminal recidivism. *Journal of Criminal Law, Criminology and Police Science* 57:35–38.

Mannheim, H., and Wilkins, L. T. (1955). *Prediction methods in relation to borstal training.* London: Her Majesty's Stationery Office.

Metzner, R., and Weil, G. (1963). Predicting recidivism. *Journal of Criminal Law, Criminology and Police Science* 54:307–16.

Miles, D. (1957). The validity of clinical judgment. *Journal of Social Psychology* 45:75–79.

Mueller, P., and Coon, D. (1964). *Parole outcome prediction for male opiate users in Los Angeles area.* Sacramento: Department of Corrections, Research Report 18.

Nuttall, C. P., et al. (1977). *Parole in England and Wales.* London: Her Majesty's Stationery Office.

Ogden, D. A. (1954). A borstal typology study (Camp Hill). *British Journal of Delinquency* 5:99–111.

Ohlin, L. E. (1951). *Selection for parole.* New York: Russell Sage.

Ohlin, L. E., and Lawrence, R. (1952). A comparison of alternative methods of parole prediction. *American Sociological Review* 17:268–74.

O'Leary, V., and Glaser, D. (1972). The assessment of risk in parole decision making. In *The future of parole,* ed. D. J. West. London: Duckworth.

Panton, J. H. (1962). The use of the MMPI as an index to successful parole. *Journal of Criminal Law, Criminology and Police Science* 53:484–88.

Rose, A. G. (1954). *Five hundred borstal boys.* Oxford: Blackwell.

Saden, S. J. (1962). Correctional research at Jackson prison. *Journal of Correctional Education* 15(4):22–26.

Schnur, A. (1949). Prison conduct and recidivism. *Journal of Criminal Law, Criminology and Police Science* 40:36–42.

——— (1951). The validity of parole selection. *Social Forces* 29:322–28.

Sealy, A. P., and Banks, C. (1971). Social maturity, training, experience and recidivism amongst borstal boys. *British Journal of Criminology* 11:245–64.

Seashore, M.; Haberfield, S.; Irwin, J.; and Baker, K. (1976). *Prisoner education.* New York: Praeger.

Simon, F. H. (1971). *Prediction methods in criminology.* London: Her Majesty's Stationery Office.

Takagi, P. (1965). *Criminal types and parole prediction.* Sacramento: Department of Corrections, Research Report 14.

Taylor, A. J. W. (1967). Prediction for parole. *British Journal of Criminology* 7:418–23.

Tennenbaum, D. J. (1977). Personality and criminality. *Journal of Criminal Justice* 5:225–35.

Tibbitts, C. (1931). Success or failure on parole can be predicted. *Journal of Criminal Law, Criminology and Police Science* 22:11–50.

Vichert, B., and Zahnd, W. (1965). Parole: Low and high risk parolees. *Canadian Journal of Corrections* 7:39–48.

Vold, G. B. (1931). *Prediction methods and parole.* Hanover, NH: Sociological Press.

Waller, I. (1974). *Men released from prison.* Toronto: University of Toronto Press.

Ward, P. G. (1968). The comparative efficacy of differing techniques of prediction scaling. *Australian and New Zealand Journal of Criminology* 1:109–12.

Warner, S. B. (1923). Factors determining parole from the Massachusetts reformatory. *Journal of Criminal Law, Criminology and Policy Science* 14:172–207.

Wisconsin (1964). *Adult base expectancies.* Madison: Division of Corrections, Research Bulletin C8.

—— (1965). *Juvenile base expectancies, Wisconsin School for Girls.* Madison: Division of Corrections, Research Bulletin C9.

CHAPTER 6

Predicting Absconding From Young Offender Institutions

DAVID THORNTON AND SHEILA SPEIRS

SUMMARY

Custodial institutions for young offenders differ in the levels of physical security they provide: closed establishments are designed to make it difficult for trainees to abscond, whereas it is relatively easy to run away from open establishments. Clearly, it would be advantageous to allocate to closed establishments those young offenders who would be particularly likely to abscond if placed in open conditions. Early attempts to distinguish those young offenders who were likely to abscond were largely unsuccessful, however, and the emerging theoretical model suggested that the only substantive predictor of absconding was previous absconding (Clarke and Martin, 1971). A few recent studies (notably Laycock, 1977) have given more promising results. Encouraged by this, we attempted in the present research to derive and cross-validate a scale for predicting absconding from open institutions. It is shown that on the basis of a few items of simple background information it is possible effectively to grade trainees in terms of their proneness to abscond. The theoretical and practical implications of this capability are discussed.

INTRODUCTION

When offenders are placed in open conditions it is inevitable that some will abscond. The actual level of absconding is determined partly by aspects of the institution (for example, its location and degree of security) and partly by the type of people it is supposed to contain. Many aspects of individual institutions are fixed, but it is possible to alter the intake by manipulating allocation criteria. The population considered here is that of young offenders between the ages of 15 and 20 years (inclusive) sentenced to borstal training (a semi-indeterminate custodial sentence). The aim is to explore to what extent it is possible to identify those trainees who are the more likely to abscond, given only the characteristics that would be known at the time of allocation.

There are two reasons for trying to predict absconding. The first is its obvious practical importance. Abscondings often lead to further crime. They cause fear in the local community and they consequently reduce the prison department's ability to make use of open conditions. A high absconding rate can also make it difficult to run an effective training regime, and it is possible that it reduces the deterrent value of a custodial sentence. The second reason for trying to predict absconding derives from the possibility of interpreting absconding as a delinquent act. Considered as a target for criminological study, absconding has a number of advantages over other types of offense: the dark number of undetected offenses is believed to be comparatively low; absconding occurs in an environment that is easily studied and can even be experimentally manipulated; and it is comparatively easy to compare the characteristics of absconders and nonabsconders (Clarke and Martin, 1971; Laycock, 1977). Thus the study of absconding allows one to test general criminological theories with a rigor that is not possible for other types of offense. Considerations of this type have led some to attach a special theoretical weight to the results of research into absconding.

Early attempts to identify trainee characteristics that predicted absconding were remarkably unsuccessful. The most comprehensive and influential of these early studies was that by Clarke and Martin (1971). At the time of their research, an approved-school order was the main custodial disposal open to the courts for offenders aged between 10 and 16. (An approved school is roughly equivalent to a training school in North America.) Many of those sentenced to an approved school spent a few weeks in a classifying school for assessment prior to allocation. Clarke and Martin tried to identify trainee characteristics, known at the classifying-school stage, that predicted subsequent absconding. A comprehensive range of trainee characteristics was investigated. Most of the better-known and validated personality questionnaires were included, together with measures of trainees' attitudes, psychiatric history, criminal history, home background, and behavior in the classifying schools.

Of all these variables only three showed significant predictive power. Absconders from approved schools were more likely to have absconded from another institution, they tended to be younger at the time of their first conviction, and they appeared to have committed offenses more frequently. Previous absconding behavior was the most powerful predictor and, among trainees with a prior history of absconding, criminal-history variables failed to distinguish those who went on to abscond from approved schools from the remainder. Naturally enough, these results discouraged Clarke and Martin from trying to develop a prediction scale for absconding. Instead, they went on to demonstrate the importance of factors in the institutional environment as determinants of absconding. The theoretical model to emerge from this work was an "environmental learning theory." Applied to absconding, the theory (in its extreme form) holds that initially trainees are equally likely to abscond and that whether they do so is entirely determined by the current environment. However, once trainees have absconded their likelihood of doing so again depends upon the consequences they experience. Thus, trainees who find absconding enjoyable become more inclined to abscond. In sum, then, not only did Clarke and Martin fail to discover trainee characteristics predictive of absconding, but they also developed a theory suggesting that the search for such characteristics was inherently futile.

Later research has qualified this picture. Laycock (1977), in a study of open-borstal trainees, distinguished those who absconded alone from those who absconded in a group, and she broke the "group absconders" down into "leaders" and "followers". Her results suggested that trainees who absconded as followers tended to be intropunitive extraverts. Similarly, Brown, Druce, and Sawyer (1978) found that trainees who absconded as members of a group tended to score as "group dependent" on a personality questionnaire. These results are theoretically important in suggesting that a trainee's absconding behavior is related to more general modes of functioning rather than being the specific habit postulated by environmental learning theory. Other research has confirmed this conclusion. Both Laycock (1977) and Banks, Mayhew, and Sapsford (1975), the latter in a study of adult male prisoners allocated to open conditions, found that the nature of offenders' current convictions distinguished absconders from nonabsconders. The effects identified by Banks, Mayhew, and Sapsford, were quite small. (For example, burglars had an absconding rate of 4.7 percent, whereas men convicted for fraud had a risk of 1.7 percent.)

In her study of male trainees allocated to open borstals, Laycock obtained more impressive results. Trainees with a current conviction for a motor vehicle offense had an absconding rate of 32 percent, whereas those without such a conviction had an absconding rate of 16 percent. It is difficult to see how the environmental learning model can account for such a result, since the consequences of absconding do not vary with the nature of current offense. It is, of course, possible to postulate that committing a motoring offense (for example, "joy riding") is in some important way similar to absconding. Both, for example, involve putting oneself at risk for an extended period of time, whereas other delinquent acts can normally be completed fairly quickly. But to accept that similarities at this level of abstraction are the units of personal consistency is in effect to return to the sort of trait theory of personality to which environmental learning theory was designed to be an alternative. In any case, Laycock's results make it clear that previous absconding behavior is not the only effective predictor of absconding. Thus her study reopens the possibility of discovering enough trainee characteristics predictive of absconding from which to derive an effective prediction scale.

Despite the more positive results obtained by later researchers, only one has actually gone on to try to develop a prediction scale. In a study of borstal trainees allocated to open conditions in the prison department's midland region, Blanchard (1977) used a Bayesian method to construct a prediction equation based on some thirty variables, most of them trainee characteristics. Unfortunately, Blanchard did not apply his scale to a validation sample. It is essential to estimate predictive efficiency in a validation sample, because of the problem of shrinkage (see chapter 1). Shrinkage does not always occur (see Nuttall et. al., 1977), but it can be quite dramatic (Simon, 1971). Since shrinkage results from discrepancies between the construction sample and the population from which the sample is drawn, it can be lessened by the increasing the sample size. For this reason a very large construction sample was used in the present research.

The possibility of shrinkage must also be taken into account when assessing the predictive power of a scale. This is usually done by using a second sample (the validation sample) to assess the degree to which shrinkage has taken place. If shrinkage is large, then best estimates of the scale's predictive power should be obtained from the validation sample alone. On the other hand, if shrinkage is small or nonexistent, then best estimates may be obtained by combining the validation and construction samples. In this second case the improved representativeness resulting from enlarging the sample will more than compensate for any slight degree of bias that is entailed by including the construction sample.

Estimating the degree of shrinkage that has occurred by comparing a construction sample with a validation sample is more difficult than may at first appear. The problem is that an apparent decrease (or increase) in predictive power may reflect extraneous changes in either—such as in how open borstals are run (altering the overall rate of absconding), in the allocation policy (altering the relative frequency in open borstals of trainees falling into the different risk categories), or in recording practices (altering the recorded frequency of absconding)—rather than genuine shrinkage. It is important therefore to choose an index of predictive power that is, as far as possible, independent of both the overall rate of absconding and the proportion of trainees falling into the different risk categories. In addition, small differences between the scale's predictive power in the construction sample and in the validation sample can be expected to arise from sampling error. It is therefore desirable to be able to test the null hypothesis that these differences are due merely to sampling error. The technique adopted here meets all these requirements.

The proportion of trainees absconding at each level on the prediction scale was calculated separately for both construction and validation samples. If the scale works, then as risk scores increase so the proportion of trainees absconding should also increase. Plotting risk level against proportion of trainees absconding will give a graph whose shape indexes the power of the prediction scale (figure 6.1). Changes in the overall rate of absconding will affect the graph's height but not its gradient (figure 6.2). The proportion of trainees obtaining a given risk score will affect only the precision with which the absconding rate for that risk category can be estimated. Thus the gradient of the graph of percentage absconding versus risk score indexes the power of the prediction scale in a way that is unbiased by these factors. If the power of the prediction scale declines from the construction sample to the validation sample, then the construction-sample graph should be steeper than the validation-sample graph (figure 6.3).

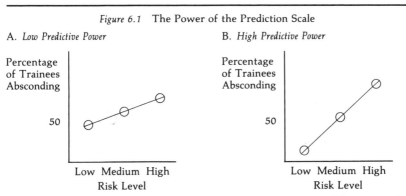

Figure 6.1   The Power of the Prediction Scale

A. *Low Predictive Power*

B. *High Predictive Power*

Note: If the scale has low predictive power (A), there will be little difference in the proportions of trainees absconding at each level of risk and the graph will be almost flat. The more the proportion of trainees absconding changes across risk levels, the steeper the graph will be and the higher the predictive power of the scale (B).

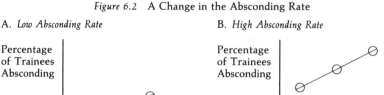

Figure 6.2   A Change in the Absconding Rate

A. *Low Absconding Rate*   B. *High Absconding Rate*

Note: With a higher overall rate of absconding, the proportion of trainees absconding is higher for each risk level, but the change in proportion from one risk level to another remains the same.

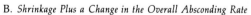

Figure 6.3   Detecting Shrinkage

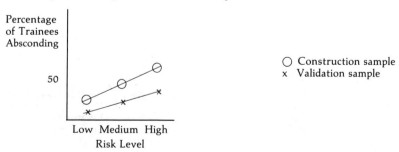

A. *Pure Shrinkage*

B. *Shrinkage Plus a Change in the Overall Absconding Rate*

Comparing the steepness of the two graphs could be difficult if the shape of the slope was complex. However, the relationship between risk score and absconding rate might be expected to be approximately linear. Thus the relationship can be described by a linear regression equation where the regression coefficient will index the steepness of the slope. A test for the parallelism of the construction- and validation-sample graphs can then be made by:

    a. fitting a regression model estimating the two regression lines that assumes that they are parallel; or
    b. fitting a model that allows the two to have different slopes.

If the second model fits significantly better than the first and the slope of the construction-sample graph is steeper than the slope of the validation-sample graph, then we may infer that shrinkage has occurred.

THE STUDY

The original motivation behind the present research was the purely practical concern to develop a prediction scale for identifying those male borstal trainees who would be particularly likely to abscond if allocated to open conditions.* Regardless of our success in this practical enterprise, however, the results have implications for the plausibility of rival theoretical accounts of the importance of individual differences in absconding. In particular, if trainee variables other than a history of absconding make an independent contribution to the prediction of absconding from open borstals, then the extreme form of the environmental learning theory account of individual differences would be called into question.

Construction Sample

Information on male trainees allocated to open borstals between 1 May 1977 and 31 December 1978 was extracted from the Young Offender Psychology Unit (YOPU) data base. This gave a construction sample of 4,583 cases. Missing data meant that not all of these cases could be used for all analyses. In particular, previous criminal-history data was available for only 3,761 cases. To

---

*The present research, in common with most other studies, focused only on absconding by male trainees. A study of female open-borstal trainees would be of interest. However, the small number of female trainees in open conditions (about fifty at any one time) makes research difficult.

determine whether they absconded, cases were followed up for a minimum of nine months after reception.*

Definition of an Absconding

An absconding was defined as an incident where a trainee had run away directly from the institution. Certain other unauthorized absences—namely, absconding from an outside working party, failure to return from home leave, or temporary release—were not counted as absconding. These were excluded because their circumstances are rather different, and only selected trainees are given such opportunities. Overall, 23 percent of the sample absconded during the follow-up period.

Procedure

Eighty variables (covering previous criminal and institutional history, family background, occupational status, ethnic origin, and indicators of psychiatric and physical disorder) were cross-tabulated against absconding from open borstals. Thirty-one of these proved to be significantly ($p < 0.05$) predictive. However, variables were retained as potential contributors to the prediction scale only if they were very significantly ($p < 0.001$) predictive of absconding. This precaution was intended to reduce the possibility of basing the scale on chance associations. Each of the 25 variables surviving this test was then reduced to categories with absconding rates that differed by at least 5 percent. In practice, this reduced variables to two or, at the most, three categories. The most predictive variable was (not surprisingly) previous absconding behavior, so the sample was divided into three groups on the basis of this variable, as follows:

> *Group A:* those trainees who had previously absconded from Home Office custody (that is, from the police or from a remand center, detention center, borstal, or prison). Only 3 percent of the sample fell into this group, but they had a 57 percent absconding rate.
>
> *Group B:* those trainees who had previously absconded from noncustodial situations (that is, from other than Home Office custody). About 13 percent of the sample fell into this group, and they had an absconding rate of about 36 percent.
>
> *Group C:* trainees who had no recorded previous absconding behavior. This group had an absconding rate of 21 percent.

*Borstal training is of variable (discretionary) length. However, we found that the average training time for trainees allocated to open conditions tended to be about 34 weeks. Absconding from open borstals tends to occur toward the beginning of the sentence; about half within the first month, according to Laycock. Borstal was replaced by a sentence of "youth custody" in 1983.

Group A is too small to subdivide, and its absconding rate is high enough to justify assigning it to a high-risk category without further ado. Groups B and C are sufficiently large to warrant subdivision. Accordingly, variables were sought that distinguished absconders within these two groups. Two variables, age and the number of occasions on which the trainees had been convicted for motor theft (taking and driving away) were particularly successful at doing this. Groups B and C were therefore further subdivided by these variables (giving 18 subgroups). The remaining variables were then examined to identify features that consistently distinguished absconders from nonabsconders within these subgroups. Being unemployed on arrest consistently discriminated absconders within all the subgroups. Color (coded as "white" versus "nonwhite") powerfully discriminated absconders from nonabsconders among the subgroups composing Group C. Accordingly, nonwhite trainees in Group C were assigned to a low-risk category. Log-linear models were then used to verify that, for the remaining trainees, previous noncustodial absconding, age, motor theft, and employment status on arrest all independently contributed to the prediction of absconding from open borstals.

Having selected variables for the prediction scale, we found the next problem was to decide how to weight them. It would have been possible to use weights from the (all two-way associations) log-linear model. However, such a weighting scheme would be arithmetically too complicated to be applied routinely by borstal staff. Instead the (two-way associations) log-linear model was used to generate expected absconding rates for each combination of the predictor variables. A simple weighting scheme was then devised that approximately corresponded to these expected absconding rates. This made it possible to operationalize the prediction scale as the algorithm depicted in table 6.1. Table 6.2 shows the absconding rate associated with each risk category for the construction sample. Scores of 7 or greater were placed in category 7, and scores of 0 or less were placed in category 0.

Validation Sample

Information on male trainees allocated to open borstals between 1 January 1979 and 31 March 1980 was extracted from the Young Offender Psychology Unit data base. Eliminating cases with missing data ($N = 692$) gave 2,387 cases for analysis. The follow-up for data on absconding was as in the construction sample. The overall absconding rate was 20 percent.

Procedure and Results

The algorithm from table 6.1 was applied to the validation sample. Table 6.3 gives the absconding rates associated with each risk

Table 6.1 Algorithm for Categorizing Trainees According to Levels of Risk

	Points				
	+20	+2	+1	0	−20
1. Any previous custodial abscondings?	Yes			No	
2. Any previous noncustodial abscondings?		Yes		No	
If no, is trainee colored?				No	Yes
3. Was trainee employed at time of arrest? (N.B. at school=not employed)			No	Yes	
4. How many separate convictions for TADA?*		Two or more	One	None	
5. What age was trainee on date of sentence?		15 or 16	17 or 18	19 or 20	

*Taking and driving away vehicles.

Table 6.2 Absconding Rates by Risk Category for the Construction Sample

	Risk Category							
	0	1	2	3	4	5	6	7
Number of Absconders	49	69	133	198	163	77	56	106
Number of Trainees in Category	548	485	715	874	570	241	138	190
Percent of Cases that Absconded	9	14	19	23	29	32	41	56

category for the validation sample. Logistic analysis (Fienberg, 1980) was used to test the statistical significance of the relationship between risk categories and absconding rates in the validation sample. Regression models were fitted with the computer program GLIM (Baker and Nelder, 1978). The linear trend was significant (x^2 = 106.2, with one degree of freedom; $P < 0.001$). Departures from linearity were not significant (x^2 = 9.9, with six degrees of freedom). Thus the risk categories appear to form a straightforward linear index of proneness to abscond.

A logistic analysis was conducted to test for the presence of shrinkage. Risk category and sample (construction versus validation) were the two independent variables. The proportion absconding for each combination of these two variables was the input to the logistic analysis. As described in the introduction, if shrinkage has taken place the linear relationship of risk category to absconding rate should have a steeper gradient in the construction sample than in the validation sample. If shrinkage is absent, the two slopes should (except for chance variation) be parallel. Thus a test for the

Table 6.3   Absconding Rates by Risk Category for the Validation Sample

	Risk Category							
	0	1	2	3	4	5	6	7
Number of Absconders	29	48	87	116	81	44	36	37
Number of Trainees in Category	421	312	474	518	333	151	91	87
Percent of Cases that Absconded	7	15	18	22	24	29	40	43

Table 6.4   Absconding Rates for the Combined Sample

	Risk Category							
	0	1	2	3	4	5	6	7
Percent of Cases that Absconded	8	15	19	23	27	31	40	52
Number of Trainees in Category	969	797	1,189	1,392	903	392	229	277

interaction between the sample and the linear component of risk category is a pure test for shrinkage. This effect was small and within the range of expected chance fluctuations (χ^2 = 1.3, with one degree of freedom).

Given that shrinkage appears to be negligible in the present case, best estimates of the absconding rate associated with each risk category can be obtained by combining validation and construction samples. Table 6.4 shows the absconding rates observed for the combined sample.

DISCUSSION

Our data indicate that on the basis of a few pieces of simple background information it is possible effectively to grade trainees in terms of their proneness to abscond from open borstals. The theoretical and practical issues raised by this capability are discussed in the final two sections.

Theoretical Issues

The purpose of this section is to consider possible explanations for the predictiveness of the various components of our prediction scale. The scale has six components, two of which refer to previous absconding. That these should be important predictors of future absconding is hardly surprising, since a correlation between past and future absconding is suggested by most theoretical perspectives. According to the traditional trait theory of personality, for example, a person with an "absconding personality" (a complex of traits that collectively predispose a trainee to abscond), if there is such a thing, should have been predisposed to abscond in the past and should be predisposed to abscond in the future. Indeed, from this perspective, the most direct available index of the relevant combination of traits might be past absconding. Clarke and Martin's (1971) research led them to reject traditional trait theory. Instead they proposed a learning theory model of absconding according to which the rewarding quality of a first absconding experience makes the trainee more inclined to abscond in the future. Yet another possibility has been proposed by Millham, Bullock, and Hosie (1978). Discounting both trait and learning theory, they propose what they call an interactionist account. They argue that the effect of having absconded is to make life in the institution after recapture more unpleasant (because of official punishment, loss of privileges, staff hostility, loss of status with inmates, and the like). Thus the institutional reaction to the recaptured absconders provides them with an even stronger motive to abscond than they started with. At present both the learning theory account and the interactionist account are compatible with the evidence. Clarke and Martin's failure to find traits predictive of absconding would count against the trait theory, though later work (Laycock, 1977; Brown, Druce, and Sawyer, 1978) using more sophisticated methodology has suggested that the trait approach may have some application to absconding.

It is less easy to explain the predictive value of the other four components of the risk scale. Laycock (1977) had previously noted the relationship of motoring offenses to absconding from open borstals. She considered a number of possible explanations: that absconders hope to use this behavior (stealing a car) in their absconding; that they are risk takers or excitement seekers; or that they are particularly inclined to miss their family. It is not clear how plausible these accounts are. Car theft is not a particularly common method of absconding and it is not obviously more useful to someone on the run than burglary or theft (absconders are, after all, short of such things as food, money, and civilian clothing). Further, motoring offenses are by no means the most risky type of offense; offenses against the person probably carry a greater chance of conviction, and housebreaking might be as exciting. It is possible, however, that the form of risk taking involved in motoring offenses is similar to that involved in absconding. Specifically, both involve being in an illegal, risky state for an extended period of time (the period of being on the run for absconding and the period of driving around in the stolen car for motor offending). No other offense commonly committed by juveniles shares this feature. A willingness to tolerate being at risk for an extended period of time may be a key element in absconding.

As far as we are aware, no previous published work has identified the predictive value of age, employment on arrest, or color, and so no explanations for these have been put forward. We ourselves can suggest only some tentative explanations for their predictive value. We assume that absconding is an attempt to escape from noxious features of the institutional environment. Absconding should therefore be more likely for trainees who are being bullied or who have an antagonistic relationship with staff and less likely for trainees who receive social support from other inmates or who get on well with staff. Age, employment on arrest, and color all seem relevant to these hypothesized mediating variables. Thus, older trainees are probably better at handling relationships with authority and are less likely to be bullied (because they are bigger and have more prestige). Younger trainees are more vulnerable to bullying and more likely to have got into the borstal system because they proved unmanageable in community homes (and hence are more likely to develop an antagonistic relationship with staff in the borstal). Unemployment may relate to absconding because difficulty in relating to authority figures contributes to both. Finally, black trainees (the majority of nonwhite trainees are of West Indian origin) may form a more cohesive social group within borstal and so may protect each other from bullying and in general cushion each other against the stresses of institutional life.

Regardless of whether these speculations are correct, the present results do have one clear theoretical implication. About half the predictive power of the scale is accounted for by variables other than previous absconding. It is difficult to see how this result can be accommodated within the extreme form of environmental learning theory, at least as it was originally formulated. No doubt some form of learning theory could be used to explain the data, but the claim that the only real predictor of a behavior is having previously engaged in the same behavior would have to be abandoned. Apart from requiring a liberalized notion of "similar behavior", such a revised learning theory model would probably also have to incorporate the notion that the environments to which individuals are exposed are partly determined by the individual's own characteristics.

Practical Issues

The borstal system for males in England and Wales comprises eleven closed (secure) establishments and nine open establishments. Allocation procedures are designed to place in closed conditions trainees who are likely to (a) abscond, (b) cause public alarm if they absconded, (c) commit serious offenses if they absconded, and (d) abuse open conditions by smuggling in illicit items (for example, drugs). One practical issue, then, is whether our prediction scale might be used to improve these allocation procedures.

At a minimum, we would suggest that trainees falling into absconding risk categories 6 and 7 should be allocated to closed conditions. Nearly half this group will abscond and therefore end up in closed conditions eventually. For each extra place required in closed conditions, this procedure would save about one absconding. Absconders often commit offenses while on the run. We estimate that for each extra closed place required nearly one and a half known absconding-related offenses would be saved.*

It is much less clear whether trainees falling into the low-risk categories (say, categories 0 and 1) should automatically be allocated to open conditions. Present allocation procedures place great emphasis on excluding "dangerous" trainees from open conditions. This practice can be justified on the grounds that it avoids public alarm and diminishes the frequency of serious offenses being committed by absconders. The current practice does, however, have certain limitations. In particular, it assumes that borstal trainees can be sensibly categorized into two groups: "the dangerous" and "the not-dangerous". It is more likely that there is a continuum of dangerousness and that some of those trainees currently allocated to closed conditions are only marginal cases. For example, having two previous convictions for minor violence will get a trainee allocated to closed conditions in most geographical regions, but having only one such conviction will allow him to be allocated to open conditions. In such marginal cases it would make sense to pay more attention to the absconding risk category. Thus we would suggest that cases with two convictions for minor violence who fall into risk category 0 (who have an 8 percent chance of absconding) are better candidates for open conditions than cases with one conviction for minor violence who fall into risk categories 4 or 5 (with a risk of absconding that is nearly four times greater). Essentially the point is that, for cases that are marginal in terms of dangerousness, whether they will abscond is much more predictable than whether they will commit a serious offense if they abscond. Thus, if our aim is to minimize those

---

*According to Laycock (1977) about a quarter of absconders are charged as the result of offenses committed while on the run. The average number of offenses associated with each trainee charged was 5.5. The number of known offenses resulting from absconding is therefore roughly 1.4 per absconding. Allowing for undetected offenses, the true figure could easily be ten times as high.

absconding incidents which result in serious offenses, we can achieve this aim more effectively by allocating in terms of absconding risk than by allocating in terms of the seriousness of trainees' previous convictions.

Another possibility is selective allocation between open establishments. There is considerable variation between open borstals in their absconding rates. Some reduction in the overall absconding rate might be obtained by placing those high-risk trainees who are allocated to open conditions in borstals having low absconding rates. However, the scope for doing this is limited by the concern to place trainees within a reasonable traveling distance of their homes (to facilitate visits).

A procedure that might be effective would be to leave the allocation system unaltered but to attach to trainees' documentation some explicit indication of their absconding proneness. Most theories of absconding give some role to institutional events and in particular to trainees' relations with staff. Thus it may be that staff could be trained to respond to high-risk trainees in a way that would reduce their inclination to abscond. On the other hand, flagging high-risk trainees might have negative consequences. Labels can sometimes turn into self-fulfilling prophecies. It should be possible to test this experimentally. Certainly, if flagging were shown to be effective in containing high-risk trainees, it would be a very simple and cheap procedure.

In conclusion, we have shown that, contrary to some previous attempts, it is possible to identify trainees who are particularly likely to abscond from open borstals. Moreover, this was done on the basis of a small number of individual characteristics known at the time of allocation. The practical implications include the possibility of making wider use of open conditions and the more effective control of potential absconders.

REFERENCES

Baker, R. J., and Nelder, J. A. (1978). *The GLIM system.* Oxford: Numerical Algorithms Group.

Banks, C.; Mayhew, P.; and Sapsford, R. (1975). *Absconding from open prisons.* Home Office Research Study No. 26. London: Her Majesty's Stationery Office.

Blanchard, A. J. (1977). *Midland region borstal allocation project, Part II.* DPS Series II, No. 50. London: Home Office.

Brown, R. J.; Druce, N. R.; and Sawyer, C. E. (1978). Individual differences and absconding behavior. *British Journal of Criminology* 18:62–70.

Clarke, R. V. G., and Martin, D. N. (1971). *Absconding from approved schools.*

Home Office Research Study No. 12. London: Her Majesty's
Stationery Office.
Fienberg, S. E. (1980). *The analysis of cross-classified categorical data.* 2d ed.
Cambridge, MA: MIT Press.
Laycock, G. K. (1977). *Absconding from borstal.* Home Office Research Study
No. 41. London: Her Majesty's Stationery Office.
Millham, S.; Bullock, R.; and Hosie, K. (1978). *Locking up children.* Farnborough,
Hants: Saxon House.
Nuttall, C. P. et al. (1977). *Parole in England and Wales.* Home Office Research
Study No. 38. London: Her Majesty's Stationery Office.
Simon, F. H. (1971). *Prediction methods in criminology.* Home Office Research
Study No. 7. London: Her Majesty's Stationery Office.

CHAPTER 7

Prediction and Treatment of Self-Injury by Female Young Offenders

J. ERIC CULLEN

SUMMARY

The phenomenon of deliberate self-injury in a closed institution for female young offenders was studied. In three phases, the author explored (a) a wide range of variables to determine what might discriminate self-injurers from noninjurers, (b) whether ratings based on apparently predictive variables were useful in the subsequent identification of high-risk offenders, and (c) whether a systematic approach to treating self-injurers would reduce the frequency of this behavior. The new ratings were found to have better predictive capacity than chance or existing procedures, and following practical intervention the rates of self-injury fell significantly.

INTRODUCTION

There are a large number of theoretical interpretations of deliberate self-injury. Rosenthal et. al. (1972) explained self-injury by women as a means of dealing with genital conflict and trauma centering around menstruation. They reported that the histories of young women who had repeatedly cut their wrists revealed a significant incidence of early physical illness and surgery and markedly abnormal patterns of menstruation. They hypothesized that adults in helpless and overwhelmingly passive situations often identify with their oppressor and act out against themselves the aggression of which they feel themselves the victims. Cookson (1977) and McKerracher, Loughnane, and Watson (1968), however, found no evidence to support the contention that self-injury is related to premenstrual tension or irregular menstruation.

Several authors (Ping-Nie Pao, 1969; Kafka, 1969; Graff and Mallin, 1967; Rosenthal et al., 1972) reported a process of depersonalization leading to self-injury. Patients appeared to enter "an altered state of consciousness" in which they progress to numbness, feel flat and withdrawn, and report that the self-injury was effective as a means of reintegration. Matthews (1968) suggested that adolescent girls were more likely to express their difficulties under stress by withdrawal, depression, and preoccupation than were boys, who tended to engage in "other-directed activity, especially of the aggressive type."

One of the most frequently reported characteristics of self-injury is the absence of pain. Grunebaum and Klerman (1967) suggest that this loss of feeling may represent a special form of isolation or dissociation. McKerracher, Loughnane, and Watson (1968) reported that only 28 percent of unstable patients said that they felt pain during the act of self-injury and that 73 percent agreed that pain was experienced later, the time lapse varying widely from a few hours to several days.

Another aspect of self-injury related to the absence of pain and dissociation is the sense of tension release. Ping-Nie Pao (1969) reported a female patient feeling "very tense; following a period of tenseness she decided to be by herself; while alone, the tension mounted; then, all of a sudden, she discovered she had already cut herself." He interpreted this pattern as entering "a regressed ego state with surrendering of autonomous ego functioning to a drive-dominated act which was simultaneously sadistic and masochistic." Simpson (1975) put the case more simply, arguing that patients tend to feel "depressed, angry and tense and want to express the extent of their feelings but feel unable to do so in words. Tension becomes the predominant affect. . . . As the increasing tension becomes unbearable a transition to a depersonalized state occurs. . . . They become increasingly isolated and self-absorbed, withdrawn and dissociated, and suddenly they cut." The act of cutting is apparently therapeutic and they even describe cutting with a sense of relief and pleasure after which they were often able to sleep.

More recently a number of authors have explained self-injury in behavioral terms. Robbins (1977), in providing a teacher's guide to the treatment of self-injurious behavior in mentally handicapped children, referred to the work of Sandow (1975). Sandow described the behavior as usually being performed by children with poor communication skills. There was often an increasing tolerance to pain and a related increase in the severity of the injuries. The children were found to use the behavior to modify adult behaviors, sometimes to gain attention or other rewards and sometimes to escape or avoid unwanted or unpleasant attention. Brewster et. al. (1977) responded to this conclusion by cautioning that "self-injury is not necessarily a behaviour that is simply caused and maintained by attention." They go on to suggest "it is very important to record and objectively analyse self-injury in terms of setting, conditions and consequences before deciding on the method of treatment."

Perhaps any attempt at an all-embracing explanation of self-injury is inappropriate, the range of factors and the variety of behavior encompassed being so great. "In the long term, an effective means of reducing a problem behaviour can only be discovered from the basis of a careful and precise analysis of the behaviour and its possible causes" (Brewster et al., 1977). Self-injury in a closed institution, especially a borstal for girls, presents a unique combination of factors, the understanding of which forms the basis of this research. Bullwood Hall is the only closed (secure) borstal for female young offenders in the United Kingdom. Trainees are committed to a borstal for an indeterminate custodial sentence of between six months and two years, with the majority in practice serving between six and nine months.

STUDY 1: THE IDENTIFICATION OF VARIABLES THAT DISCRIMINATE SELF-INJURERS FROM THOSE WHO DID NOT SELF-INJURE

Method

A sample of 95 female trainees at Bullwood Hall Borstal aged 15 to 21 were assessed during the six months from April to October 1979. Of these, 50 were trainees who did not injure themselves during training and 45 were trainees who had injured themselves (of which 34 injured themselves, 4 attempted suicide, and 7 did both). All persons who had injured themselves or attempted suicide were rated on a large number of variables within one of four categories:

1. *Historical information*, including age, history of broken home, having been the subject of a Care Order, previous criminal history, previous institutional experience, marital status, having had children, psychiatric history, and number of previous self-injuries or suicide attempts.

2. *Personality information* was derived from four questionnaires: the Eysenck Personality Questionnaire (Eysenck and Eysenck, 1975); Blackburn's Aggression Scale (Blackburn, 1977); and two brief inventories by Eysenck and Wilson concerning self-esteem and happiness (Eysenck and Wilson, 1975). Descriptions of these are available from the author on request.

3. *General environment*, based on staff and trainees' accounts of the training house environment in which they were resident.

Assessments were made via the Moos Correctional Institutions Environment Scale (CIES), which purports to assess perception in terms of the extent of expressiveness, involvement, autonomy, support, personal-problem orientation, practical-problem orientation, order and organization, clarity and control (Moos, 1968).

4. *Immediate circumstances,* including the trainee's description of events before, during, and after the self-injury as well as a self-report of her emotional state, sense of pain, and the like. Information was obtained via a standard interview form and was substantiated whenever possible by comments from hospital or house staff using comparable interview forms.

Results

Analysis of variance and nonparametric trend tests were applied to the data comparing the characteristics of those who self-injured or attempted suicide with the noninjuring group. Table 7.1 gives a summary of the results of the statistical analyses.

History. Trainees who attempted suicide but did not injure themselves were significantly ($p < .01$) more likely to describe their family as being intact, to have had previous violent offenses ($p < .05$), and not to have children ($p < .05$). The 34 trainees who had self-injured only were significantly more likely than those who had not to have had previous custodial experience ($p < .005$) and to have previously injured themselves ($p < .001$). Both groups, the attempted suicides and the self-injurers, were significantly more likely than those who had not injured themselves to have had psychiatric treatment on a regular basis ($p < .02$) and to have had previous suicide attempts ($p < .002$). There were no significant differences in marital status or age.

Personality. Trainees who attempted suicide or injured themselves while at Bullwood Hall were significantly more likely to describe themselves as aggressive ($p < .05/.001$), unhappy ($p < .001$), nervous ($p < .002/.01$), and as having a low self-opinion ($p < .05/.01$) than were the noninjurers. The self-injurers only were also more likely to describe themselves as "psychotic" or tough-minded ($p < .01$), while suicide attempters tended to see themselves as introverted ($p < .05$).

General Environment. Trainees who attempted suicide were significantly more likely to describe their training house environment as more supportive ($p < .02$), encouraging open expression of feelings ($p < .05$), and oriented toward helping them with personal problems ($p < .05$). Self-injurers, however, found the environment significantly less supportive ($p < .05$) and lacking in order and organization ($p < .05$). The self-injurers were further distinguished from both the non-

Table 7.1 Significant Correlations between Self-Injury and Suicide Attempts and Historical, Personality, and Environmental Variables

	Current Suicide Attempts		Current Self-Injury	
	Level of Significance	*Direction of Correlation*	*Level of Significance*	*Direction of Correlation*
Historical Variables				
1. Family intact	$p < .01$	(+)	N.S.	
2. Previous self-injury	N.S.		$p < .001$	(+)
3. Previous suicide attempt	$p < .002$	(+)	$p < .001$	(+)
4. Previous violence	$p < .05$	(+)	N.S.	
5. Previous custody	N.S.		$p < .005$	(+)
6. Previous psychiatric treatment	$p < .02$	(+)	$p < .02$	(+)
7. Had children	$p < .05$	(−)	N.S.	
Personality Variables				
8. Aggression	$p < .05$	(+)	$p < .001$	(+)
9. Self-esteem	$p < .05$	(−)	$p < .01$	(−)
10. Happiness	$p < .001$	(−)	$p < .001$	(−)
11. Psychoticism	N.S.		$p < .01$	(+)
12. Neuroticism	$p < .002$	(+)	$p < .01$	(+)
13. Extraversion	$p < .05$	(−)	N.S.	
General Environmental Variables				
14. Supportive	$p < .02$	(+)	$p < .05$	(−)
15. Encouraging expression	$p < .05$	(+)	N.S.	
16. Personal-problem oriented	$p < .05$	(+)	N.S.	
17. Having order and organization	N.S.		$p < .05$	(−)
18. Controlled	N.S.		$p < .02$	(+)

Note: Statistics used were raw and corrected χ^2 and Kendall's τ.

injurers and the attempted suicides in that they felt their training houses, although lacking order and organization, to be overcontrolled by staff ($p < .02$). Trainees who repeatedly self-injured were significantly ($p < .01$) more likely to receive Governor's Reports for serious institutional rule violations. The training house that had a "therapeutic regime" model and group counseling as the central element of its program had by far the lowest rate of self-injury (1) and suicide attempts (0) during the study period, and both staff and trainees described it in overwhelmingly favorable terms. Staff and trainees rated support, expression, involvement, and personal-problem orientation the most important aspects of this injury-free environment.

Immediate Circumstances. Complete interview information was available for 45 incidents of self-injury. Over two-thirds (70 percent) of all incidents of self-injury or attempted suicide were committed in the trainee's cell between 6 P.M. and midnight, while the trainee was alone. A large number (16 of 45) occurred between 6 and 7:30 P.M., the period when most informal socializing would normally occur. Nineteen of the 35 trainees interviewed shortly after the incidents reported feeling no pain, and another 14 reported feeling only slight discomfort. The remaining two reported a pleasant physical sensation. When asked what reasons they had at the time for injuring themselves, the main reasons given were feelings of depression (25), homesickness for family (12), manipulation in order to escape from or avoid problems (8), desire for sympathy (5), or feelings of guilt (5). By far the most preferred methods for self-injuring were multiple lacerations (usually of the forearms), done with glass from broken windows or metal from toothpaste or tobacco tins, and "strangulation," by tying a ligature (usually a torn sheet or mattress cover) around the neck. These two methods accounted for 40 of the 45 incidents recorded in the assessment.

Conclusion

Self-injury within the borstal appeared to follow relatively clear patterns, and the results indicated that self-injurers differed from noninjurers on a number of variables. Nine of the best discriminating variables were then used in an attempt to predict those trainees most likely to injure themselves or attempt suicide.

STUDY 2: THE VALIDATION OF RISK RATINGS ON A SAMPLE OF BULLWOOD HALL RECEPTIONS

Method

All receptions over a four-month period (March–June 1980) were tested and interviewed and then given "risk ratings" based on nine factors:* (1) previous psychiatric treatment, (2) previous institutional experience, (3) previous self-injury or suicide attempt, (4) a neuroticism score over 18, (5) an aggression score over 24, (6) a self-esteem score under 14, and (7) a happiness score under 11, plus (8a) previous commitment to a borstal, and (9a) a psychoticism over 8 (for self-injurers only), or (8b) previous violent offenses and (9b) an extraversion score under 10 (for those who attempted suicide only.) Each variable was scored 0 or 1, and the cut-off point in each case was determined by applying χ^2 tests to the scores for the 95 trainees from

*Alternative prediction instruments are currently being examined: see Appendix.

study 1 and accepting a significance level of $p < .05$. Risk scores were then obtained for 92 receptions and later compared with incidences of self-injury or attempted suicide among the sample. The trainees were not told the purpose of the testing, and interview questions were conducted as part of a routine induction procedure.

Results

A risk rating of 5 or higher accurately predicted 83 percent of all self-injurers. The results of trend tests confirmed that this differentiation was significant (χ^2 = 10.6, with one degree of freedom; $p < .01$). Only 8 percent of those scoring 5 or higher were false positives (noninjurers), and there were only two false negatives, or trainees with low risk scores who subsequently injured themselves. An additional comparison was made between the scores and the only existing procedure for identifying risks, the *F* classification. This standard prison procedure identifies receptions who have attempted suicide at any time in their lives and is not intended to predict self-injury. The *F* classification was recorded for just over half (55 percent) of the self-injurers, suggesting that the new scores might substantially improve our predictive capability.

STUDY 3: THE PREVENTION AND TREATMENT OF SELF-INJURIES

Method

An analysis of the results obtained from the above two studies suggested the direction that treatment might most effectively take. Risk ratings were collected weekly on all receptions during their first week in the borstal and were circulated to all relevant staff. Any trainee with a high (5 or more) rating was interviewed to explore possible problems amenable to practical solutions or individual counseling. Examples of practical help were phone calls to the trainee's family, special letters or visits, and arrangements for the trainee to share a room with another girl with whom she could relate. The hospital staff, who were responsible for recording and treating all reported injuries, agreed to circulate confidential lists of all self-injuries on a weekly basis as well as maintaining a daily link with the psychologist, who counseled all self-injurers personally.

Intervention

Viewed as an operant behavior, self-injury appeared to perform one or more of a limited number of functions:

1. to reduce the physical sensation of tension and anxiety;

2. to attract positive attention in the form of sympathy and comfort;

3. to punish oneself for perceived failings, such as being a disappointment to one's family;

4. to manipulate the environment for overt escape or avoidance (for example, transfer to another house).

The appropriate intervention strategies were dictated by assumptions as to which of these objectives were in operation, bearing in mind that they were not mutually exclusive. Where positive attention was an apparent cause of injuring, staff were encouraged to control their sympathetic responding after self-injury and to behave as neutrally as possible. Trainees were advised to take preventive steps, such as ringing the cell bells and talking to staff or asking to see the psychologist, before the act. Increasing injury-free periods were then reinforced with such rewards as attention, practical help, and cigarettes, as the situation warranted.

When trainees with a high risk rating indicated during their induction week that they were depressed and feeling guilty toward or missing their parents and family, arrangements were often made to allow special telephone calls or visits. A high risk rating followed by one or more self-injuries within a few days or weeks of arrival at the borstal frequently warranted allowing the trainee priority in being bunked-up, or sharing a room, with a more stable and favorably perceived trainee. These practical interventions would be complemented by individual counseling from the psychologist or psychiatrist, depending on the approach deemed most appropriate. If manipulation was apparently part or all of the cause for self-injuring, staff were advised to ignore consistently the trainees' entreaties and to advise them of the official channels through which they could obtain redress, such as house changes.

Self-injury as a new behavior in the closed borstal setting has many of the characteristics of an "escape" mode of behavior. The trainee, confined within the "apparatus" (borstal generally, cell specifically), is subjected to aversive stimuli (oppressive confinement, abuse from peers, guilt reactions, "reactive depression," and the like). Under normal circumstances she could escape or avoid the aversive stimuli through flight, the comforting of family or friends, or perhaps the use of alcohol or drugs. None of these are available to her in the borstal; having little or none of the deterrent anticipation of pain that normally helps to prevent injury, she may opt for the tension relief afforded by self-injury. Most recorded behavioral treatment of self-injury takes the form of either aversion therapy (essentially punishment) or extinction (essentially withholding praise or punishment). There are serious limitations to applying either to the present population. The main relevant application of aversion therapy has been with retarded children who showed a high frequency of self-injury such as face-beating or banging their heads against the wall. These acts occurred in public places such as classrooms and were usually of a high-frequency, low-interval nature: more amenable to punishment techniques. The main limitation of practicing extinction is that the withholding of attention would need to be practiced consistently and immediately from the first incident by all concerned or a variable schedule of reinforcement would be established. Whether this approach was warranted would depend on the circumstances of each case.

Results

The rates of self-injuring and attempted suicide were compared for the periods October 1979–June 1980 and October 1980–June 1981, inclusive—that is, before and after the implementation of the new screening procedures, which were introduced on 1 October 1980. χ^2 tests (corrected for continuity), applied to the total numbers who injured themselves or attempted suicide as proportions of the total numbers at risk, proved significant for both self-injurers (χ^2 = 11.4, with one degree of freedom; $p < .001$) and attempted suicides (χ^2 = 9.7, with one degree of freedom; $p < .01$). Table 7.2 provides the results, using a number of comparisons, all of which show appreciable decreases in the second period. This is true despite the fact that the history of previous self-injury and other predictive variables had continued at comparable levels since the beginning of the research. The frequency of attempted suicides declined so substantially that they were dropped from subsequent analyses.

Possible design limitations

The reduction in self-injury may have come from: (1) changes in the composition of the population, (2) differences in recording procedures, (3) other factors, such as seasonal shifts or changes in staff in crucial positions, as well as (4) the success of the "treatment." In order to clarify the first point, all the variables collected in the first study were monitored continuously. There were no significant changes in the nature of the population in terms of such factors as a history of self-injury or of psychiatric treatment. The recording procedures were those used by the hospital staff consistently since before 1978, well before the research began.

The possibility of a seasonal pattern to self-injuries was suggested by the similarity between the 1979 and 1980 monthly rates (see figure 7.1). To control for this, a comparable nine-month period was

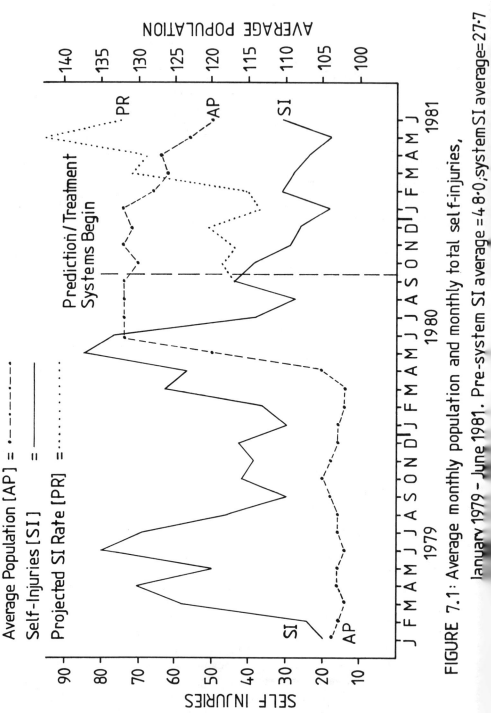

FIGURE 7.1: Average monthly population and monthly total self-injuries, January 1979 – June 1981. Pre-system SI average = 48·0; system SI average=27·7

Table 7.2 Summary of Results

	1 October 1979–1 July 1980	1 October 1980–1 July 1981	Percentage Change
Total trainees at risk during nine-month periods	296	308	+4%
Average monthly population	116	126	+9%
Percentage of receptions having history of self-injury	40%	43%	+8%
Total number of self-injuries*	465	249	−46%
Total number of suicide attempts	21	5	−76%
Total number of trainees who self-injured	103	68	−34%
Average number of self-injuries per month	51.7	27.7	−46%
Monthly rate of injuries per trainee (including noninjurers)	.33	.16	−52%
Average number of self-injuries per self-injurer	4.5	3.7	−18%

*These figures were taken from the borstal hospital log of self-inflicted injuries. For the purposes of this research, tattooing and a small number of other behaviors (such as jumping into the swimming pool or shaving the head) recorded in the log were excluded from consideration.

monitored. Figure 7.1 also has a line indicating the rate of self-injury expected had the previous rate continued, including the changes in trainee numbers by month. As for the efficacy of "treatment," the methodological requirement of randomly allocating girls to differential treatments or no treatment was operationally impossible due to the institution's allocation system, which required trainees to be placed in training houses on a space-available basis. An additional limitation was the selective requirements of special facilities, such as the "therapeutic community" and Day Training Centre. Necessity dictated that these limitations be accepted in any attempt to understand and reduce self-injuries.

DISCUSSION

Risk ratings developed for a secure institution for female young offenders appear to be an effective means of identifying those girls most likely to injure themselves (or attempt suicide) while so contained. There were also a number of personality variables that discriminated but that did not necessarily improve the predictive power of such ratings. The ratings used had the additional value of also identifying those trainees most likely to be repeat injurers. These ratings are not intended to be applicable to all populations, as the predictive criteria will presumably vary according to both the nature of the population and the environment in which it exists.

There was some evidence that those girls who attempted suicide were discernibly different from those who only injured themselves. Having children may be a deterrent influence in the contemplation of suicide, and it would seem that self-injurers are rather more experienced in terms of custodial confinement. The results of assessing their perceptions of the general environment of the wing on which they lived suggest that those girls who attempted suicide were dealt with more sympathetically after the event and subsequently saw their house environment as more supportive and helpful than did the self-injurers. There was some evidence, albeit equivocal, that a regime geared toward the open expression of feelings, mutual support, and counseling had a positive effect on the incidence of self-inflicted injury.

There appeared to be two relatively discrete types of self-injurer in this sample. The first group, by far the larger in number, were those girls who injured themselves within a few weeks of their arrival, did so only once or twice, and then only relatively superficially. These girls responded well to practical interventions and advice and seldom persisted with their injuring. The second group, much smaller in number, were identified as a result of the number of injuries they committed and their apparent immunity to most efforts at positive intervention. Girls in this second group are the subject of current research being carried out beyond the scope of this work.

In summary, a simple system of predictive risk ratings was found effectively to identify those female young offenders most at risk of self-injuring or attempting suicide. Following practical intervention and counseling, the incidence of both injuring and suicide attempts fell significantly.

APPENDIX

After the system of risk ratings had been in force for several months, a logistic regression was applied to the data to determine whether a more parsimonious predictive model could be derived. The results of these analyses implied that the main effects S (self-injury or attempted suicide in history) and H (other historical variables, for example, previous institutional experience or psychiatric treatment) made significant independent contributions to predicting self-injury but that the questionnaire scores did not. Consequently, a modified rating scale was devised to reflect these results. The new scale was calculated as follows:

RATING	DESCRIPTION
0	No history of self-injury or attempted suicide. The rating remains 0 even when one or more other historical variables apply.
1	A history of self-injury or attempted suicide.
2	A history of self-injury/suicide attempt plus *one* other historical predictor.
3	A history of self-injury/suicide attempt plus two or more other predictors.

The question of the efficacy of this modified rating system forms part of ongoing research.

REFERENCES

Blackburn, R. (1977). *The development and validation of scales to measure hostility and aggression.* Special Hospitals Research Report No. 12. London: Department of Health and Social Security.

Brewster, L.; Hattersley, J.; Hope, R.; and Tennant, L. (1977). Self-injurious behaviour—A few words of caution. *APEX* 5:4–7.

Cookson, H. M. (1977). A survey of self-injury in a closed prison for women. *British Journal of Criminology* 17:332–47.

Eysenck, H., and Eysenck, S. (1975). *Manual of the Eysenck Personality Questionnaire.* London: Hodder and Stoughton.

Eysenck, H., and Wilson, G. (1975). *Know your own personality.* Harmondsworth: Penguin.

Graff, H., and Mallin, R. (1967). The syndrome of the wrist cutter. *American Journal of Psychiatry* 124:36–42.

Grunebaum, H. U., and Klerman, G. L. (1967). Wrist slashing. *American Journal of Psychiatry* 124:527–34.

Kafka, J. S. (1969). The body as transitional object: A psycho-analytic study of a self-mutilating patient. *British Journal of Medical Psychology* 42:207–12.

Matthews, P. C. (1968). Epidemic self-injury in an adolescent unit. *International Journal of Social Psychiatry* 14:125–33.

McKerracher, D. W.; Loughnane, T.; and Watson, R. A. (1968). Self-mutilation in female psychopaths. *British Journal of Psychiatry* 114: 829–32.

Moos, R. (1968). The assessment of the social climates of correctional institutions. *Journal of Research in Crime and Delinquency* 5:174–88.

Ping-Nie Pao (1969). The syndrome of delicate self-cutting. *British Journal of Medical Psychology* 42:195–206.

Robbins, E. S. (1977). Self-injurious behaviour—A teacher's guide to treatment. *APEX* 5:8–9.

Rosenthal, R. J.; Rinzler, C.; Walsh, R.; and Klansner, E. (1972). Wrist-cutting syndrome: The meaning of a gesture. *American Journal of Psychiatry* 128:1363–68.

Sandow, S. (1975). A study of informal aproaches to the treatment of self-injurious behaviour in the severely subnormal. *British Journal of Mental Subnormality* 21:10–17.

Simpson, M. A. (1975). The phenomenology of self-mutilation in a general hospital setting. *Canadian Psychiatric Association Journal* 20:429–33.

IV
Other Criminological Applications

CHAPTER 8

Predicting Self-Reported and Official Delinquency

DAVID P. FARRINGTON

SUMMARY

In the Cambridge Study in Delinquent Development, 411 boys have been followed up from age 8 to age 25. In this chapter, the prediction of juvenile convictions (between ages 10 and 16), adult convictions (between ages 17 and 20), juvenile self-reported delinquency (at age 14–15), and adult self-reported delinquency (at age 18–19) is studied. The extent to which these four measures can be predicted by data obtained from records, from parents, from teachers, from peers, and from the boys themselves by age 10 is investigated. Five methods of selecting and combining variables were compared, and the boys were divided into construction and validation samples. It was difficult to identify a group with much more than a 50 percent chance of delinquency and, conversely, to identify more than 50 percent of the delinquents. The more sophisticated multiple regression, predictive attribute analysis, and logistic regression techniques were, if anything, worse than the simpler Burgess and Glueck methods, although (except in the case of juvenile self-reported delinquency) the Burgess and Glueck methods were not markedly more efficient than the best single predictor. It is suggested that it is more feasible to predict not delinquency in general but the most persistent or "chronic" offenders, who account for a significant proportion of all crime.

INTRODUCTION

The primary aims of this chapter are as follows: (1) to investigate to what extent it is possible to predict offending by juveniles (age 10–16) and young adults (age 17–20) in a prospective longitudinal survey; (2) to compare the predictions of self-reported and official delinquency; (3) to compare the efficiency of five of the most commonly used methods of combining variables into a prediction instrument—the Burgess points score, the Glueck method, multiple linear regression, predictive attribute analysis, and logistic regression; and (4) to investigate some of the practical implications of the results, especially in relation to incapacitation.

Some of the previous attempts to predict delinquency have been reviewed in the introduction to this volume by Farrington and Tarling, which also shows that most criminological prediction studies have aimed to predict recidivism among officially criminal groups (especially of parolees) rather than the onset of delinquency in a relatively normal sample. As stated in the introduction, the best-known attempt to predict delinquency was carried out by Glueck and Glueck (1950), who claimed remarkable success in identifying future delinquents. However, the Gluecks' research was retrospective rather than prospective, with the result that the measures could have been biased by a knowledge of who was delinquent; used rather extreme groups of delinquents and nondelinquents; had an artificially high prevalence of delinquents (50 percent); and capitalized heavily on chance, by not having both construction and validation samples. All four of these pitfalls are avoided here.

In any research with official delinquents, it is difficult to know whether delinquent behavior, or selection for official processing of delinquent behavior, is being predicted. In an attempt to separate out these two factors, this chapter investigates the prediction of delinquency as measured by (1) official convictions and (2) self-reports. The self-report method has been used extensively in recent years, and most modern delinquency research (and theorizing) is based on it. The key question with both self-reports and official convictions is the extent to which they are valid measures of delinquent behavior. Unfortunately, the major method of investigating validity has been to compare self-reports with official convictions (see, for example, Farrington, 1973; Hindelang, Hirschi, and Weis, 1981). Generally, juveniles who have been arrested or convicted have a high likelihood of admitting the offenses involved. For example, West and Farrington (1977) found that only 5 percent of convicted youths denied having been convicted, and only 2 percent of unconvicted youths claimed to have been convicted. Furthermore, among unconvicted youths, large numbers of admitted offenses predicted future convictions (Farrington, 1973).

It seems plausible to argue that self-reports and official convictions are both reasonably valid measures of delinquent behavior, although subject to different biases. If a factor predicts both, it might be argued that it is a predictor of offending behavior rather than of the willingness to self-report or of the likelihood of being selected for official processing. It is a pity that validation studies have not yet been attempted comparing both self-reports and official records with a more direct measure of offending, for example, one based on observation (see Buckle and Farrington, 1984). The present research is the first study of the prediction of self-reported offending in comparison with the prediction of official convictions. As stated in the introduction, criticisms of the Gluecks induced many criminologists (and especially delinquency researchers) to treat the prediction of delinquency as a taboo topic. Virtually all modern delinquency research emphasizes explanation rather than prediction.

The present chapter is the first comparison of the major methods of selecting and combining variables into a prediction instrument using delinquency data. All the existing comparisons (reviewed in the introduction) are based on recidivism data, and there is no guarantee that results obtained in predicting recidivism will hold in predicting delinquency. A comparison of two methods (the Glueck technique and multiple regression) was carried out by La Brie (1970), who concluded that they were equally efficient. However, LaBrie did not have a validation sample. The five methods used here are described more fully in the introduction and in the chapter by Tarling and Perry.

A simple measure of predictive efficiency is used in this chapter. The simplest prediction problem is a comparison of predicted and nonpredicted groups with delinquent and nondelinquent outcomes. In this case, percentages might be used to measure predictive efficiency, but it is difficult to know which percentages to choose. For example, should the focus be on the percentage of the predicted group who became delinquents or on the percentage of delinquents who were predicted? These two percentages may be negatively related. It may be possible to achieve a high percentage of the predicted group becoming delinquents by predicting a small extreme group, but this will probably be at the cost of a low percentage of delinquents being predicted.

In the present research, as far as possible, approximately the same proportion of the sample was predicted to be delinquents as actually became delinquents (about one-quarter). This meant that the percentage of the predicted group who were delinquents was about the same as the percentage of delinquents who were predicted. All predictor variables and prediction instruments were dichotomized into the "worst" quarter and the remaining three-quarters, in the interests of comparability and to avoid capitalizing on chance in the selection of cutoff points (compare, Simon, 1971). The ϕ correlation (derived from χ^2, adjusted for sample size) was used as the major summary measure of predictive efficiency, but the percentage of the predicted group becoming delinquents is also given, since this is often more meaningful.

THE CAMBRIDGE STUDY IN DELINQUENT DEVELOPMENT

The present analyses use data from the Cambridge Study in Delinquent Development, which is a prospective longitudinal survey of 411 males. Data collection began in 1961–62, when most of the boys were age 8, and ended in 1980, when the youngest person was aged 25 years 6 months*. The major results of the survey can be found in four books (West, 1969, 1982; West and Farrington, 1973, 1977), and a concise summary is also available (Farrington and West, 1981).

At the time they were first contacted in 1961–62, the boys were all living in a working-class area of London, England. The vast majority of the sample was chosen by taking all the boys of age 8–9 who were on the registers of six state primary schools within a one-mile radius of a research office that had been established. There were other schools in the area, including a Roman Catholic school, but these six were the ones which were approached and which agreed to cooperate. In addition to 399 boys from these six schools, 12 boys from a local school for the educationally subnormal were included in the sample, in an attempt to make it more representative of the population of boys living in the area.

The boys were almost all white Caucasian in appearance. Only 12, most of whom had at least one parent of West Indian origin, were black. The vast majority (371) were being brought up by parents who had themselves been reared in the United Kingdom or Eire. On the basis of their fathers' occupations, 93.7 percent could be described as working class (categories III, IV, or V on the Registrar General's scale), in comparison with the national figure of 78.3 percent at that time. This was, therefore, overwhelmingly a white, urban, working-class male sample of British origin.

The boys were interviewed and tested in their schools at about 8, 10, and 14 years of age, by male or female psychologists. They were interviewed in the research office at about 16, 18, 21, and 24, by young male social science graduates. On each occasion, up to and including age 18, the aim was to interview the whole sample, and it was always possible to trace and interview a high proportion. For example, at age 18–19, 389 of the original 411 (94.6 percent) were interviewed. Of the 22 youths missing at this age, one had died, one could not be traced, 6 were abroad, 10 refused to be interviewed, and in the other 4 cases the parent refused on behalf of the youth. The interviews at later ages were with subsamples only.

In addition to interviews and tests with the boys, interviews

*Since this chapter was written, a further attempt to interview the whole sample at age 31-32 has begun.

with their parents were carried out by female social workers who visited their homes. These interviews with parents took place about once a year from when the boy was about 8 until he reached the age of 14–15 and was in his last year of compulsory education. The primary informant was the mother, although the father was also seen in the majority of cases. Most of the parents were cooperative. At the time of the final interview, when the boys were 14–15, information was obtained from the parents of 399 boys (97.1 percent). The boys' teachers also filled in questionnaires about their behavior in school for each boy at ages 8, 10, 12, and 14. Again, the teachers were very cooperative, and at least 94 percent of questionnaires were completed at each age.

It was also possible to make repeated searches in the central Criminal Record Office in London to try to locate findings of guilt sustained by the boys, by their parents, by their brothers and sisters, and (in recent years) by their wives. These searches continued until March 1980, when the youngest sample member was aged 25 years 6 months. The criminal records of the boys who have not died or emigrated are believed to be complete from the tenth birthday (the minimum age of criminal responsibility in England and Wales) to the twenty-fifth birthday.

The Cambridge Study is unique in having such frequent contacts with the subjects and their families over such a long period and in measuring a large number of variables derived from a wide variety of sources (the boys themselves, their parents, their teachers, their peers, and criminal, educational, employment, social services, and medical records). Many variables were measured before any of the boys were officially convicted, therefore avoiding the problem of retrospective bias. This rich data set is ideal for investigating the extent to which delinquency can be predicted.

MEASURES OF DELINQUENCY

The emphasis in the present chapter is on juvenile delinquency (age 10–16) and young adult offending (age 17–20), since interview information for the whole sample is available only up to age 18–19. About 20 percent of the boys (84) became juvenile official delinquents—that is, were found guilty in a court of an offense normally recorded in the Criminal Record Office and committed between their tenth and seventeenth birthdays. Slightly more boys (94) were convicted as young adults—that is, for offenses committed between their seventeenth and twenty-first birthdays. Minor nonindictable offenses (such as, motoring infractions) were excluded in arriving at these figures. The included offenses were mainly crimes of dishonesty, principally theft, burglary, and taking motor vehicles. As might have been expected, these two convicted groups overlapped considerably; 51 of the juvenile official delinquents were also adult official delinquents. (After these analyses were completed, one further adult official delinquent was discovered.)

In an attempt to obtain information about delinquent behavior as well as about convictions, the boys were given self-reported delinquency questionnaires at various ages. At ages 14 and 16, each boy was asked to say whether or not he had committed each of 38 delinquent and fringe-delinquent acts. As a measure of juvenile self-reported delinquency, each boy was scored according to the total number of different acts he admitted at either or both ages. For ease of comparison with the 84 juvenile official delinquents, the 80 boys with the highest self-report scores, all of whom admitted at least 21 different acts, were grouped together and called the juvenile self-reported delinquents. The 97 adult self-reported delinquents were defined according to those who admitted the most acts in the questionnaire given at age 18–19, for ease of comparison with the 94 adult official delinquents. Just about half of the juvenile self-reported delinquents (41) were also juvenile official delinquents, and just about half of the adult self-reported delinquents (49) were also adult official delinquents.

PREDICTORS OF DELINQUENCY

Unlike most criminological prediction studies, the choice of predictor variables in this research was determined not by their availability in official records but by their alleged theoretical importance (in 1961) as causes of delinquency (see Farrington and West, 1981). Twenty-five variables were included in this analysis. These were all factors measured by the time a boy was age 10–11, and so they were genuinely predictive of the four criterion variables, juvenile and adult official delinquency and juvenile and adult self-reported delinquency. As mentioned earlier, each variable was dichotomized. A predictor variable was included in the analysis only if the proportion of boys coded "not known" on it was 5 percent or less. On most variables, there were no missing cases. Because this was a predictive rather than a theoretical exercise, no attempt was made to use variables that were all theoretically independent. (For theoretical analyses, see Farrington, 1985.)

Three of the predictors were derived from records, namely, criminality of parents, sibling delinquency, and secondary school allocation (a measure of educational achievement). Four were behavioral measures, namely, troublesomeness (rated by teachers and peers), conduct disorder (rated by teachers and parents), daring (rated by peers and parents), and nervous-withdrawn (rated by parents and supplemented by medical records). Seven family background variables were based on the home interviews with parents carried out by psychiatric social workers, namely, family income, housing, family size (supplemented by school records and interviews with the boys), social class (rated on the Registrar General's scale), parental child-rearing behavior (which reflected cruel, passive, or neglecting attitudes, erratic or harsh discipline, and marital disharmony), temporary or permanent separations (for reasons other than death or hospitalization), and the uncooperativeness of the parents toward the social workers. Six variables were derived from tests completed by the boys, namely, extraversion, neuroticism and lying (from the New Junior Maudsley Inventory), vocabulary (from the Mill Hill test), nonverbal IQ (from the Progressive Matrices test), and psychomotor clumsiness (from the Porteus Mazes, the Spiral Maze, and the Tapping Test). A measure of the popularity of each boy was obtained from a peer rating, and his height and weight were also measured. Finally, there were two combined ratings constructed by the researchers in advance of knowledge about delinquency, namely, "acting out" and "social handicap" (see West, 1969, pp. 54, 67).

CONSTRUCTION AND VALIDATION SAMPLES

As explained in the introduction by Farrington and Tarling, the estimate of predictive efficiency obtained in the sample used to construct a prediction instrument is usually misleadingly high. It is desirable to obtain a more accurate estimate of the predictive efficiency in the population by applying the prediction instrument to a different (validation) sample. For the purposes of the present chapter, the total sample of 411 boys was divided into two halves using a table of random numbers, producing a construction (C) sample of 205 and a validation (V) sample of 206.

It had been anticipated that the C and V samples would not differ significantly in proportions of delinquents. This was true with juvenile official delinquency (19.1 percent in C, 22.1 percent in V), juvenile self-reported delinquency (20.5 percent in C, 18.6 percent in V), and adult official delinquency (21.6 percent in C, 24.5 percent in V). However, 19.9 percent of the C sample became adult self-reported delinquents, in comparison with 30.1 percent of the V sample, a statistically significant difference ($\chi^2 = 4.83$, $p < .05$; all values of χ^2 quoted in this chapter have one degree of freedom). The random allocation, therefore, was not very satisfactory in the case of adult self-reported delinquency, although it is only to be expected that one in 20 randomly chosen pairs of samples would be significantly different at $p = .05$.

RELATIONSHIP BETWEEN PREDICTORS AND DELINQUENCY

Table 8.1 summarizes the relationship between each of the 25 predictors and each of the four delinquency measures, separately for the construction (C) and validation (V) samples. In addition to the 25 variables described above, juvenile official and self-reported delinquency were used as predictors with the criteria of adult official and self-reported delinquency. The strength of each relationship was measured by the ϕ correlation, which was derived from the value of χ^2 (corrected for continuity) calculated from the 2×2 table relating the predictor to the criterion. The maximum value of ϕ depends on the marginal totals and is often considerably less than 1 (see Farrington, 1985). Hence, seemingly low values of ϕ often reflect considerable differences between delinquent and nondelinquent groups. For example, in the C sample, 42.9 percent of 49 boys rated troublesome became juvenile official delinquents, in comparison with 11.6 percent of the remaining 155 ($\chi^2 = 21.5$, $p < .001$, $\phi = .32$). Turning the percentages around, we find 53.8 percent of 39 juvenile official delinquents were rated troublesome, in comparison with 17.0 percent of the remaining 165.

There was a considerable amount of variation between the two samples. To take an extreme case, low IQ was significantly related to juvenile official delinquency in the C sample ($\phi = .24$, $p < .001$), but not in the V sample ($\phi = .05$). Relationships in the total sample have been given elsewhere (for example, West and Farrington, 1973, pp. 209–14, for juvenile official delinquency).

Eight variables were significantly related to juvenile official delinquency in both samples (troublesomeness, conduct disorder, acting out, daring, criminal parents, social handicap, low income, and low vocabulary), but only three to juvenile self-reported delinquency (troublesomeness, daring, and social handicap). Apart from delinquency measures, eight variables were significantly related to adult official delinquency in both samples (troublesomeness, acting out, criminal parents, delinquent siblings, social handicap, large family size, poor housing, and low school allocation), but only two to adult self-reported delinquency (troublesomeness and daring). The fact that social background measures such as low family income and large family size are more closely related to official convictions than to self-reported delinquency has been noted elsewhere (Farrington, 1979a). Nearly 40 percent of the relationships examined in this study

Table 8.1 Significance Levels (p) of ϕ Correlations between Predictors and Delinquency Measures

Predictors at Age 8–10	Juvenile Official Delinquency		Juvenile Self-Reported Delinquency		Adult Official Delinquency		Adult Self-Reported Delinquency	
	C	V	C	V	C	V	C	V
Troublesomeness	.001	.001	.01	.01	.001	.001	.05	.01
Conduct disorder	.001	.05	N.S.	.05	.001	N.S.	N.S.	N.S.
Acting out	.001	.05	N.S.	.05	.05	.01	.01	N.S.
Daring	.001	.001	.01	.001	N.S.	.001	.01	.05
Criminal parents	.001	.01	.001	N.S.	.001	.001	.01	N.S.
Delinquent siblings	.05	N.S.	N.S.	.001	.01	.001	N.S.	N.S.
Social handicap	.001	.05	.05	.01	.01	.01	N.S.	.01
Low family income	.05	.05	N.S.	.05	N.S.	.001	N.S.	N.S.
Large family size	N.S.	.01	N.S.	N.S.	.01	.001	N.S.	N.S.
Poor housing	.01	N.S.	N.S.	N.S.	.01	.05	N.S.	N.S.
Poor parental behavior	.001	N.S.	N.S.	.05	N.S.	.05	N.S.	N.S.
Separations	.01	N.S.	N.S.	N.S.	.05	N.S.	N.S.	N.S.
Uncooperative family	.01	N.S.	N.S.	N.S.	.05	N.S.	N.S.	N.S.
Low IQ	.001	N.S.	.01	N.S.	N.S.	.05	N.S.	N.S.
Low vocabulary	.01	.05	.001	N.S.	N.S.	.05	N.S.	N.S.
Low school allocation	.05	N.S.	N.S.	N.S.	.01	.05	N.S.	N.S.
High extraversion	N.S.	N.S.	N.S.	.05	N.S.	N.S.	N.S.	N.S.
High lie score	N.S.	N.S.	N.S.	N.S.	N.S.	.05*	N.S.	N.S.
Psychomotor clumsiness	N.S.	.001	N.S.	N.S.	N.S.	N.S.	N.S.	N.S.
Juvenile official delinquency†					.001	.001	.001	.001
Juvenile self-reported delinquency†					.001	.001	.001	.001

*Negative correlation. All other significant correlations were positive (the boys in the "worst" quarter were more likely to be delinquent than were the remainder).
†Juvenile official and self-reported delinquency, of course, were not measured at age 8–10.
Note: The following predictors were not significantly related to any criterion variable in any sample: nervous-withdrawn, low social class, high neuroticism, unpopularity, low height, low weight.
C=Construction sample, V=Validation sample.

were statistically significant (80 out of 208), far in excess of the chance expectation of 5 percent.

METHODS OF COMBINING PREDICTORS

As mentioned earlier, the aim in this chapter is to compare the efficiency in predicting delinquency of five of the most commonly used methods of selecting and combining predictors, namely, the Burgess method, the Glueck method, multiple regression, predictive attribute analysis, and logistic regression. It is not argued that these methods are the best that could be used, nor even that in all cases their use with these kinds of criminological data is justifiable. The selection and combination of predictors (often to produce an "experience" or "base expectancy" table) is based on the assumption that a composite variable will predict a criterion more efficiently than will a single predictor, but this assumption has rarely been subjected to empirical test (compare Brown, 1978). For example, the best predictor of reconviction is usually the number of previous convictions, and it is important to know the extent to which the prediction could be improved by combining previous convictions with other variables. This kind of question will be investigated here.

THE BEST SINGLE PREDICTOR

Table 8.2 shows the results of all the prediction exercises, beginning with the best single predictor. In order for the selection and combination of predictors to be judged worthwhile, a composite prediction instrument should be considerably more efficient than the best single predictor. The best predictor of juvenile official delinquency in the C sample was troublesomeness (see table 8.1). As already mentioned, 42.9 percent of those rated troublesome became juvenile official delinquents, leading to a ϕ correlation of 0.32. These figures are shown in table 8.2. In the V sample, 47.6 percent of 42 boys rated troublesome became juvenile official delinquents, in comparison with 15.4 percent of the remaining 162 ($\chi^2 = 18.3$, $p <$ .001, $\phi = .30$). The best single predictor of juvenile official delinquency in the V sample was not troublesomeness but daring.

In the case of juvenile self-reported delinquency, the best single predictor in the C sample was criminal parents. Of the 55 boys with criminal parents, 38.2 percent became juvenile self-reported delinquents, in comparison with 14.0 percent of the remaining 150 ($\chi^2 = 13.0$, $p < .001$, $\phi = .25$). However, parental criminality was not significantly predictive in the V sample (28.6 percent of 49 as opposed to 15.5 percent of 155: $\chi^2 = 3.39$, not significant, $\phi = .13$). As might perhaps have been expected, the best predictor of adult official delinquency in the C sample was juvenile official delinquency (64.1 percent of the 39 juvenile delinquents being adult delinquents, in comparison with 11.5 percent of the remaining 165: $\chi^2 = 48.5$, $p <$ .001, $\phi = .49$). Juvenile official delinquency was also a highly significant predictor in the V sample, but the best predictor of adult official delinquency in this sample was juvenile self-reported delinquency. Again, as expected, the best predictor of adult self-

Table 8.2 The Efficiency of Predicting Delinquency

Method	Juvenile Official Delinquency		Juvenile Self-Reported Delinquency		Adult Official Delinquency		Adult Self-Reported Delinquency		Average Over Delinquency Measures	
	19.1 C	22.1 V	20.5 C	18.6 V	21.6 C	24.5 V	19.9 C	30.1 V	20.3 C	23.8 V
Best Single Predictor	42.9 (.32)	47.6 (.30)	38.2 (.25)	28.6 (.13)	64.1 (.49)	57.8 (.40)	51.2 (.39)	61.1 (.31)	49.1 (.36)	48.8 (.29)
Burgess Method	46.9 (.38)	45.1 (.31)	42.2 (.27)	37.5 (.25)	52.7 (.45)	58.3 (.42)	45.5 (.33)	52.4 (.24)	46.8 (.36)	48.3 (.31)
Glueck Method	46.0 (.38)	46.0 (.32)	46.0 (.34)	36.0 (.24)	54.0 (.44)	60.0 (.46)	48.1 (.41)	53.1 (.28)	48.5 (.39)	48.8 (.33)
Multiple Regression	54.0 (.49)	33.3 (.14)	45.3 (.35)	35.3 (.23)	55.6 (.43)	56.9 (.42)	49.1 (.43)	57.7 (.35)	51.0 (.43)	45.8 (.29)
Predictive Attribute Analysis	42.9 (.39)	41.1 (.27)	48.0 (.37)	24.5 (.09)	64.1 (.49)	57.8 (.40)	46.6 (.42)	55.7 (.38)	50.4 (.44)	44.8 (.29)
Logistic Regression	50.0 (.43)	27.5 (.06)	40.4 (.26)	38.0 (.27)	62.5 (.48)	59.1 (.41)	55.3 (.48)	56.0 (.32)	52.1 (.41)	45.2 (.27)

Note: The figure in each cell shows the percentage of the identified group who became delinquents (official or self-reported). In all cases, the identified group are about 50 of about 200 in each of the construction (C) and validation (V) samples. The correlations are given in parentheses. With $N = 200$, $\phi = .14$ is significant at $p = .05$, and $\phi = .23$ is significant at $p = .001$.

reported delinquency in the C sample (but only just) was juvenile self-reported delinquency (51.2 percent of 41 as opposed to 11.6 percent of 155: χ^2 = 29.5, $p < .001$, ϕ = .39). However, it was again true that the best predictor in the C sample was not also the best predictor in the V sample. The best predictor of adult self-reported delinquency in the V sample was juvenile official delinquency.

THE BURGESS METHOD

The simplest method of selecting and combining predictors is that generally ascribed to Burgess (1928). In the Burgess method, each person is given a score of 1 or 0 on each of a number of predictors, depending on whether he falls into a category with an above- or below-average delinquency rate. In using this method, the most important questions to be resolved center on the number of predictors to be chosen and on what to do about predictors that are closely intercorrelated. The method used here was something of a compromise between Burgess and Ohlin. Each prediction score was based on the half-dozen or so factors most closely related to each criterion, disregarding intercorrelations between them. Each boy was scored 1 or 0 on each variable, depending on whether the category in which he fell was associated with an above- or below-average delinquency rate. If a boy was not known on one or more variables, his score on the others was increased pro rata. For example, if a boy scored 3 points on 5 variables and was not known on the other, his final score would be 3 x (6/5) or 3.60.

The 7 best predictors of juvenile official delinquency in the C sample (all significant at $p \leq .001$) were troublesomeness, conduct disorder, acting out, criminal parents, social handicap, low IQ, and poor parental behavior (in that order). Each variable was given a weight of 1.0 in arriving at a prediction score. Two boys in the construction sample had the maximum score of 7, and both were juvenile official delinquents, as were 6 of the 8 boys with the next highest score of 6. As with all other variables, the prediction scores were dichotomized into the "worst" quarter (the group identified as potential delinquents) and the remaining three-quarters. Of the 49 boys in the C sample with prediction scores of more than 2 points, 46.9 percent became delinquents, in comparison with 10.3 percent of the remainder (χ^2 = 30.0, $p < .001$, ϕ = .38).

Table 8.2 shows that, in the C sample, the Burgess method was a slight improvement on the best single predictor of troublesomeness, since the percentage of the identified group becoming delinquents⌄ increased from 42.9 to 46.9 and the ϕ correlation increased from .32 to .38. Of the 51 boys in the V sample scoring more than 2 points, 45.1 percent became delinquents, in comparison with 14.4 percent of the remainder (χ^2 = 19.2, $p < .001$, ϕ = .31). Table 8.2 shows that this was very little improvement over the predictive power of troublesomeness alone in the V sample. Of the 7 best predictors in the C sample, poor parental behavior and low IQ were not significantly predictive in the V sample. Two of the three best predictors in the V sample, daring and psychomotor clumsiness, were not among the 7 best predictors in the C sample, and in fact psychomotor clumsiness was not significantly predictive in the C sample.

These analyses were repeated with juvenile self-reported delinquency, adult official delinquency, and adult self-reported delinquency. Table 8.2 shows that the Burgess method was a considerable improvement over the best single predictor in predicting juvenile self-reported delinquency in the V sample. This was because the best single predictor in the C sample (criminal parents) was not significantly related in the V sample. Of the 6 best predictors chosen to make up the prediction score on the basis of their relationships with juvenile self-reported delinquency in the C sample (criminal parents, low vocabulary, daring, low IQ, troublesomeness, and social handicap), three were still significantly predictive in the V sample (see table 8.1). The Burgess method was little better than the best single predictor in predicting adult official delinquency and somewhat worse in predicting adult self-reported delinquency.

These results suggest that, where there is known to be a good single predictor (as juvenile official delinquency is known to be a good predictor of adult official delinquency), little is gained by the Burgess method. When the existence of a good single predictor is less obvious, the Burgess method is likely to be better than the best single predictor. On the other hand, it must be pointed out that, apart from juvenile official and self-reported delinquency, no factors measured between ages 10 and 16 were included in the prediction of adult official and self-reported delinquency. It is possible that later factors combined with the best single predictor by the Burgess method might have produced an improved prediction.

THE GLUECK METHOD

The method of selection and combination of factors used by Glueck and Glueck (1950) is somewhat more complex than the Burgess method, although Kirby (1954) reported that Burgess and Glueck prediction scores correlated at a level of 0.9. The Gluecks advocated that a prediction table should be based on about five factors that most significantly distinguished between delinquents and nondelinquents. If possible, the factors should be mutually exclusive and independent, although the Gluecks (1950, p. 259) said that "even if there is some overlapping of the factors, the value of the resulting instrumentality for prediction purposes is not impaired." In deriving prediction scores, each category of each variable is weighted according to the percentage of boys in that category who are delinquents.

In my use of the Glueck method, exactly the same predictors were chosen as in the Burgess method. Only the weightings were different. For example, in deriving a prediction score for juvenile official delinquency, a boy's total would be incremented by .116 if he was rated not troublesome and by .429 if he was rated troublesome. This was because, in the C sample, 11.6 percent of the non-troublesome group and 42.9 percent of the troublesome group became delinquents. As explained in the previous section, where a boy was not known on one or more of the factors contributing to the prediction score, his total on the other factors was increased pro rata.

Table 8.2 shows the efficiency of the Glueck predictions. For example, 46.0 percent of the 50 boys with the highest prediction scores in the C sample became juvenile official delinquents, in comparison with 10.4 percent of the remaining 154 (χ^2 = 28.7, $p <$ .001, ϕ = .38). The comparable figures in the V sample were 46.0 percent of 50 in comparison with 14.3 percent of 154 (χ^2 = 20.3, $p <$ .001, ϕ = .32). Looking at the values of ϕ in the V sample, one sees that the Glueck method is generally superior to the Burgess method and to the best single predictor, although whether the improvement in predictability justifies the extra effort involved in weighting according to percentages is doubtful.

MULTIPLE LINEAR REGRESSION

The Burgess and Glueck methods have been criticized for being subjective and arbitrary and for not taking sufficient account of the intercorrelations between predictors. With the increasing availability of statistical packages of computer programs such as SPSS, the most common technique now used for selecting and combining predictors is probably multiple linear regression, popularized by Mannheim and Wilkins (1955). With a dichotomous dependent variable, this technique is mathematically identical to discriminant analysis (see, for example, Feldhusen, Aversano, and Thurston, 1976). As stated in the introduction, the problem with multiple regression is that its statistical assumptions are often violated by criminological data.

The forward stepwise multiple regression technique available in SPSS was used to obtain weights here. In this procedure, predictor variables are added one at a time, at each stage adjusting the weights of all the variables in the equation to produce the greatest possible increase in the multiple correlation between the actual and predicted values of the criterion. The multiple correlation approaches its maximum possible value when only a small number of predictors are included in the equation and the addition of more predictors does not greatly increase it. As an example, in predicting juvenile official delinquency in the C sample, the multiple correlation was 0.58 with all predictors in the equation. However, a multiple correlation of 0.51 was achieved with only five predictors, and one of 0.55 with eight predictors. The analysis was carried out under two conditions: (1) allowing all variables to enter the equation and (2) adopting an arbitrary stopping point, such that a predictor was included in the equation only if its addition produced an increase in the multiple correlation of at least 0.01. (This corresponded to an increase significant at the 0.10 level.) The figures shown in table 8.2 are for the multiple regression with a stopping point. For juvenile delinquency in the C sample, only eight predictors were included.

Multiple regression was more efficient than the Burgess or Glueck methods in predicting delinquency in the C sample. For example, 54.0 percent of the 50 boys with the highest prediction scores based on only the eight predictors included in the equation up to the stopping point became juvenile official delinquents, in comparison with 7.8 percent of the remaining 154 (χ^2 = 49.2, $p <$ .001, ϕ = .49). The efficiency was even greater for multiple regression without a stopping point (ϕ = .52). However, predictions in the V sample based on multiple regression were usually inferior to those based on the Glueck method, and this was especially true for multiple regression without a stopping point. It seems likely that multiple regression is too sensitive to variations that are specific to a particular sample and that probably reflect error or essentially chance effects. Allowing more variables to enter the equation merely adds more error to it.

PREDICTIVE ATTRIBUTE ANALYSIS

Predictive attribute analysis is a hierarchical splitting technique that can be used with dichotomous variables, and it has been described by MacNaughton-Smith (1965). Its advantages over multiple regression are that it does not depend on such restrictive statistical assumptions about the variables involved and that nonlinear interactions are automatically investigated. If a factor was positively related to the criterion in one part of the sample and negatively related in another, this would be detected by predictive attribute analysis but not easily by multiple regression, at least not in its standard usage. There seems to be no readily available computer program to carry out predictive attribute analysis, and so it has not been used a great deal (see Gottfredson, Gottfredson, and Garofalo, 1977; Wilkins and MacNaughton-Smith, 1964). It is described in the chapter by Tarling and Perry in this volume.

In assessing the value of predictive attribute analysis, it is interesting to investigate the incidence of nonlinear interactions, which in the Cambridge Study in Delinquent Development were extremely rare. In the C Sample, each of the four criteria was related to each of the 25 predictors, separately at both values of each of the other predictors. In only 39 out of 2,400 cases was there a ϕ correlation greater than +0.10 at one value of a third variable and less than –0.10 at the other. In only 4 cases were the two ϕ correlations greater than +0.15 and less than –0.15. These results agree with those of Beverly (1964) in showing the rarity of nonlinear interaction effects.

The clearest example of an interaction was the relationship between juvenile self-reported delinquency and secondary school allocation, controlling for vocabulary. When vocabulary was low, the boys with low secondary school allocation were less likely to become juvenile self-reported delinquents (25.0 percent of 36 as opposed to 52.0 percent of 25: $\chi^2 = 3.57$, $p < .10$, $\phi = -.24$). In contrast, when vocabulary was high, the boys with low secondary school allocation were more likely to become juvenile self-reported delinquents (40.0 percent of 20 as opposed to 10.1 percent of 119; $\chi^2 = 10.1$, significance test not valid, $\phi = .27$). If these results are not to be attributed to chance, they may reflect (a) an association between underachievement (high vocabulary and low school allocation) and delinquency and (b) the inability of those with the lowest verbal skills (low vocabulary and low school allocation) to report accurately.

As usual, an attempt was made to identify about 50 boys as potential delinquents by choosing the categories that included the highest percentages of delinquents. For example, for juvenile official delinquency in the C sample, these were (1) 8 troublesome boys with delinquent siblings, (2) 22 troublesome boys with no delinquent siblings but who were said to be acting out, and (3) 33 boys who were not troublesome but who had criminal parents. This produced a total of 63 identified boys, of whom 27 were delinquents (42.9 percent).

Table 8.2 shows that the efficiency of predictive attribute analysis was rather similar to that of multiple regression. Predictive attribute analysis was usually superior to the Glueck method in the C sample and inferior in the V sample. The results obtained with adult official delinquency are artifactual in the sense that the identified group were all juvenile official delinquents. There was a very large shrinkage between the C and V samples for juvenile self-reported delinquency, which agrees with Simon's (1971) finding that this technique can have very large or very small shrinkages in comparison with others.

LOGISTIC REGRESSION

As pointed out in the introduction, logistic regression has rarely been used in criminology, although it is more suitable than multiple regression, for example. One practical problem in using it arises from the available computer package (GLIM) used here, which is far less developed than SPSS. While using GLIM, it is necessary to investigate the contribution of each predictor to the equation rather laboriously, whereas the analogous testing procedure in stepwise multiple regression is done automatically by SPSS. Fortunately, with dichotomous variables, multiple and logistic regression tend to select the same predictors for the equation. Therefore, in order to reduce the time taken over the logistic regression analyses, they were carried out only with variables identified (as significant at $p = .10$) in the multiple regression analyses.

Table 8.2 shows that, on the basis of the average ϕ correlation in validation samples, the logistic regression was the least efficient technique, despite its theoretical attractions. This was primarily because of the large shrinkage seen in the analysis of juvenile official delinquency. It seemed that logistic regression became less efficient in the validation sample as the number of predictors included in the equation increased, and the same phenomenon was observed with multiple regression. These techniques may capitalize too heavily on chance when more than four or five predictors are included in the equation. However, the difference between the best technique (Glueck, average ϕ in V samples equal to 0.33) and the worst (logistic regression, 0.27) was not very great.

FURTHER COMPARISONS

It was recommended in the introduction that researchers should not just present summary measures of predictive efficiency but should give some indication of the distribution of the criterion variable over different prediction scores. Table 8.3 shows the percentage of delinquents in various percentile ranges of prediction scores. The percentile ranges reflect the skewed (J-shaped) distributions of most prediction scores, with a large number bunched at the bottom end (boys not identified as potential delinquents on any predictor making up the instrument). For example, 9 of the 20 boys (45.0 percent) with the highest scores according to the Burgess technique in predicting juvenile official delinquency in the validation

Table 8.3 Percentage Delinquent Versus Prediction Scores in Validation Samples

Criterion and Method	Percentage of Delinquents in Percentile Scores			
	0–50	51–75	76–90	91–100
Juvenile Official Delinquency				
Burgess	11.8	19.6	45.2	45.0
Glueck	9.8	23.5	41.9	50.0
Multiple Regression	13.7	27.5	29.0	40.0
Predictive Attribute				
Analysis	10.8	25.5	35.5	50.0
Logistic Regression	17.6	25.5	22.6	35.0
Juvenile Self-Reported				
Delinquency				
Burgess	8.8	17.6	35.5	45.0
Glueck	11.8	15.7	29.0	45.0
Multiple Regression	9.8	19.6	25.8	50.0
Predictive Attribute				
Analysis	13.1	20.0	23.3	30.0
Logistic Regression	8.8	19.6	35.5	40.0
Adult Official Delinquency				
Burgess	7.8	25.5	51.6	65.0
Glueck	4.9	27.5	51.6	75.0
Multiple Regression	8.8	23.5	54.8	60.0
Predictive Attribute				
Analysis	21.8	14.0	26.7	60.0
Logistic Regression	9.8	25.5	41.9	70.0
Adult Self-Reported				
Delinquency				
Burgess	16.5	33.3	41.4	73.7
Glueck	15.5	35.4	44.8	68.4
Multiple Regression	19.6	20.8	55.2	68.4
Predictive Attribute				
Analysis	18.6	25.0	58.6	57.9
Logistic Regression	19.6	25.0	51.7	63.2

sample were delinquents, in comparison with 14 of the next 31 (45.2 percent), 10 of the next 51 (19.6 percent), and 12 of the lowest 102 (11.8 percent). (Where scores were tied, boys were selected in order of identification number.)

The interest in table 8.3 is to see the extent to which extremely high prediction scores identify a vulnerable group. Even with an extreme category, it seems to be impossible to identify a group of whom more than 50 percent become juvenile delinquents. The predictions of adult delinquency were better, but this was probably because of the availability of measures of juvenile delinquency as predictors.

IMPLICATIONS FOR DELINQUENCY PREVENTION

To a statistically significant degree, although with perhaps a 50 percent false-positive rate, juvenile delinquency can be predicted.

What can be done to prevent it? Any attempt to prevent delinquency should be based on explanatory rather than predictive research. Our study involved both and placed most emphasis on early environment and upbringing. The educationally retarded children from poor, socially handicapped, criminal families were especially at risk of committing delinquent acts. This suggests that, even at the cost of taking a little away from the more fortunate members of society, scarce welfare resources should be concentrated on this vulnerable group. It can be argued that current attempts to prevent and treat delinquency occur much too late in a person's life. If delinquency is part of a larger syndrome beginning in childhood and continuing into adulthood, as our research suggests, special help and support in the first few years of life is most likely to be successful.

What options are there for the criminal justice system? Our research suggests that convictions do not have their intended (individual deterrent or reformative) effects. Boys who were first convicted between ages 14 and 18 had significantly increased delinquent behavior (as measured by self-report) by the later age, in comparison with unconvicted boys matched on delinquent behavior at age 14. A similar result was obtained for first convictions between ages 18 and 21 (see Farrington, 1977; Farrington, Osborn, and West, 1978).

As pointed out in the introduction, there has been a great deal of recent interest in incapacitation as a penal policy. The Cambridge Study data are useful in investigating incapacitation, because of the availability of self-reports of offending and official convictions of a fairly representative sample (as opposed to a sample of detected offenders, on which most of the existing incapacitation research is based).

During the interview at age 18–19, the boys were asked how many of certain specified crimes they had committed in the previous three years. For example, the 389 boys interviewed reported a total of 342 burglaries. During this three-year period, 28 of the boys (7.2 percent) had been convicted of a total of 35 offenses of burglary, suggesting that the probability of a burglary leading to a conviction was 10.2 percent. These 28 convicted boys reported committing 136 burglaries, or 39.8 percent of the total admitted by the whole sample. They also reported 223 acts of damaging property (35.7 percent of the total of those admitted), 111 of stealing from vehicles (24.3 percent of the total), 88 of taking and driving away vehicles (20.8 percent), and 194 of shoplifting (16.0 percent).

It might therefore be predicted that, if there had been a mandatory sentence of 3 years incarceration for every convicted burglar of age 15–18, the total numbers of crimes in these categories would have decreased substantially. There are methodological problems with this argument (see, for example, Blumstein, Cohen, and Nagin, 1978). There is also a substantial practical problem. Of the 28 boys convicted of burglary, only 7 were given institutional sentences for it. Of the remainder, 9 received probation, 6 received a fine, and 6 were given a discharge. Of the 7 institutionalized youths, 4 were sent to a detention center, which would have involved 2 months incarceration each. The other 3 (two going to borstal and one to approved school) probably were incarcerated for a total of 36 months (see Langan and Farrington, 1983). The total incarceration actually experienced by these 28 burglars, therefore, was about 44 months. To incarcerate all 28 for 3 years each would mean increasing the average daily population incarcerated by a factor of about 22, which is clearly impossible.

Slightly more realistically, imagine that the total amount of incarceration for burglary could be doubled from 44 to 88 months. Each boy convicted of burglary committed an average of about 1.6 burglaries per year. Therefore, doubling the incarceration might possibly have prevented about 6 of the total 342 burglaries reported—less than 2 percent. The implications of this analysis are that the probability of conviction for burglary is too low and the number of burglaries committed by unconvicted boys is too high for a penal policy of incapacitation to be effective in reducing the burglary rate significantly.

THE CHRONIC OFFENDERS

Incapacitation is likely to have its greatest effect on the crime rate if it is applied selectively to the most persistent offenders, as Greenwood (1982) argued. The research of Wolfgang, Figlio, and Sellin (1972) showed that about 6 percent of their fairly representative sample were responsible for 52 percent of all the recorded offenses up to age 18. Each of these boys, called the "chronic" offenders, had been arrested at least five times. They accounted for even greater proportions of the violent crimes (71 percent of the homicides, 73 percent of the forcible rapes, 70 percent of the robberies, and 69 percent of the aggravated assaults). The key question is the extent to which the chronic offenders can be predicted at an early age (see Blumstein and Moitra, 1980).

In the present study, the boys were divided into those with 0, 1, 2, 3, 4–5, and 6 or more convictions between the tenth and twenty-fifth birthdays (see Farrington, 1983). The 23 chronic offenders with 6 or more convictions (5.8 percent of the sample, or 17.4 percent of all the convicted youths) amassed a total of 230 convictions, an average of 10 each. They accounted for almost exactly half (49.1 percent) of the total number of 468 convictions of this sample. They also accounted for substantial proportions of the self-reported offenses at age 18–19 (32.2 percent of all taking and driving away vehicles, 30.4 percent of all burglaries, 23.7 percent of all shopliftings, and 20.8 percent of all thefts from cars).

How well could the chronic offenders have been predicted at age 10? The number in this group is really too small to carry out special predictive analyses with construction and validation samples. However, all the chronic offenders were first convicted as juveniles, and they might be regarded as extreme examples of juvenile official delinquents. Therefore, the previously completed predictive analyses of juvenile official delinquents should give a reasonable indication of the predictability of the chronic offenders. The Burgess method was scrutinized, since it was the simplest, least likely to capitalize on chance, and about as efficient as any other. As stated earlier, the Burgess scale was based on seven predictors, each weighted 1.0. Three were measures of bad behavior (troublesomeness, conduct disorder, acting out), one reflected a deprived background (social handicap), and the others were criminal parents, poor parental child-rearing behavior, and low IQ.

Taking the construction and validation samples together, 55 boys scored 4 or more out of 7 points on this scale. These included the majority of the chronic offenders (15 of the 23), 22 other convicted boys (up to the twenty-fifth birthday), and 18 unconvicted ones. The predictive efficiency was quite similar in the construction and validation samples. In the construction sample, 30 boys scored 4 or more, comprising 8 chronic offenders, 11 other convicted boys, and 11 unconvicted ones. In the validation sample, 25 boys scored 4 or more, including 7 chronic offenders, 11 other convicted youths, and 7 unconvicted ones. These results suggest that, to a considerable extent, the chronic offenders can be predicted at age 10 (see also Blumstein, Farrington, and Moitra, 1985).

CONCLUSIONS

To return to the major aims of this chapter, it was difficult to identify a group with much more than a 50 percent chance of juvenile delinquency and, conversely, this meant that it was difficult to identify more than 50 percent of the juvenile delinquents. It was easier to predict official convictions than self-reported delinquency, and easier to predict adult offending than juvenile delinquency. The more sophisticated multiple regression, predictive attribute analysis, and logistic regression techniques were if anything worse than the simpler Burgess and Glueck methods, although in most instances the Burgess and Glueck methods were not markedly more efficient than the best single predictor.

There are several possible reasons for the relative inefficiency of delinquency prediction. One is that relevant predictor variables were not measured. However, as already mentioned, attempts were made in this project to measure all variables that were alleged (in 1961) to be causes of delinquency, and information was obtained from the boys themselves, from their parents, from their teachers, from their peers, and from official records. A second possible reason is that the measures of the predictor and criterion variables contained too much error and, because of the dichotomizing, were too insensitive. A third possible reason is that delinquency depends on events that occur after age 10 or that are essentially unpredictable or due to chance.

How could the efficiency of delinquency prediction be improved? The comparisons of different prediction methods suggest that it will not be improved by devising and using more sophisticated mathematical methods of selecting and combining variables into a prediction instrument, at least with our present methods of measurement. It may be that advances in predictive efficiency will only follow the development of more valid, reliable, and sensitive measurement techniques. Whether predictive efficiency would be greater, and whether the more sophisticated methods would perform better, in larger samples is uncertain. The results of Babst, Gottfredson, and Ballard (1968), with a construction sample of over 3,000, and of Ward (1968), with a construction sample of 1,600, are not in favor of this proposition.

It seems to be more realistic and feasible to predict not delinquency in general but the most persistent or chronic offenders, who account for a significant proportion of all crime. If these people could be identified at the time of their first convictions, they could be subjected to special preventive measures. A policy of incapacitation could not be pursued, because it would require an enormous increase in the institutional population to have a significant effect on the crime rate. It would be cheaper, and it might be more effective, to provide more welfare help and support for these boys and their families at the earliest possible stage.

REFERENCES

Babst, D. V.; Gottfredson, D. M.; and Ballard, K. B. (1968). Comparison of multiple regression and configural analysis techniques for developing base expectancy tables. *Journal of Research in Crime and Delinquency* 5:72–80.

Beverly, R. F. (1964). *Base expectancies and the initial home visit research schedule.* Sacramento: California Youth Authority Research Report 37.

Blumstein, A.; Cohen, J.; and Nagin, D., eds. (1978). *Deterrence and incapacitation.* Washington, DC: National Academy of Sciences.

Blumstein, A.; Farrington, D. P.; and Moitra, S. (1985). Delinquency careers: Innocents, desisters, and persisters. In *Crime and justice,* ed. M. Tonry and N. Morris, vol. 6. Chicago: University of Chicago Press, in press.

Blumstein, A., and Moitra, S. (1980). The identification of "career criminals" from "chronic offenders" in a cohort. *Law and Policy Quarterly* 2:321–34.

Brown, L. D. (1978). The development of a parolee classification system using discriminant analysis. *Journal of Research in Crime and Delinquency* 15:92–108.

Buckle, A., and Farrington, D. P. (1984). An observational study of shoplifting. *British Journal of Criminology* 24:63–73.

Burgess, E. W. (1928). Factors determining success or failure on parole. In *The workings of the indeterminate-sentence law and the parole system in Illinois,* ed. A. A. Bruce, A. J. Harno, E. W. Burgess, and J. Landesco. Springfield, IL: Illinois State Board of Parole.

Farrington, D. P. (1973). Self-reports of deviant behavior: Predictive and stable? *Journal of Criminal Law and Criminology* 64:99–110.

———(1977). The effects of public labelling. *British Journal of Criminology,* 17:112–125.

———(1979a). Environmental stress, delinquent behavior, and convictions. In *Stress and anxiety,* eds. I. G. Sarason and C. D. Spielberger, vol. 6. Washington, DC: Hemisphere.

———(1979b). Longitudinal research on crime and delinquency. In *Crime and justice,* eds. N. Morris and M. Tonry, vol. 1. Chicago: University of Chicago Press.

———(1983). Offending from 10 to 25 years of age. In *Prospective studies of crime and delinquency,* ed. K. Van Dusen and S. A. Mednick. Boston: Kluwer-Nijhoff.

———(1985). Stepping stones to adult criminal careers. In *Development of antisocial and prosocial behavior,* ed. D. Olweus, J. Block, and M. R. Yarrow. New York: Academic Press, in press.

Farrington, D. P.; Osborn, S. G.; and West, D. J. (1978). The persistence of labelling effects. *British Journal of Criminology* 18:277–84.

Farrington, D. P., and West, D. J. (1981). The Cambridge Study in Delinquent Development. In *Prospective longitudinal research,* ed. S. A. Mednick and A. E. Baert. Oxford: Oxford University Press.

Feldhusen, J. F.; Aversano, F. M.; and Thurston, J. R. (1976). Prediction of youth contacts with law enforcement agencies. *Criminal Justice and Behavior* 3:235–53.

Glueck, S., and Glueck, E. T. (1950). *Unraveling juvenile delinquency.* Cambridge, MA: Harvard University Press.

Gottfredson, D. M.; Gottfredson, M. R.; and Garofalo, J. (1977). Time served in prison and parole outcomes among parolee risk categories. *Journal of Criminal Justice* 5:1–12.

Greenwood, P. W. (1982). *Selective incapacitation.* Santa Monica, CA: Rand Corporation.

Hindelang, M. J.; Hirschi, T.; and Weis, J. G. (1981). *Measuring delinquency.* Beverly Hills, CA: Sage.

Kirby, B. C. (1954). Parole prediction using multiple correlation. *American Journal of Sociology* 59:539–50.

La Brie, R. A. (1970). Verification of the Glueck prediction table by mathematical statistics following a computerized procedure of discriminant function analysis. *Journal of Criminal Law, Criminology, and Police Science* 61:229–34.

Langan, P. A., and Farrington, D. P. (1983). Two-track or one-track justice? Some evidence from an English longitudinal survey. *Journal of Criminal Law and Criminology* 74:519–546.

MacNaughton-Smith, P. (1965). *Some statistical and other numerical techniques for classifying individuals.* London: Her Majesty's Stationery Office.

Mannheim, H., and Wilkins, L. T. (1955). *Prediction methods in relation to borstal training.* London: Her Majesty's Stationery Office.

Ohlin, L. E. (1951). *Selection for parole.* New York: Russell Sage.

Simon, F. H. (1971). *Prediction methods in criminology.* London: Her Majesty's Stationery Office.

Ward, P. G. (1968). The comparative efficiency of differing techniques of prediction scaling. *Australian and New Zealand Journal of Criminology* 1:109–12.

West, D. J. (1969). *Present conduct and future delinquency.* London: Heinemann.

———(1982). *Delinquency: Its roots, careers, and prospects.* London: Heinemann.

West, D. J., and Farrington, D. P. (1973). *Who becomes delinquent?* London: Heinemann.

———(1977). *The delinquent way of life.* London: Heinemann.

Wilkins, L. T., and MacNaughton-Smith, P. (1964). New prediction and classification methods in criminology. *Journal of Research in Crime and Delinquency* 1:19–32.

Wolfgang, M. E.; Figlio, R. M.; and Sellin, T. (1972). *Delinquency in a birth cohort.* Chicago: University of Chicago Press.

CHAPTER 9

Predicting Outcomes of Mentally Disordered and Dangerous Offenders

TONY BLACK AND PENNY SPINKS

(with statistical assistance from Roger Tarling)

SUMMARY

The Mental Health Act (1959) for England and Wales raised special problems of prediction for the small but important group of violent offenders who are also mentally disordered. The study described here demonstrates that the problem is intensified by the low rate of reoffending, which, although it may be encouraging for both the institutions concerned and the public whose safety is at risk, is still a cause for concern when the offenses are often horrifying and the offenders notorious.

The sample retrospectively studied was selective in that it represented those who, according to the criteria used at the time, were considered fit for discharge; it was, therefore, not representative of the population from which it was drawn. Three main types of failure (subsequent assaults, reconvictions and readmissions) and one measure of success (period spent living in the community) were used for deriving prediction instruments. The results demonstrated that it is possible to match or improve on existing prediction instruments and to add to "previous record" as a criterion for future behavior in the case of three of the four selected categories of outcome.

The results of the study raise some interesting implications for discriminating offenders and providing appropriate treatment programs and settings; for the assessment methods associated with these; and, crucially, for information and data-processing requirements (including hitherto restricted sources) that will need to be used to provide in the future both the best protection for public safety and individual rights and the optimum settings for care and treatment services.

INTRODUCTION

The topic of dangerousness and the dangerous offender has received considerable attention recently from criminologists. Academic interest in the United States is reflected in the series of volumes resulting from the Ohio Dangerous Offenders Project and in the National Academy of Sciences' Panel on Research on Deterrent and Incapacitation Effects, which commissioned a methodological critique of the subject and a prospectus for further research (Monahan, 1978). In Britain, dangerousness has recently been considered by the Floud Committee (Floud and Young, 1981) set up under the auspices of the Howard League for Penal Reform. A summary of the report, reactions to it, and other opinions on dangerous offenders are contained in a special number of the *British Journal of Criminology* (vol. 22, no. 3, July 1982).

The interest in dangerousness has arisen for many reasons. A rise in violent crimes has focused attention on these crimes and on the perpetrators of them. But the concept of dangerousness and the dangerous offender also assumes importance in the context of changes in sentencing policy and the continuing debate about the role of prisons. A move toward shorter or determinate sentences or an appraisal of the preventive effects of imprisonment—its so-called incapacitation effect—raises the particular issue of how to deal with the small group of exceptional offenders from whom the public especially desires protection. The role of protective sentencing in regard to dangerous offenders was a prime interest of the Floud Committee.

But what is dangerousness and can dangerous offenders be identified? The term *dangerousness* is often equated with violence, and at least implicit in most definitions is some aspect of mental illness or mental instability. Yet there is no satisfactory legal definition or scientific measure, either psychological or medical, of dangerousness. Furthermore, dangerous events (however defined) are rare, making any attempt to identify dangerous offenders or predict dangerous events notoriously difficult. Results of empirical research testify to the difficulty in overcoming this so-called base-rate problem.

For example, Brody and Tarling (1980) considered detailed information from many sources about a representative sample of 811 adult males serving prison sentences in Britain. They identified a subgroup of 77 men who could be thought of as possibly dangerous. Within the follow-up period of five years, 18 "dangerous" offenders had still not been released from prison and information on 7 others was not available. Of the remaining 52, 13 (25 percent) were convicted of a further assaultive crime; and 9 (17 percent) of a more serious assaultive crime consistent with an assessment of dangerousness. An equal number of dangerous offenses (9) were committed by the other group of released prisoners who could not have been previously identified as dangerous. Brody and Tarling concluded that their findings "offer little encouragement for a policy which aims to reduce serious assaults by selective incapacitation of those with violent records" and also that the public is as well protected as it can expect to be. American studies—for example, Wenk, Robinson, and Smith (1972), Cocozza and Steadman (1974), and Schlesinger (1978)—have reached broadly similar conclusions.

The difficulty in identifying dangerous offenders in predicting dangerous events has persuaded some commentators (Conrad and Dinitz, 1977; Megargee, 1976; Bottoms, 1977) to reject the use of predictive devices or even of expert opinions in sentencing decisions. The Floud Committee commented that

> "the critics are being nihilistic, rather than merely pessimistic, in urging the unqualified hopelessness of the enterprise of assessing dangerousness and in insisting that, in facing the fact that some serious offenders do present an unacceptable risk of serious harm, we can hope for no expert help of any kind which could materially improve the validity of our predictive judgments. Such nihilism seems unrealistic."

In practice, offenders convicted of particularly serious offenses under the terms of the Mental Health Act of 1959 are sent to special (secure) hospitals. As long as this procedure exists, decisions have to be taken about the appropriate moment to discharge these people back into the community. It is the assessment of this decisionmaking process that is the subject of the present paper. It should be pointed out that Brody and Tarling's research excluded this category of offender; their study was confined to convicted people in prisons. The only study to assess a similar group of offenders was that of Walker and McCabe (1973; see also Payne, McCabe and Walker, 1974). Walker and McCable analyzed information about a sample of offender-patients who were admitted to National Health Service and special hospitals under hospital orders made by criminal courts. However, their study was restricted to "first-year leavers"—that is, those who were released within one year of being admitted—and so they excluded the more serious cases. Nor did their study include the detailed social and psychological data of the present study. Nevertheless, their results are of interest.

About one-third of their effective sample of 334 was reconvicted during the follow-up period of two years. The number of previous convictions proved to be the most powerful predictor. The next most powerful predictor was the type of offense that had led to the initial hospital order. Offenders convicted of dishonesty—theft, fraud, burglary, or robbery—were two-and-a-half times more likely to be reconvicted than those convicted of other crimes, such as violence, sexual offenses, vagrancy, and public disturbance. A rather poor third predictor was the diagnostic grouping, categorized as (1) schizophrenia, (2) subnormality, psychopathic disorder, and (3) all other diagnoses, most involving affective labels. The schizophrenic offender-patients had the lowest probability of reconviction, and the subnormal or psychopathic group the highest. In commenting on their results, the researchers pointed out that their prediction model was better at picking out low-risk groups than high-risk ones, but a large proportion of the sample (56.9 percent) had middle-range probabilities for which prediction was not satisfactory.

BACKGROUND TO THE PRESENT STUDY

Broadmoor is one of five special hospitals in Great Britain to which mentally disordered offenders are sent. (These special hospitals also take nonoffenders, such as violently behaved psychiatric patients unsuitable for the conventional open hospital.) The offenders mainly come directly from the courts on a hospital order, although a small proportion are sentence-serving prisoners transferred as being in need of psychiatric treatment. In general, offender-patients have committed the kinds of offenses from which it is deemed the public need protection, and the hospital order reflects the acceptance by the court that there is some psychiatric disorder that needs treatment. Hospital orders are in effect "indeterminate sentences," in that the patients remain in hospital until they are thought to be fit for discharge.

This study has grown naturally out of psychological work done at Broadmoor since the Psychology Department was established in 1960. In the 1960s assessment formed a large part of the clinical work. Research was mainly concerned with relating the clinical findings to demographic data, identifying the social, psychological, and psychiatric characteristics of the various offender groups within the patient population (for example, Black, 1973). Later it was decided to collect follow-up data on men who had left the hospital in the period 1960–1965. In the 1970s there were several well-publicized incidents of discharged Broadmoor patients committing further violent offenses, emphasizing the need for these data to become the subject of a study to investigate the success or failure of the discharge process. A general report of this study is given in Black (1982), and this chapter presents selected findings in greater detail, in particular the attempt to develop prediction instruments.

THE SAMPLE

In the early 1960s, Broadmoor had a population of about 850 patients, some 730 men and about 120 women. (The population is now down to some 600—500 men and 100 women—mainly due to the opening of Park Lane Hospital and rebuilding work at Broadmoor.) The present sample included all 128 men discharged directly into the community during the period 1960-65, who comprised 21 percent of all men leaving the hospital. Of the other men leaving the hospital, 50 percent left by transfer to other hospitals in England and Wales, a small proportion were returned to their country of origin, some went back to prison (but only those who were transferred from prison in the first place), others were transferred to other special hospitals, and a few died in hospital.

Initially, this community-discharge group was selected because these releasees were the only ones for whom postdischarge supervision was arranged directly from Broadmoor. All the remainder became the responsibility of another authority and were thought likely to be more difficult to follow up. The average age on admission for the sample of 128 men discharged into the community was 34 years and the average age on discharge was 41-1/2 years. The average length of stay in Broadmoor was therefore 7-1/2 years. Table 9.1 summarizes some other basic information about the sample.

It should be pointed out that the sample is not representative of either incoming patients or of those resident in the hospital at any given date. The discharge process is, of course, selective. For

Table 9.1 General Description of the Sample (N = 128)

	Number	Percent
Previous History		
With previous convictions	77	60
With previous hospital admissions	63	49
With previous Broadmoor admissions	14	11
Type of Offense		
Homicide (murder and manslaughter)	62	48
Other violence against the person	33	26
Sexual offenses	4	3
Property offenses — damage (including arson)	6	5
Property offenses — acquisitive	23	18
*Psychiatric Diagnoses**		
Schizophrenic	33	26
Affective disorder	41	32
Psychopathic (or similar diagnosis)	54	42
Organic	14	11
Subnormal	5	4

*A second or third diagnosis occurred sometimes: hence the total of 147 diagnoses for the sample of 128.

example, 20 percent of those admitted between 1963 and 1970 had committed homicide, whereas 33 percent of the resident population in 1970 and in 1976 had committed homicide. Similarly, the hospital population in 1970 was 56 percent schizophrenic, compared with 26 percent in the sample. By contrast, there is a higher proportion of psychopaths in the sample (42 percent), as against only 25 percent of the resident population. Furthermore, 6 percent of the resident population had affective disorders, as against 32 percent of this discharge group. The results of this study, therefore, should be taken as referring to this sample only and not as any indication of how an equivalent number of new admissions or residents would fare if they were unselectively discharged at some later date.

PREDICTOR VARIABLES

All measures constituting possible predictor variables were obtained from case notes, Broadmoor medical office files, Psychology Department files and/or card indexes. In addition to the descriptive variables discussed above (age, type of offense, and psychiatric diagnosis), table 9.2 lists the other possible predictor variables that were available in the study.

Table 9.2   Variables Constituting Possible Predictors Available for Analysis

Variable	
1	Year of discharge
2	Age at admission
3	Age at discharge
4	Length of stay in Broadmoor
5	Psychiatric diagnosis
6	Mental Health Act (1959) classification
7	Type of offense
8	Form of admission (the pre-1959 Mental Health Act equivalent of the section under which patient was committed to Broadmoor)
9	Form of discharge (conditional or unconditional)
10	Initiator of discharge (Responsible Medical Officer or Mental Health Review Tribunal)
11	Residence on discharge (hostel or private)
12	Relationship to victim (no victim, well known, stranger)
13	Previous convictions
14	Previous psychiatric admissions
15	Previous special hospital admissions
16	Education
17	Previous occupation
18	Marital status
19	WAIS (Wechsler Adult Intelligence Scale)
20	Raven's Progressive Matrices
21	Mill Hill Vocabulary Scale
22	MMPI Scales (Minnesota Multiphasic Personality Inventory)
23	Porteus Maze Test
24	Psychological Report Prognosis

Some of the variables listed require a brief description. The Mental Health Act (1959) defines four groups of mental disorder: mental illness, psychopathic disorder, subnormality, and severe subnormality.* The classification that offenders had been given (variable 6) under the provisions of this Act constitute a broad psychiatric classification for purposes of committal by the court to a hospital. The psychiatric diagnosis (variable 5) is a more specific and clinical classification made after the patient's arrival in Broadmoor hospital.

The majority of the sample, 100 (78 percent), were discharged conditionally (variable 9); that is, they could be recalled if their behavior suggested that they might constitute a danger to themselves or to others. The other 28 (22 percent) could not be recalled in this way. The introduction of the Mental Health Act enabled patients (or their families) to apply for discharge to a Mental Health Review Tribunal (variable 10). During the period under review, 19 patients were successful in obtaining discharge by this means but, for the majority, discharge proceedings were initiated by their Responsible Medical Officer.

The psychological predictor variables (variables 19 to 23) derive mainly from various cognitive tests and personality questionnaires, which formed part of both the baseline clinical assessment program and the research enquiries throughout the period. WAIS (variable 19), Raven's Progressive Matrices (variable 20), and the Mill Hill Vocabulary Scale (variable 21) were all used to measure some aspect of intelligence.

To avoid assembling what seemed likely to be much redundant data, not all MMPI scales (variable 22) were included but only those which had been shown to be useful in previous clinical work and other research at Broadmoor or which seemed relevant to the problem of outcome following discharge (Blackburn, 1968, 1971, 1972, and 1975; Welsh, 1956; Giedt and Downing, 1961). Three validity scales were included; F, K, and L. The standard clinical scales included were D (depression), Pd (psychopathy), Mf (sex-role), Pa (paranoia), Sc (schizophrenia), and Ma (hypomania). Factor scales A (anxiety), R (repression), Ex (extraversion), Dn (denial), and Im (impulsivity) were also constructed. Two scores from the Foulds, Caine, and Creasy (1960) scales were also included; total hostility and direction of hostility.

The ability to solve mazes is associated with cognitive ability, but specifically with the ability to plan and use foresight. It also yields measures of motor control (Porteus, 1945; Gibbens, 1963). Porteus maze data (variable 23) were therefore collected for the sample. As well as the usual Test Age and Q Score, also included were the

*These definitions were changed by the Mental Health Act (1983).

components of the Q Score and the Q Score expressed as a proportion of the maze distances successfully traced. The final variable included was the opinion expressed in the psychological report made prior to discharge on the patient's likely success following discharge (variable 24).

INTERRELATIONSHIPS BETWEEN PREDICTOR VARIABLES

Many of the predictor variables were interrelated, and examination of these relationships revealed one important pattern, in that men who had committed homicide differed from other offenders in many respects. They tended to have had fewer previous convictions: 40 (64 percent) had none, whereas only 10 (15 percent) of other kinds of offender had no previous convictions. They also tended to have had fewer previous psychiatric admissions: 42 (68 percent) had none, compared with half that proportion (22, or 34 percent) of other kinds of offender. Ninety percent of those who had committed homicide were categorized as "mentally ill" within the legal definitions of the Mental Health Act. These men's psychiatric diagnosis was not usually psychopathic, but most often in this sample "affective disorder." On the MMPI, a high proportion (72 percent) of those who had committed homicide scored very low or low on the Im scale (impulsivity) and very low on the Pd (psychopathy) scale; they also tended to have low scores on the total hostility scale. This is consistent with the findings of Megargee (1966), Blackburn (1971), and Howells (1983) that a large proportion of homicides tend to be overcontrolled and less impulsive and that their offenses tend to be isolated violent events. The associations also showed that those who committed homicide tended to attract indeterminate sentences, stayed longer in Broadmoor (82 percent stayed for over six years), were older when discharged, and were discharged conditionally.

Furthermore, there was a good deal of overlap between variables, which enabled some to be omitted. All those who were classified as psychopathic under the Mental Health Act were also clinically diagnosed as psychopathic while at Broadmoor. Because of this and the fact that many who were admitted before the implementation of the Act did not have a classification, the Mental Health Act category was dropped from subsequent analyses. In addition, the type of offense on admission and the relationship to the victim were associated. The relationship to the victim was thus excluded. The form of the discharge was related to the form of the admission, in that the "sentence", in many cases, predetermined the form of release. Life-sentence prisoners transferred to hospital would be conditionally discharged if ever they left. Offenders subject to indeterminate hospital orders would also be discharged conditionally, whereas those transferred to hospital from prison while serving determinate sentences would be released unconditionally if recommended for discharge on the expiry of their sentences. Type of "sentence" was therefore omitted and only form of discharge retained.

Outcome after Discharge

The sample was followed up for a period of five years after being discharged from Broadmoor. Details of subsequent behavior during this period were available from various sources: Broadmoor hospital records, Special Hospitals Research Unit records, and the Department of Health and Social Security Mental Health Index. Information on subsequent criminal behavior was obtained from the first two of these sources. However, two of the sample could not be traced, and one returned to the West Indies during this period, so the following analysis was based on the 125 men for whom the information was complete. Various indices of success and failure were derived and are presented in table 9.3.

Whether the patient committed further assaults is the most stringent criterion of success or failure. The general opinion at Broadmoor is that, since the hospital accepts dangerous, violent patients who have committed grievous assaults (including sexual offenses and homicide), the principal aim is that patients will not commit similar offenses after release. Table 9.3 shows that only 13 out of 125 subsequently committed assaults of a dangerous kind. In addition, however, events occurring after the five-year follow-up period (in many cases up to 15 or more years) are known, and use of this information increases the number of assaultive reoffenders to 17 known at the present time. None committed a homicide in the five-year follow-up period, but two, who had already committed assaults during the follow-up period, have since committed homicide. One of the later homicides was of a fellow prisoner in an institution where the ex-patient, already a reoffender, was

Table 9.3 Outcome Measures

Criterion	Failure Number	Failure Percent	Success Number	Success Percent
Committed further assaults	13	10.4	112	89.6
Subsequent court appearances	49	39.2	76	60.8
Subsequent psychiatric admissions or readmissions to Broadmoor	36	28.8	89	71.2
Remained in the community for the entire five years	61	48.8	64	51.2

subsequently detained. It is perhaps not unreasonable to suggest that the public would still regard themselves as adequately protected if any further offenses were committed while the offender was being detained in another secure place.

Although the number of subsequent assaults was reassuringly small, any subsequent reoffending is, in some sense, a failure, even if it is less serious than the original offense. Forty-nine of the sample (39.2 percent) appeared in court for a criminal offense during the follow-up period. Although this sample is a very distinctive group and comparisons with others not strictly valid, presentation of other reconviction rates does serve to put this finding in some context. Payne, McCabe, and Walker (1974) found that 35 percent of their "first-year leavers" were reconvicted within two years. The Home Office Prison Statistics (1980) give a reconviction rate of 51 percent for all men released from prison and a rate of 33 percent for those serving longer sentences (over four years) for more serious offenses. Phillpotts and Lancucki (1979) found that 71 percent of the 693 males given custodial sentences in their sample were reconvicted within six years. Of the 435 males who were convicted of violence (not necessarily serious), 49 percent were reconvicted during the follow-up period. Therefore, the reoffending rate in the present study was not unduly high.

It will be remembered that, in addition to committing serious criminal offenses, members of the sample were also suffering from some form of psychiatric disorder at the time of admission to Broadmoor. Therefore, subsequent rehabilitation in the community and the absence of further admissions to psychiatric hospitals are also desirable outcomes. Twenty-four patients had further psychiatric admissions, while 24 were readmitted to Broadmoor; 12 had both outcomes, so a total of 36 (28.8 percent) were either readmitted to Broadmoor or to some other psychiatric hospital (or both) during the follow-up period.

Just under half, 61 (48.8 percent), did not spend the entire five years out in the community; that is, they were readmitted to a special or a psychiatric hospital or given a custodial sentence. (A further 10 were reconvicted during that time and given noncustodial sentences.) Therefore, 64 men (51.2 percent) were neither too ill nor too dangerous to require removal from the community. In terms of Broadmoor's *raison d'être*, this measure is probably as good an overall index of success as can be found.

Details of other possible outcome measures (such as subsequent imprisonment), the number of fail events (rather than just the proportion who failed), and the time interval before failure are given in Black (1982).

RELATIONSHIP BETWEEN OUTCOME AND PREDICTOR VARIABLES

Not unexpectedly, previous convictions, previous psychiatric admissions, and type of offense were the most highly related to the four outcome measures. Previous history is almost unanimously found to be a good predictor in criminological research. In the discussion of the interrelationship between predictor variables (above), it was pointed out that the sample fell into two distinct groups; those who had committed homicide and those who had committed other kinds of offense. This distinction persisted when performance after discharge was assessed, and hence the type of offense was important. Once previous history and type of offense were taken into account, the significance of other variables in predicting outcome was much reduced.

Social background, education, previous occupation, and marital status were not related to any of the outcome measures. Neither were the IQ measures and many of the psychometric scales. Black (1982) discusses these interrelationships in greater detail; it is sufficient for present purposes to record the overall success and failure tendencies, which are given in table 9.4.

Table 9.4 Success and Failure Tendencies

Success Tendencies
No previous "history" (offending or psychiatric)
Currently homicide offender
Older
Been in Broadmoor longer
Diagnosed as "affective disorder"
Under indeterminate "sentence" (hospital order now)
Victim family or well known
On psychological assessment prior to discharge:
Less emotional disturbance
More social conformity and control
More uncertainty on nonverbal problem-solving tasks

Failure Tendencies
With previous convictions
Currently property offender or nonhomicide assault
Younger
Been in Broadmoor shorter
Classified as "psychopathic disorder"
Under fixed sentence (Section 72 of M.H. Act)
Victim stranger or casual acquaintance
On psychological assessment prior to discharge:
Psychiatric readmissions:
　More thinking and sensory disturbance ("psychotic")
　More hostile attitudes
Reoffenders in general:
　More impulsive and extraverted ("psychopathic")
Subsequently committed assaults:
　More impulsive and emotionally disturbed

PREDICTION INSTRUMENTS

For each of the four outcome measures various prediction instruments were developed, the procedure being to select from initial analyses the most highly associated predictor variables. Stepwise multiple regression was employed in this process. Having thus derived a subset of the variables, alternative logistic regression models were applied to the data to construct prediction equations and risk classifications. Goodman and Kruskal's γ was calculated to measure predictive power (Tarling, 1982).

Committed Further Assaults

The prediction instrument for the outcome measure "committed further assaults" included type of offense, age at discharge, and MMPI scales F and Ex. The resulting risk classifications are presented in table 9.5. It can be seen from the table that the instrument satisfactorily identified successes, but only about half of those who failed could be predicted to fail with any certainty. Nevertheless, one compensation of the instrument is that it identified only one false positive, that is, an offender predicted to fail but who actually succeeded. Of the five with a high predicted probability of failure (p = 0.7 or above), none had committed homicide, their age at discharge was well below average, and all had above-average scores on MMPI scales F and Ex. Predictive power was high (γ = .94), but this may be somewhat misleading. The high value is attributable to the instrument's ability to predict the large number of successes rather than to its ability to detect failures.

Subsequent Court Appearances

As expected, number of previous convictions and type of offense were the most important variables in predicting subsequent court appearances. In addition to these two variables, MMPI scale Ex, age at discharge, and the psychological report prognosis were also significantly related to outcome and were included in the prediction equation. The risk classifications for subsequent court appearances are given in table 9.6. Discrimination was fairly good and the

Table 9.5 Risk Classifications for Outcome Measure "Committed Further Assaults"

Risk Class (p)	Success (Number)	Failure (Number)	Failure Rate (Percent)
0 to .3	105	4	3.7
.3 to .5	6	3	33.3
.5 to .7	1	1	50.0
.7 to 1.0	0	5	100.0

Note: γ = .94; p = predicted probability of failure.

instrument correctly identified 55 successes and 28 failures, in all 66.4 percent of the sample. Predictive power was therefore high (γ = .90). The prediction instrument compares favorably with that developed by Payne, McCabe, and Walker (1974) in that it identified more high-risk offenders and in that a smaller proportion (24.0 percent) fell into categories with middle-range probabilities (0.3 to 0.7).

Subsequent Psychiatric Admissions

The three variables type of offense, previous psychiatric admissions, and length of stay in Broadmoor were used to predict subsequent psychiatric admissions. It can be seen from table 9.7 that the model was generally poor. Only 4 patients were identified as having a high probability of being readmitted to a psychiatric hospital, and the outcome for a larger proportion (34.4 percent) could not be predicted with any accuracy. Predictive power was correspondingly lower (γ = .70).

Total Time in the Community

Total time in the community, as stated above, is the best measure of success and failure after discharge. Once again, previous history (defined in this case as previous convictions and/or previous psychiatric admissions) together with type of offense were the most powerful predictors. In addition, the two MMPI scales Ex and Pd were also found to be predictive. The prediction instrument derived from these four variables did accurately predict the outcome for 97

Table 9.6   Risk Classifications for Outcome Measure "Subsequent Court Appearances"

Risk Class (p)	Success (Number)	Failure (Number)	Failure Rate (Percent)
0 to .3	55	10	15.4
.3 to .5	12	5	29.4
.5 to .7	7	6	46.2
.7 to 1.0	2	28	93.3

Note: γ = .90; p = predicted probability of failure.

Table 9.7   Risk Classifications for Outcome Measure "Subsequent Psychiatric Admissions"

Risk Class (p)	Success (Number)	Failure (Number)	Failure Rate (Percent)
0 to .3	67	11	14.1
.3 to .5	13	9	40.9
.5 to .7	8	13	61.9
.7 to 1.0	1	3	75.0

Note: γ = .70; p = predicted probability of failure.

(77.6 percent) of the sample (see table 9.8). Predictive power was therefore high (γ = .94). Of the 46 individuals most likely to fail, only four did not have previous convictions or previous psychiatric admissions. Nearly 78 percent of the property offenders were present in this group, compared with 36 percent of those convicted of "other assaults" and 18 percent of homicide offenders. The group was generally above average on MMPI scales Pd and Ex.

DISCUSSION

In the introduction to this study it was pointed out that dangerous offenses were rare and often spontaneous, with little forewarning of their occurrence. This makes it difficult to identify, prospectively, dangerous offenders and to predict dangerous offenses. The results of this study show that subsequent dangerous acts are infrequent even among a sample who by their previous acts would, under any criteria, be assessed as potentially dangerous. Only 13 out of 125 committed a violent offense within five years following discharge from Broadmoor, none resulting in death (although during the next ten years four more committed violent offenses and two of the original 13 violent reoffenders offended again fatally). Nevertheless, it should be remembered that this sample is not representative of all patients in Broadmoor, since those thought to be the more serious risks are not discharged. What the results do show is the relative success of the discharge process, confirming Brody and Tarling's (1980) point that the public is as well protected as it can expect to be. The instrument developed to predict subsequent assaultive offenses for this discharge group did identify about half of those who became reoffenders. Other outcomes, subsequent court appearances and whether the patient spent the entire five-year follow-up period in the community, could be predicted more accurately, although this could not be said about the patient's likelihood of being readmitted to a psychiatric hospital (arguably a less disastrous outcome for the former patient and a less dangerous outcome for the public).

The results of this retrospective prediction exercise suggest that

Table 9.8   Risk Classifications for Outcome Measure "Total Time in the Community"

Risk Class (*p*)	Success (Number)	Failure (Number)	Failure Rate (Percent)
0 to .3	52	5	8.8
.3 to .5	7	7	50.0
.5 to .7	4	4	50.0
.7 to 1.0	1	45	97.8

Note: γ = .94; *p* = predicted probability of failure.

the development of prediction instruments could have some utility in at least identifying those patients particularly prone to fail. Application of such findings could be of benefit not just in influencing discharge decisions but also in developing treatment programs within the hospital in order to prepare patients for discharge and in allocating after-care resources to those most in need.

Discriminating between Treatment Needs

The different patterns of past history, offending, psychological variables, and postdischarge behavior tend to confirm the experience of the hospital staff, namely, that the same treatment program is not appropriate for all groups of patients. Type of offense was strongly related to all outcome measures and featured in all prediction equations. None of those who had committed homicide subsequently committed a violent offense. Members of this group were also less likely to be reconvicted or readmitted to a psychiatric hospital and were more likely to complete five years in the community successfully. It has been suggested that the homicidal offender who shows an overcontrolled pattern of behavior would benefit from therapy aimed at overcoming excessive inhibitions about aggression and hostility (Black, 1981). This program is the converse of that required by undercontrolled offenders (in this sample predominantly the nonhomicidal group), who need to increase these same inhibitions. Most custodial institutions provide the latter program but at a general, institution-oriented level. This is valuable as far as it goes, because so many patients of the psychopathic type lack controls generally. For patients who are violent only in very specific circumstances (including many sexual offenders), or who are so habitually inhibited that they have no behaviors in their repertoire for coping with provocation until, under extreme stress, they react with catastrophic behavior, the implication is that special units designed for specific treatment requirements tailored to particular groups of patients need to be set up, either independent of current institutions or, if possible, within them. Even then, there are the usual well-known limitations of institutions (for example, Goffman, 1961) resulting from the fact that a natural environment replicating the pressures and problems of the outside world is almost impossible to create. The alternative is a series of graded environments, from a secure institution through to the open community.

The Differential Assessment Problem

Much has been written in criticism of personality questionnaires in general and the MMPI in particular (see, for example, Britton and

Savage, 1966). Yet, the present results and past research at Broadmoor, notably by Blackburn (1983), suggest that there are good reasons for continuing with this type of assessment technique; MMPI scales Ex, Pd, and F were significantly related to outcome even after controlling for type of offense and past history. However, much of the information yielded by the MMPI was redundant for the purpose of investigating differences in the Broadmoor population and outcome after discharge. This suggests that many scales could be eliminated, thereby reducing the size of the questionnaire. A start has been made with the SHAPS—Special Hospitals Adjustment and Personality Schedule—largely derived from the MMPI, but this has yet to be used in prediction research, and so comparison with the MMPI is questionable. Nevertheless, the SHAPS contains the Ex and Pd scales from the MMPI in their entirety.

The meaning of these discriminating MMPI scales is of interest here. Ex is an extraversion measure additional to the standard array (Giedt and Downing, 1961). Pd is the standard scale 4 designated "Psychopathic deviate", which features in many studies of offender groups. Together with scale 9 it constitutes the classic so-called 49 profile associated with the aggressive "primary psychopath" (Hare, 1970). In factor studies the Pd scale actually has a moderate loading on the first or emotionality factor of the inventory (Kassebaum, Couch, and Slater, 1959). Blackburn (1974) comments that it has sufficient independence of other scales, however, to be worth retaining in the SHAPS. Groups not identified by other measures of "maladjusted extraversion" often score highly on the Pd scale, and its items appear to be associated with deprived background and perception by the patient of unsatisfactory personal, familial, and social relationships.

The F scale is one of the MMPI's standard validity scales, usually said to indicate "faking bad". Usage suggests, however, that high scores can occur in both neurotic and psychotic patients who are reporting high levels of subjectively experienced distress. As such it is worth considering as a clinical variable and not merely an indicator of invalid responding. McKegney (1965) has reported the identification of a significant number of F-scale items associated with the MMPI profiles of delinquent groups.

The particular combination of the MMPI scales Ex, Pd, and F therefore looks strongly reminiscent of a condition sometimes described as "maladjusted extraversion". Individuals displaying this MMPI profile are emotionally unstable and have a poor tolerance to stress. Being extraverted, however, they tend not to internalize such stress, as does a person in a classic anxiety state or a depressive, but to externalize it in the form of hostility and aggression toward people and objects in the environment. Again, as extraverts, they are sensitive to external more than to internal stimuli and so they abuse their main source of stimulatory satisfaction.

In clinical practice, it is unlikely that these MMPI scores would be considered in isolation, but rather as an adjunct to an idiopathic approach. The development of this comprehensive approach to the assessment of Broadmoor patients in the last decade is reviewed by Black (1981).

IMPLICATIONS FOR THE FUTURE

It is worth reemphasizing that this is the first systematic follow-up study of men discharged from Broadmoor using data collected in the course of clinical assessment. There is, therefore, a need to test the prediction instrument on a second, validation, sample. There is also a need for a procedure to provide consistent feedback on discharged patients about significant events, such as psychiatric readmissions, court appearances, subsequent offenses, and later imprisonment. Such information would enable prospective studies to be carried out. Criteria identified could then be applied predictively and continuously to patients under consideration for discharge. This information would also allow some evaluation of treatment programs. Meanwhile, the presently reported research represents a start in investigating the problem of dangerousness and public protection; human factors such as public safety and individual liberty are involved, as well as the high cost of treating a patient in a secure institution.

REFERENCES

Black, D. A. (1973). *A decade of psychological investigation of the male population of Broadmoor: General demographic information.* Special Hospitals Research Report No. 8. London: Department of Health and Social Security.

———(1981). Implications for sentencing of psychological developments in behavioural assessment and treatment. In *Law and psychology*, ed. S. Lloyd-Bostock. Oxford: Centre for Socio-Legal Studies.

———(1982). A five year follow-up study of male patients discharged from Broadmoor Hospital. In *Abnormal offenders, delinquency and the criminal justice system*, ed. J. Gunn and D. P. Farrington. Chichester: Wiley.

Blackburn, R. (1968). Personality in relation to extreme aggression in psychiatric offenders. *British Journal of Psychiatry* 114:821-28.

———(1971). Personality types among abnormal homicides. *British Journal of Criminology* 11:14-31.

———(1972). Dimensions of hostility and aggression in abnormal offenders. *Journal of Consulting and Clnical Psychology* 38:20-26.

————(1974). *Development and validation of scales to measure hostility and aggression.* Special Hospitals Research Report No. 12. London: Department of Health and Social Security.

————(1975). An empirical classification of psychopathic personality. *British Journal of Psychiatry* 127:456–60.

————(1983). Psychometrics and personality theory in relation to dangerousness. In *Dangerousness: Problems of assessment and prediction,* ed. J. Hinton. London: Allen and Unwin.

Bottoms, A. E. (1977). Reflections on the renaissance of dangerousness. *Howard Journal* 16:70–96.

Britton, P., and Savage, R. D. (1966). The Minnesota Multiphasic Personality Inventory. In *Readings in clinical psychology,* ed. R. D. Savage. Oxford: Pergamon.

Brody, S., and Tarling, R. (1980). *Taking offenders out of circulation.* Home Office Research Study No. 64. London: Her Majesty's Stationery Office.

Cocozza, J., and Steadman, H. (1974). Some refinements in the measurement and prediction of dangerous behavior. *American Journal of Psychiatry* 131:1012–14.

Conrad, J. P., and Dinitz, S. (1977). *In fear of each other: Studies of dangerousness in America.* Lexington, MA: Lexington Books.

Floud, J., and Young, W. (1981). *Dangerousness and criminal justice.* London: Heinemann Educational Books.

Foulds, G. A.; Caine, T. M.; and Creasy, M. A. (1960). Aspects of extra- and intro-punitive expression in mental illness. *Journal of Mental Science* 106:599–610.

Gibbens, T. C. N. (1963). *Psychiatric studies of borstal lads.* Maudsley Monographs No. 11. London: Oxford University Press.

Giedt, F. H., and Downing, L. (1961). An extraversion scale for the MMPI. *Journal of Clinical Psychology* 17:156–59.

Goffman, E. (1961). *Asylums.* Harmondsworth: Penguin.

Hare, R. D. (1970). *Psychopathy: Theory and research.* New York: Wiley.

Home Office (1980). *Prison statistics.* London: Her Majesty's Stationery Office.

Howells, K. (1983). Social construing and violent behaviour in mentally abnormal offenders . In *Dangerousness: Problems of assessment and prediction,* ed. J. Hinton. London: Allen and Unwin.

Kassebaum, G. S.; Couch, A. R.; and Slater, P. E. (1959). The factorial dimensions of the MMPI. *Journal of Consulting and Clinical Psychology* 23:226–36.

McKegney, F. P. (1965). An item analysis of the MMPI F scale in juvenile delinquents. *Journal of Clinical Psychology* 21:201–05.

Megargee, E. I. (1966). Undercontrolled and overcontrolled personality types in extreme antisocial aggression. *Psychological Monographs* 80, no. 611.

————(1976). The prediction of dangerous behavior. *Criminal Justice and Behavior* 3:3–22.

Monahan, J. (1978). The prediction of violent criminal behavior. In *Deterrence and incapacitation: Estimating the effects of criminal sanctions on crime rates,* ed. A. Blumstein, et al. Washington, DC: National Academy of Sciences.

Payne, C.; McCabe, S.; and Walker, N. (1974). Predicting offender-patients' reconvictions. *British Journal of Psychiatry* 125:60–64.

Phillpotts, G. J. O., and Lancucki, L. B. (1979). *Previous convictions, sentence and reconvictions.* Home Office Research Study No. 53. London: Her Majesty's Stationery Office.

Porteus, S. D. (1945). Q Scores, temperament and delinquency. *Journal of Social Psychology* 21:81–103.

Schlesinger, S. E. (1978). Prediction of dangerousness in juveniles—A replication. *Crime and Delinquency* 24:40–48.

Tarling, R. (1982). Comparison of measures of predictive power. *Educational and Psychological Measurement* 42:479–87.

Walker, N. D., and McCabe, S. F. (1973). *Crime and insanity in England,* vol. 2. Edinburgh: Edinburgh University Press.

Welsh, G. S. (1956). Factor dimensions A and R. In *Basic readings on the MMPI in psychology and medicine,* ed. G. S. Welsh and W. G. Dahlstrom. Minneapolis: University of Minnesota Press.

Wenk, E. A.; Robinson, J. O.; and Smith, G. W. (1972). Can violence be predicted? *Crime and Delinquency* 18:393–402.

CHAPTER 10

Modelling a Criminal Justice System

R. GORDON CASSIDY

SUMMARY

The last two decades have seen an increasing utilization of computers and of the systems approach to assist decisionmakers in physical and technical systems. A more recent development has been the simulation approach to social systems. The present paper describes a systems simulation approach to the total criminal justice process and analyzes the ways in which it has been, and may in the future be, useful in criminal justice system decisionmaking. Such a model can be used to predict the effects of policy changes on different elements of the system. The paper concludes with some suggestions for better methods of assisting decisionmaking in the criminal justice system and for different methods of implementing computer modelling approaches.

INTRODUCTION

Criminal justice systems consist of at least the three formal agencies of police, courts, and corrections. There are often many additional components such as prevention programs, after-care agencies, halfway houses, and other private agencies that interface directly and indirectly with the criminal justice system. However, the majority of system resources are usually contained in the three agencies above. The operations of these three agencies are inter-related most simply through the processing of the same offenders. For this reason alone, decisions made in one agency or subsystem are directly related to, and will affect, other parts of the criminal justice system (for a more detailed examination of this interrelationship, see Cassidy and Turner, 1978). For example, the decision to release an offender on parole is a function of the types of offenders available for parole as well as of the likelihood of rearrest and prosecution of such an offender. It both implicitly and explicitly involves decisionmaking in other parts of the criminal justice system.

At a policy level, then, it is necessary for any decisionmaker within a subsystem of the criminal justice system to take into account decisions made by others and the effects of his own decision on the other subsystems. This is particularly important in an area such as parole decisionmaking, since the decision to release offenders in the community, and thus reexpose the community to the risk of their committing offenses, is one that will undoubtedly involve the police in the future and that has involved both courts and corrections up to that moment.

One way to take into account or allow for the effect that parole decisions have on other subsystems and vice versa is to use a systems approach to study the broader criminal justice system and its influence on parole decisionmaking. The systems approach discussed here is a *perspective* for examining problems and phenomena. At the present time it is widely touted as *the* method, or one of the most important methods, for understanding processes (human, physical, and technical) and for beginning to analyze and evaluate them. However, the approach is only as effective as the user, and the systems analysis is only as useful as the analytic effort put forward by the user and the researcher together.

For the purpose of this paper, the term *system* shall mean a relatively simple, conceptual framework for describing a process. A more complete discussion of this approach can be found in Ackoff (1973), Churchman (1968), Hare (1967), Morris (1967), and Wagner (1971). An excellent critique of the approach, especially in the area of social processes, is given in Hoos (1972, 1974).

The simplest method of representing a system is shown in figure 10.1. The system operates with a certain *function* or objective. In the case of the criminal justice system, one might assume this function would be to reduce the total social cost of crime and crime control, or perhaps to "protect" society. Given that the function can be defined,* the analyst can then identify particular controllable variables, such as number of parole officers, size of courts, and size of prisons; uncontrollable variables, such as crime rate (although, as crime prevention assumes a larger part or proportion of the system objectives, this may be viewed as partially controllable); and constraints, such as "due process" for suspected offenders. Given a

---

*One of the most interesting indirect uses of the systems approach is that in asking questions such as, "What is the function of the system?" discussion is usually stimulated to try to rationalize current and proposed activities. The approach itself then provides a framework for investigating objectives and goals of the system and relating these to actual operations.

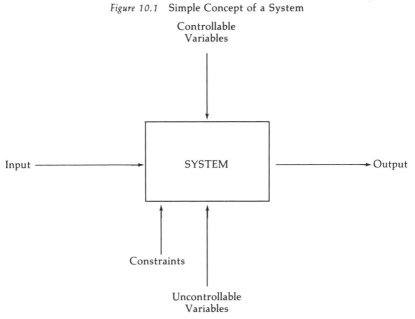

Figure 10.1   Simple Concept of a System

Note: Measure of effectiveness = f (output).

function of the system, it may then be possible to define a measure of effectiveness of the system dependent on its output.

In a social system such as the criminal justice system, it is extremely difficult to measure the outputs and to make trade-offs between their different dimensions. For example, two dimensions characterizing the output are those of equity and efficiency. Thus, the most efficient method for the regulation of criminals might simply be to arrest any person suspected of a crime and to separate the suspect immediately from society. However, this is usually unsuitable in terms of "fair" adjudication of cases, or protecting the rights of the accused offender. Consequently, these trade-offs must be made, often qualitatively, but at least they must be articulated *explicitly* as basic assumptions in the measurement of any system.

Systems can also be described at many different *levels*. One might look at the total societal system of which the criminal justice system is simply one small part. Or one might observe the parole decisionmaking system, wherein the number of parolees, number of parole officers, and the hours and locations worked are controllable, although total budgetary allocations, in relation to other subsystems such as courts and police, are all given as constraints or uncontrollable variables. When one moves to the modelling of the larger system, including police, courts, and corrections as three components or subsystems, then budgets and the relationships between subsystems may become controllable. Depending on the level of the systemic model being constructed, there will be different definitions of function, controllable and uncontrollable variables, constraints, output, and measures of effectiveness.

However, we believe that, before telling administrative and political decisionmakers what "ought" to happen in crime control or a subsystem, one should know what is *presently* happening in the system. Only then can one state how present initiatives should be changed to accommodate changing values or objectives of the system or society.

ADVANTAGES OF SYSTEMS/SIMULATION MODELS

In trying to assess whether a systems and/or simulation model might be applied to a given social system, Brewer and Hall (1973) describe some of the possible reasons for using computer simulation:

1. it is either impossible or extremely costly to observe certain processes or the results of certain policies in the real world;
2. the observed system is too complex to be described by a "closed form" analytic model;
3. no straightforward analytical technique exists for solving the problems found in such a system;
4. the social process under investigation is subject to continuous change and is highly nonlinear in its behavioral patterns.

However, traded off against these reasons is the difficulty of obtaining good data on the system and of knowing exactly the context of the kinds of policy analysis for which such a model might be used. Beause of this difficulty, in developing a simulation model of the criminal justice system the trade-offs must be assessed by the modellers and from this assessment a "reasonable" model formulated within the described purposes. The original JUSSIM model developed by Blumstein allows a high interactive capability while putting a *relatively* minimal dependence on data. Blumstein (1976, personal communication) has articulately described this trade-off:

Any model of a system is only a limited characterization of that system. It is only a definite set of variables, and these are reflected in a limited set of relationships. The fundamental modelling issue is how one trades off complexity, and its associated virtues of greater realism, against simplicity, and *its* virtues of low cost, ease of interpretation, and lesser data and relational requirements. This issue goes beyond questions of computer size (which one might impose as an additional constraint in order to increase accessibility of a given model to a wider class of users) but serves further to force the necessity for dealing with those tradeoffs.

It is precisely for this reason that we felt Blumstein's JUSSIM model was most applicable for modelling the total Canadian criminal justice system. JUSSIM was therefore converted into a Canadian model, CANJUS, and we will use this in our discussion on the use of system models.

DESCRIPTION OF THE CANJUS MODEL

The systems model we describe here is clearly only a first step in beginning a quantitative analysis of a criminal justice system. However, as we have said, it is necessary to describe the way in which the criminal justice system operates at present before suggesting ways to improve the operation of the administration of justice.

The CANJUS model for the Canadian system is based on the linear systems model originally developed by Blumstein and Larson (1969).* The JUSSIM model has been further developed by Belkin, Blumstein, and Glass (1971) at Carnegie-Mellon University. The CANJUS model provides not only a description of the flow of persons within the system, but also allows the user to incorporate costs and workload data for the different states in the criminal justice system. In concept, the CANJUS simulation model is quite similar to models of traffic flow in urban areas, in which the analyst uses the computer to simulate cars travelling on streets in an urban network. The model is basically a device for keeping track of flows within a well-defined system together with the resources applied to process the flows. The following is a brief description of the CANJUS simulation model.

The basic inputs consist of the following information:

1. A set of crime types, into which the population being processed by the criminal justice system is divided. There are 23

---

*Quite clearly, there are many other such models of the system that might be used. These include models of the total system, such as that of Abraham (1972), or of such subsystems as the police, courts, or corrections (see, for example, Hann, Bailey, and Taylor, 1974). The JUSSIM model was selected because of its simplicity of approach (a linear mean-value simulation) as well as its flexible characteristics of being easily able to incorporate better measurement of the system and increased detail in modelling.

different crime types used in the CANJUS simulation model (see Hopkinson, 1973, and Cassidy, 1974, for more detail).

2. A definition of stages in the criminal justice system. The stages presently used in the model are very much at an aggregate level. They include, for example, five different types of court stages (judge and jury, judge without jury, magistrate with consent, magistrate absolute, and superior court); stages for charging an individual; and stages for different types of sentences, penal institutions, and parole. The number of stages in the criminal justice system in the CANJUS model is approximately 35. Figure 10.2 describes these different stages.

3. A set of flows of persons among the different stages in the system. These flows, within any particular crime type, comprise, for example, the number of persons who, given that they were charged with an indictable offense, went to one of the courts; or, given that they were convicted, the number who received a suspended sentence, probation, or a fine and the number who were committed to an institution. Through the use of data on the different subsystems of the Canadian criminal justice system and making certain assumptions (see Hopkinson, 1973, for more detail), it is possible to compute the proportion of persons flowing among the different stages. This is shown in figure 10.2 for all assaults in 1971 in Canada, excluding Quebec and Alberta.

4. A set of resources, including police, judges, prosecuting attorneys, correctional officers and probation officers, and a set of costs for these resources per unit time. For an explanation of the problems and assumptions made in obtaining these costs, see Johnson and Peach (1973). These resources are then applied to the different stages where they participate in the administration of the criminal justice system.

5. A set of workloads, or times to process one person charged with a crime type, in the different stages of the system. For example, a homicide might take four judge-hours to process in a judge and jury court. Hopkinson (1973) and Dick (1974) provide further details of the problems encountered, and assumptions used, in deriving these workloads. Table 10.1 lists the workloads included in CANJUS.

Given these different inputs, the model multiplies the number of persons coming into a stage by the unit workload for that crime type and by the unit resource cost to obtain the total cost for processing that number of persons, in that crime type, in that stage of the system. The model can also aggregate the total workload requirement over the total system (or in particular parts of the system). It

Chart of the Canadian Criminal Justice System

Offences Reported 63893

Cleared by Charge 21563

30481 Cleared Otherwise

11849 Unsolved

Adults Charged 20622

Charges Dropped

Initial Appearance 20622

Preliminary Inquiry 96

Charges Dropped & Acquitted

Summary Offence 14927

Superior Court

Acquitted

County Court Judge w/o Jury 5 — 5

Acquitted 6

County Court Judge & Jury 91 — 85

Acquitted 68

Magistrate Court w/c 549 — 481

Acquitted 846

Magistrate Court Absolute 5050 — 4204

Acquitted

Convicted 4775

Suspended Sentence 276

Suspended with Probation 682

Fine 2150

Institution 1667

Fine 3690

Suspended Sentence with Probation 885

Suspended Sentence 665

Other 688

Convicted 6476

Appeal of Conviction 138

Dismissed 105

Substituted Verdict 3

New Trial 8

Acquitted 22

Conviction Upheld 1637

Appeal of Sentence 133

Varied 38

Dismissed 95

Institution 1637

Penitentiary 61

Expiration 31

Reparole 30

Parole Preparation 127

Prison 1576

Reparole

Expiration 1479

Mandatory Supervision
Forfeiture
Revocation
Expiration

Private 22 — Forfeiture, Revocation, Expiration

Public 27 — Forfeiture, Revocation, Expiration

Parole Service 72 — Forfeiture, Revocation, Expiration

Other 1 — Forfeiture, Revocation, Expiration

No Supervision 5 — Forfeiture, Revocation, Expiration

Institution 547

Appeal of Conviction 27

Dismissed 13

Substituted Verdict 13

New Trial 1

Acquitted 13

Conviction Upheld 533

Appeal of Sentence 12

Varied 8

Dismissed 4

Suspended Sentence

Jail 533

Expiration 533

Juvenile Charged 941

94 Never Appear in Court

(Transferred)

Appear in Court 847

Dismissed 79

Adjourned 216

Repatriated

No Action 55

Found Delinquent 497

Reprimand 14

Indefinite Detention 2

Probation 291

Probation (Parents) 10

Fine 49

Training School 39

Mental Hospital 2

Suspended Sentence 90

Note: The figures refer to assaults reported in 1971 in Canada (excluding Quebec and Alberta).

Table 10.1   Types of Workloads

Workload Number	Name	Unit of Time	Resources	Stage Number
1	Police Report	Hour	Police	1
2	Police Arrest	Hour	Police	2
3	Magistrate: Initial Appearance	Day	Magistrate Court	5
4	Magistrate: Preliminary Inquiry	Day	Magistrate Court	6
5	Magistrate: Trial	Day	Magistrate Court	7, 11, 12
6	Judge: Bench Trial	Day	County Court	9
7	Judge: Jury Trial	Day	County Court	10
8	Superior Court: Appeal	Day	Superior Court	8
9	Superior Court: Appeal	Day	Superior Court	15, 17, 30, 32
10	Penitentiary	Year	Penitentiary	19
11	Prison	Year	Prison	20
12	Jail	Year	Jail	33
13	Parole Preparation	Case	Parole Preparation	22
14	Parole	Case	Parole	24, 25
15	Mandatory Supervision	Case	Parole	21
16	Probation Preparation	Case	Probation Preparation	SSP*
17	Probation	Case	Probation	SSP*
18	Juvenile Court	Day	Juvenile Court	34
19	Juvenile Probation	Case	Juvenile Probation	Probation
20	Juvenile Training School	Year	Juvenile Training School	Indefinite Detention, Training School

*Suspended sentence probation, summary and indictable.

can also compute the total resources required, by crime type, in parts of the system or for the total system. When the user changes all, or part, of these quantities or the crime rate to be processed by the system, the model then computes the changes in total cost, total resource requirements, and total workloads.

Inputs can be disaggregated by stage, crime type, subsystem, or in a number of other ways (see Belkin and Blumstein, 1971, for more detail). The set of outputs can vary from very brief information on the changes in flows to very detailed information on costs, workloads, and resource requirements.

An example of the manipulation of inputs to obtain the outputs for the stage "Judge Trial" and the crime type "Robbery" would be as follows. The set of inputs are:

1. the crime type: Robbery;
2. the stage: Judge Trial;
3. the branching ratios: 0.4 probability of "acquittal", 0.6 probability of "found guilty";
4. the resources and their associated costs, workloads, and availability:

	Judge Resource	Prosecutor Resource
Unit Workload	6 hr/case	9 hr/case
Unit Cost	$50/hr	$10/hr
Annual Availability	1,000 hr	1,200 hr

5. a "reference" flow into the stage of 100 cases.

The outputs are:

1. the flows out of the stage: $0.4 \times 100 = 40$ cases acquitted, $0.6 \times 100 = 60$ cases found guilty;
2. the resource workloads and costs are:

	Judge Resource	Prosecutor Resource
Resource Workload	100 cases × 6 hr/case = 600 hr	100 cases × 9 hr/case = 900 hr
Resource Cost	600 hr +$50/hr = $30,000	900 hr × $10/hr = $9,000

3. the resource requirement for robbery per year is:

$$\frac{600 \text{ hr}}{1,000 \text{ hr.}} = 0.6 \text{ judges, and}$$

$$\frac{900 \text{ hr}}{1,200 \text{ hr.}} = 0.75 \text{ prosecutors;}$$

4. the total stage cost is \$30,000 + \$9,000 or \$39,000 to process the 100 cases of Robbery in the Judge Trial stage;

5. this process can be repeated over all crime types for this stage and over all stages and the results summed to obtain total subsystem or system costs, resource requirements, and workloads, per year.

As we have already mentioned, the model presently includes approximately 35 stages and 23 different crime types. Flow information for 8 provinces of Canada was derived from the 1970 and 1971 Statistics Canada reports, as well as from some special outputs obtained from Statistics Canada.

Information on cost has been obtained from agency reports and public accounts for the corrections system as well as for parts of the police and court systems. More court information was obtained through provincial reports and public accounts as well as by survey (see Johnson and Peach, 1973, for more detail). A more recent initiative by the federal/provincial justice agencies (1978–79) has led to publication, updated annually, of much better aggregate cost and workload information for justice activities.

Values for workloads used in modelling the court and police subsystems included Canadian data when available and otherwise were derived from similar jurisdictions where they are known. All workload data for the penitentiary system are from Canada and are given in terms of numbers of years sentenced for different crime types. Information on workloads for the police and courts systems was obtained from the agencies where available and otherwise by survey.

LIMITATIONS AND DIFFICULTIES OF SYSTEMS MODELLING

Naturally, any quantitative systems description (or simulation) has several limitations:

1. Perhaps most important is the problem of using numbers to characterize any social process. In using any particular value, such as the number of crimes committed or the percentage of persons who appear in court compared with the number of persons charged, several assumptions have to be made. In regard to the unit of count, there is a choice between cases, offenses, and offenders. There is also the problem of the relationships among these units of count, for example, in drawing conclusions about offenders from offenses and vice versa. A further problem is that the aggregation of cases conflicts with the belief held by many people in the system that each case is separate and must be adjudicated individually.

2. Quite often, in attempting to provide a quantitative description, the analyst must leave out many of the qualitative constraints and considerations inherent in the system itself. An example here is that the workloads in the courts are necessarily a lower bound and do not include the many hours spent by judges as well as other personnel thinking about, discussing, and debating issues of principle as well as specific issues relating to particular cases.

3. An important consideration in the development of any quantitative analysis (based on secondary use of data) is that it is dependent on the current reporting systems used by the different statistical agencies.

4. One of the most important problems inherent in a systemic approach such as that described above is that there is no causal link established or implied by the analysis itself. One cannot necessarily infer that changes made in one part of the system will have the impact on other parts of the system that is predicted by the model.* It is here that an important component, developed by Belkin and Blumstein (1971) in their original systems approach, has been added to allow a more detailed analysis of changes. The *interactive* component of the model (where the user actually "plays" with the model parameters) has many benefits and will be discussed later.

USES OF THE CANJUS MODEL

The model has some rather direct benefits as a *description* for many of the federal agencies in Canada. By providing a much better quantitative data base as a background description of present activity within the Canadian criminal justice system, the model assists in developing better policy and programs and in evaluating existing programs. It has been used to examine criminal justice expenditures and flows over the last hundred years in Canada (see Cassidy, 1974; Cassidy and Turner, 1978; Blanchard and Cassidy, 1975; and Cassidy, Peters, and Turner, 1981).

A major part of the role of the Ministry of the Solicitor General (and the Federal Department of Justice) is the coordination and provision of a forum for communication and liaison on information systems. These agencies also encourage cooperation, compatibility, and consistency in statistics and in statistical analysis among provinces and the federal government. The CANJUS model helps meet these goals by providing a standard format for collecting

---

*This point should also be made about more sophisticated, dynamic or feedback models, which still ignore causal links and attempt simply to simulate the process.

information. The model development is also useful for cross-national comparisons, particularly in comparing the Canadian system with similar descriptions of criminal justice systems in Norway, Sweden, England, Japan, and jurisdictions in the United States.*

The CANJUS model and its manipulation have a very specific use in the policy planning and evaluation process. By employing its *interactive* component, users can incorporate a set of new assumptions about possible policy and program changes within the Canadian criminal justice system and then calculate the implications of these changes on the administration of the system in regard to resources, costs, and flows (of offenders). This interactive component allows the administrator or manager to *quantify his intuition* about how changes in one part of the system may affect other parts of the system, which then allows him or her to make program (or parameter) changes and to predict the quantitative impact of these changes on the total system.

By "working with" the simulation model from a terminal (or other input device to a computer), the administrator becomes familiar not only with the limitations of the modelling methodology but also with its virtues and with how far it can be pushed in making quantitative predictions of particular changes within the system. The administrator can also easily test the sensitivity of many of the programmatic changes that may be considered within the system. However, the important point to be kept in mind is that the output is *only as good as the input*. The user must not only have a valid idea about the model's virtues and limitations and its uses but must also have good numerical and policy information (usually qualitative) about the present and expected future operation of the system.

An example that might be used here is the prediction of prison populations in the Canadian criminal justice system. It is useful to allow many factors to vary, such as crime rate, conviction rate, and parole rate, so that one can observe the impact of these parameters on the size of the prison population. Thus, the user gets some "feel" or "sense" of the impact of these "parameters" on the number of people in federal penitentiaries. A test of this use has been made in predicting prison populations (see Hopkinson, 1976), in view of the abolition of the death penalty and the imposition of definite 15- to 25-year sentences for murder. The model has also been used to predict the effect of different rates of immigration on crime control and the effect of different measures to control violent crime (see Cassidy, Hopkinson, and Mead, 1976).

---

*This has been done by Blumstein and Cassidy under a grant from the Ford Foundation, 1973–78.

Thus, apart from its descriptive benefit, the CANJUS model provides a possible tool for assisting policy planners to input a given set of assumptions about change to the system (derived from executive-level personnel and the decisionmakers) and then to describe the possible impact of these different assumptions on the total criminal justice system. Furthermore, it might be possible for the decisionmaker to assign his "prior probabilities" to the different possible policy changes and thereby to calculate the likely impact of the new costs, resources, and flows on the Canadian criminal justice system for both short- and long-range horizons.

The actual planning and evaluation of policy and program alternatives clearly involves more than a comprehensive quantitative description of the criminal justice system. The model provides a basic background description within the context of which alternatives can be assessed by interactive use. However, in actually carrying out planning and evaluation, many other factors must be included besides the basic quantitative tools for predicting program and policy impact throughout the total system.

An important constraint and real limitation of the project is that no criteria were developed for assessing the usefulness of the model. In addition, at the beginning, *no process* was instituted within the Solicitor General's Department itself for the regular use of the model in the planning of policy and program changes and for the regular input of informed judgments (of line and management personnel) as to future changes in system rates, workloads, and costs.

FUTURE PROSPECTS

Although the uses to which the CANJUS model have been put, we feel, have been substantial, there are important areas where more effort must be made in the future. Most important is the *need for communication* and integration of the model and its development with the prospective users within the agency. Clearly, the model, as developed, may be too aggregate in form for use by line personnel (this drawback was experienced in its use as a penitentiary prediction tool). However, for aggregate policy planning for the total criminal justice system, the model has substantial benefits, such as in the preliminary assessment of policies for the control of violent crime. Moreover, it will only be by significant communication of the model and of its limitations and virtues to relevant policy planning officials, at federal and provincial levels, that these uses can best be explored.

Second, there is a need to develop *criteria* about the model's objectives so that the model's success (or lack of it) can be measured. Although the Solicitor General's Department has distributed a great deal of information about the various analyses, relatively little solid quantitative evaluation can be made of the usefulness of the model. Thus it is almost impossible to assess the real impact it has had on the administration of the criminal justice system in Canada.

Third, there is a need to improve the *quality of the data* used in the model. There is no question that many of the data, particularly the policy reports of offenses and charges, have substantial limitations. However, we feel that the model was a first step in developing a quantitative description of the Canadian criminal justice system and that these data problems will only be improved once the specific limitations have been identified. This the model development succeeded in doing. However, an overriding consideration in model development is that there should be increased liaison with program managers and policy planners. Only then will it be possible to orient model development to *their* needs and ensure that the model outputs are useful to *them*.

ACKNOWLEDGMENTS

Dr. Alfred Blumstein has, throughout the course of the CANJUS project development, contributed generously of his time and given the author valuable advice. However, the present chapter, including any errors or omissions, is the responsibility of the author.

REFERENCES

Abraham, S. (1972). *A system dynamics model of a criminal justice system.* AIS Working Paper No. 72-15, Accounting and Information Systems Research Program, Graduate School of Management, University of California, Los Angeles.

Ackoff, R. L. (1973). Science in the systems age: Beyond IE, OR, and MS. *Operations Research* 21:661–71.

Belkin, J., and Blumstein, A. (1971). *Methodology for the analysis of a total criminal justice system.* Working Paper, Urban Systems Institute, School of Urban and Public Affairs, Carnegie-Mellon University, Pittsburgh.

Belkin, J.; Blumstein, A.; and Glass, W. (1971). *An interactive computer model for analysis of the criminal justice system.* Working Paper, Urban Systems Institute, School of Urban and Public Affairs, Carnegie-Mellon University, Pittsburgh.

Blanchard, J., and Cassidy, R. G. (1975). *Crime and the criminal process in Canada, 1880–1970 and beyond.* Statistics Division Working Paper 2/75, Ministry of the Solicitor General, Ottawa.

Blumstein, A., and Larson, R. (1969). Systems analysis of criminal justice. *Operations Research* 17:199–232.

Brewer, G. D., and Hall, O. P., Jr. (1973). *Policy analysis by computer simulation:*

The need for appraisal. Rand Corporation Report, P–4893, Santa Monica, California.

Cassidy, R. G. (1974). *Simulation of social systems: Product or process.* Statistics Division Report 12/74, Ministry of the Solicitor General, Ottawa.

Cassidy, R. G.; Hopkinson, G.; and Laycock, W. (1973). *Preliminary description of the Canadian criminal justice system.* Statistics Division, Ministry of the Solicitor General, Ottawa.

Cassidy, R. G.; Hopkinson, G.; and Mead, D. (1976). *The use of systems models in planning and evaluation.* Proceedings of the SEARCH Symposium, Philadelphia.

Cassidy, R. G.; Peters, M.; and Turner, R. E. (1981). Criminal justice system workloads and behavior. *Journal of the Canadian Operations Research Society (INFOR)* 19:91–112.

Cassidy, R. G., and Turner, R. E. (1978). Criminal justice system behavior. *Behavioral Science* 23:99–108.

Churchman, C. W. (1968). *The systems approach.* New York: Dell.

Dick, P. (1974). *Workloads in the Canadian criminal justice system.* Statistics Division Working Paper 14/74, Ministry of the Solicitor General, Ottawa.

Hann, R.; Bailey, J.; and Taylor, A. (1974). *A preliminary model of the planning process.* SDL Report on Feasibility Study for Penitentiary Prediction, Appendix II, Part I, Ministry of the Solicitor General, Ottawa.

Hare, V. C., Jr. (1967). *Systems analysis: A diagnostic approach.* New York: Harcourt, Brace and World.

Hopkinson, G., ed. (1973). *A preliminary description of the Canadian criminal justice system.* CANJUS Project Report, Ministry of the Solicitor General and Treasury Board Secretariat, Ottawa.

———(1976). *Validation of a computer simulation model of the Canadian criminal justice system.* Working Paper, School of Business, Queen's University, Kingston, Ontario.

Hoos, I. R. (1972). *Systems analysis in public policy.* Berkeley: University of California Press.

———(1974). Can systems analysis solve social problems? *Datamation,* June, 82–92.

Johnson, I. B., and Peach, L. (1973). *Information systems report on Canadian criminal justice system costs.* CANJUS Project Report, Ministry of the Solicitor General and Treasury Board Secretariat, Ottawa.

Morris, W. T. (1967). On the art of modelling. *Management Science* 13:B707–17.

Wagner, H. M. (1971). The ABC's of OR. *Operations Research* 19:1259–81.

V
Statistical Methodology

CHAPTER 11

Statistical Methods in Criminological Prediction

ROGER TARLING AND JOHN A. PERRY

SUMMARY

This chapter extends the research of Simon (1971), who compared the efficiency of seven statistical techniques of constructing prediction instruments in predicting reconvictions of men on probation. Using Simon's data, we focus on three additional methods: automatic interaction detector (AID) analysis, multiple classification analysis, and logistic regression. We also explain the assumptions underlying the methods. It is concluded that no statistical technique appeared to perform noticeably better than any other in validation samples.

INTRODUCTION

Prediction methods have occupied an important position in criminology and prediction instruments have been used extensively as aids in decisionmaking, most notably in selecting prisoners for parole (Gottfredson, Wilkins, and Hoffman, 1978; Nuttall et al., 1977) and in formulating sentencing guidelines (Gottfredson, Wilkins, and Hoffman, 1978). The potential of prediction methods has been explored in other applications; for example, in identifying those crimes which offer the most fruitful lines for investigation (Eck, 1979) and in determining whether defendants should be given bail (Kirby, 1977). More recently, as part of the debate on the incapacitating effects of imprisonment, attempts have been made to predict those offenders who pose the most serious threat to society either by the extent of their involvement in crime or because they are those most likely to commit violent crime causing severe personal injury—the so-called dangerous offenders (Blumstein, Cohen, and Nagin, 1978; Brody and Tarling, 1980). Prediction methods have also been used in research to test alternative theories and to evaluate

210

different forms of treatment (Brody, 1976; Sechrest, White, and Brown, 1979). It was toward this latter objective that Simon's (1971, 1972) work was directed. The main purpose of her study was to develop a prediction instrument that could be used to evaluate the effects of probation on young males between the ages of 17 and 21. During the course of her study a secondary aim developed, which was to compare different ways of constructing prediction instruments. It is further consideration of this secondary aim that forms the subject of the present chapter.

Simon used information about social and criminal histories, collected on two samples of probationers, to develop prediction instruments. The main dependent variable to be predicted was dichotomous: reconviction or not within a fixed period. In all, seven statistical techniques were employed: association analysis, predictive attribute analysis, configuration analysis, mean cost rating analysis, Lance's centroid predictive method, multiple regression, and simple point scoring methods. Predictive attribute analysis and multiple regression are discussed briefly below; a description of the other techniques can be found in Simon (1971) and the references quoted therein. On the basis of her results and those of other prediction studies that she reviewed, Simon argued that no method was greatly superior to any other and concluded that "from this examination of statistical methods for combining data, in practice all of them work about equally well."

Although Simon's work is generally recognized as a major contribution to prediction methodology, it has been criticized on the grounds that the statistical techniques used were inappropriate for the type of data collected. Maxwell (1972) stated that

> on the technical side one might complain that fuller use has not been made of more efficient statistical methods. Variables which are basically categorical in nature, and which give rise to multi-way contingency tables, can be analysed much more fully and effectively by the method of "fitting constants", following a suitable transformation of the data, than by the use of correlational techniques, while methods of taxonomy and clustering more efficient than those employed in this study have long since been available.

Carr-Hill (1971) similarly commented that a "dichotomous criterion poses special problems for those multivariate analyses which make assumptions about the distributions of the variables." He suggested that techniques developed in biometry, in particular logistic regression, are theoretically more appropriate.

The purpose of this paper is to answer these criticisms by

reanalyzing Simon's data using more efficient statistical techniques and to investigate the implications of the results obtained for criminological research. The analysis falls into two broad sections. The first presents Simon's results from predictive attribute analysis and a reanalysis of her data using an alternative binary segmentation technique, automatic interaction detector analysis. The second section considers related regression methods. Simon's results from multiple regression are compared with those obtained from the application of multiple classification analysis and logistic regression. In addition, a review is included of some prediction studies, completed since the publication of Simon's report, which have employed automatic interaction detector analysis and logistic regression.

THE DATA

All the additional analyses were undertaken on Simon's most important sample, which comprised 539 men of age 17–21 who were put on probation in 1958. For this sample detailed factual information was collected from case records about the probationers' family and home background, schooling and employment, health, leisure interests, and past and present criminal history. These data, which form the independent variables, applied to the probationer at or before the beginning of the probation order, that is, "pre-treatment." Further details of the sample and the 62 variables collected are given in Simon (1971).

The only dependent variable considered in this paper is the principal one used by Simon: reconvicted ($y = 1$) or not reconvicted ($y = 0$), of any but a very minor offense, within three years from the beginning of the probation order.

As this sample was extensively analyzed and the results well documented, it presented the overwhelming advantage that it enabled detailed comparison with earlier analyses. Nevertheless the criticism can be made that inferences drawn from this 1958 sample may not be relevant to current practice. To answer this charge, a later sample of 122 offenders of a comparable age given a probation order in 1971 was briefly contrasted.* Although a higher proportion of this group was reconvicted (58 percent, compared with 43 percent in the earlier sample), the pattern of criminal behavior and the direction of the relationship between each variable and reconviction was the same for each group. This seemed to suggest, therefore,

---

*The later probationers were drawn from a general sample of 5,000 convicted offenders (Phillpotts and Lancucki, 1979). No social information was available for this group; only details of their criminal histories.

that, while the use of probation may have changed slightly in the intervening period and reconviction rates have increased generally, the variables that could be identified as predictors have stayed the same.

METHOD FOR ASSESSING PREDICTION INSTRUMENTS*

Simon divided the sample into two groups by alternative allocation from a list of surnames. All prediction instruments were constructed using the first group of 270 cases (the construction sample) and tested on the remaining 269 cases (the validation sample). For this study the sample was split into the same construction and validation half-samples.

One way of assessing the performance of a prediction instrument is to consider the degree of association between the predicted and actual outcomes, which is generally termed the instrument's "predictive power." Numerous measures have been recommended in the criminological prediction literature. In this application three measures are used, the multiple correlation coefficient R, prediction error, and Goodman and Kruskal's γ. Even though R or the proportion of variance explained can be misleading when the dependent variable is dichotomous (as the assumption of a normally distributed error term is violated), R was still thought to provide an informative measure of the fit of the models developed. However, in view of its limitations, a further measure, prediction error, was also calculated. Prediction error is one of several indices proposed by Efron (1978) for use where the response variable is dichotomous, and it has been adopted in some criminological prediction studies. It indicates the proportion who are either reconvicted when they are predicted to be not reconvicted (that is, when their predicted probability of reconviction is less than .5) or not reconvicted when they are expected to be reconvicted.

The ideal prediction instrument would classify each individual as "will" or "will not" be reconvicted. In practice, a prediction instrument can merely assign a probability p to persons with certain combinations of attributes such that, of a group of such persons, a proportion p will be reconvicted. A prediction instrument with a good ability to discriminate would classify a substantial proportion of individuals as having a very low or a very high value of p, that is, belonging to very low or very high risk classes. To examine this

---

*Aitchison and Dunsmore (1975) have since set out a unified approach, essentially Bayesian, incorporating the basic statistical concepts in developing prediction instruments.

property, the risk classification is presented, which shows the number of offenders in each risk class and the proportion reconvicted. For each risk classification Goodman and Kruskal's γ was calculated to assess and compare the power of each prediction instrument.*

BINARY SEGMENTATION TECHNIQUES: A COMPARISON OF PAA AND AID

The principal aim of binary segmentation techniques, like others, is to explain as much as possible of the variation in the dependent variable, but the general procedure adopted to achieve this objective is to decompose the initial sample into subgroups by means of successive binary splits. Starting with the entire sample, each independent variable is examined to identify the one that is most predictive of the dependent variable. The sample is split into two subgroups on this independent variable (the two groups being as different as possible with respect to the dependent variable). The procedure is then repeated, each of the two subgroups being examined separately and partitioned further. The analysis continues until some stopping rule is invoked, and the results can be summarized and conveniently presented as a hierarchical tree diagram.

The particular algorithm adopted in any application is determined by the level of measurement of the dependent variable (nominal, ordinal, or interval scale), although for any type of data more than one routine is usually available. The algorithms also differ in the criterion used to induce the split, or "distance function", as it is sometimes called. Fielding (1979) presents a detailed account of most of the various binary segmentation techniques currently available.**

Binary segmentation techniques have now been extensively employed in social science research, either to perform preliminary exploratory analysis—for example, to identify a subset of the most important variables, to achieve a reduction in the data by forming homogeneous and deviant groups of cases—or to suggest possible interaction effects that can be incorporated within more formal

---

*Simon had previously used mean cost rating (MCR) for this purpose. However, Lancucki and Tarling (1978) have shown MCR to be closely related to Kendall's τ. Subsequently Tarling (1982) has compared both with two other measures of association, $P(A)$, from signal detection theory, and γ, and suggests γ is generally to be preferred because of its probabilistic interpretation and its smaller variance.

**The similarity between binary segmentation techniques and various methods of clustering and mathematical taxonomy should also be noted. Although only binary segmentation techniques are discussed here, algorithms have been developed that can result in more than two subgroups; for example, Press, Rogers, and Shure (1969).

analysis. But they have also been used to develop prediction devices in their own right. Because they impose no prior restrictive assumptions, they may be used to search the data in an uninhibited way. This characteristic makes them potentially useful in social science applications, where the data is often categorical, where many competing possible explanatory factors exist, and where interactions often occur. However, binary segmentation methods are not the panacea of survey research. Knowledge of the theoretical behavior of the criterion is, in some cases, lacking, different algorithms can produce different solutions for the same data, and results can sometimes be difficult to interpret. Fielding (1979), who generally advocates their wider application, concludes his review by cautioning against their slavish or ill-considered use.

The binary segmentation technique used by Simon was predictive attribute analysis (PAA: MacNaughton-Smith, 1965). For PAA, the predictor or independent variables and the dependent variable must be dichotomous. The independent variable selected to induce the split at any stage throughout the analysis is the one most highly associated with the dependent variable, as measured by χ^2. MacNaughton-Smith suggests as a stopping rule that a group should not be subdivided if the maximum χ^2 is less than 3.84 (the 5 percent value, with one degree of freedom). The major criticism of PAA is that it requires all variables to be dichotomous, so where no natural dichotomy occurs (as with many of the variables available for analysis here), one has to be imposed. Apart from introducing a subjective element into the analysis, this can lead to a significant loss of information.

Automatic interaction detector analysis (AID: Sonquist and Morgan, 1964), a technique not used by Simon, overcomes the problem presented by PAA. Essentially, AID proceeds by successive applications of a one-way analysis of variance. At each step an attempt is made to obtain the largest possible reduction in the unexplained sum of squares by first examining the groups to see which has the largest internal sum of squares (TSS_i). Then predictor variables, and all possible divisions of each predictor, are scanned to find the one that maximizes the between-group sum of squares (BSS_i) when this group is divided into two.* Therefore, maximum explanatory power of a split is obtained by maximizing:

---

*Later implementations of this method (AID III) allow for some modification of this procedure. Sequences of two or three splits, rather than individual splits, are considered and it is the sequence explaining the largest total sum of squares that is chosen, even though the first split may not maximize the between-group sum of squares (Sonquist, Baker, and Morgan, 1973).

$$\frac{BSS_i}{TSS_i} = \frac{N_1(\bar{Y}_1 - \bar{Y})^2 + N_2(\bar{Y}_2 - \bar{Y})^2}{\sum\limits_{i=1}^{2} \sum\limits_{j=1}^{N} (Y_{ij} - \bar{Y})^2}. \tag{11.1}$$

Fergusson et al. (1975) have in fact shown that equation (11.1), when applied to dichotomous variables produces exactly the same results as PAA. PAA, therefore, is merely a special case of AID.

Various stopping rules have been recommended for AID (Sonquist, Baker, and Morgan, 1973) to guard against spurious splits. For example, one rule holds that the total sum of squares for a group or the number in the group must be above some minimum value before the group may be partitioned. However, Kass (1975) has since developed a test statistic for this purpose, and a simple χ^2 approximation to it has been suggested by Scott and Knott (1976). (Details of these statistics together with their critical values can be found in both papers.)

It should be pointed out that, strictly speaking, AID requires the dependent variable to be continuous. When it is categorical, a related technique, THAID (Morgan and Messenger, 1973), is appropriate. However, when the dependent variable is dichotomous, as in this case, either can be used, although it should be remembered that the two techniques would not necessarily produce the same solution. An interesting recent addition to this collection of algorithms, CHAID (Kass, 1980), is also worthy of note. CHAID is applicable where the dependent variable is categorical (not necessarily dichotomous), and a χ^2 test is used as the criterion to induce the split. This would appear to have some theoretical advantages over THAID and can also be seen as something of a hybrid between PAA and AID. However, as yet, there is little empirical evidence of its performance.

Results from PAA and AID

The best prediction instrument developed by Simon using PAA was achieved on a subset of the criminal history variables plus the age of the offender and the number of jobs since leaving school. (Throughout this chapter, details of the analyses are not given, only the resulting risk classification.) The proportion of the variance in the dependent variable explained by her analysis in the construction sample was found to be 0.17, and the prediction error 33 percent. However, when this analysis was replicated on the validation sample, by dividing it into the same groups, the proportion of variance

Table 11.1 Risk Classification: Predictive Attribute Analysis and Automatic Interaction Detector

Risk Class p	Predictive Attribute Analysis				Automatic Interaction Detector			
	Construction		Validation		Construction		Validation	
	Number of Offenders	Percent Reconvicted	Number of Offenders	Percent Reconvicted	Number of Offenders	Percent Reconvicted	Number of Offenders	Percent Reconvicted
0 to .3	60	18.3	61	27.9	91	11.0	86	34.9
.3 to .5	106	39.6	95	35.8	40	45.0	50	30.0
.5 to .7	72	54.2	83	48.2	75	56.0	78	48.7
.7 to 1.0	32	87.5	30	66.7	64	78.1	55	50.9
	$\gamma = .58$		$\gamma = .35$		$\gamma = .71$		$\gamma = .22$	
	se* $\gamma = .07$		se* $\gamma = .09$		se* $\gamma = .05$		se* $\gamma = .09$	

*se = standard error.

explained fell to 0.08* and the prediction error rose to 39 percent. The results of the risk classification are shown in Table 11.1. Ninety-two offenders in the construction sample were predicted to have a "high" or "low" probability of being reconvicted during the three-year follow-up period (that is, fell in the extreme risk groups, where $0 < p < .3$ or $.7 < p < 1.0$). The value of γ was found to be 0.58. It can be seen that prediction was poor when this instrument was tested on the validation sample, and γ fell to 0.35.

Variables were selected for the AID analysis if their χ^2 value, with the dependent variable in the construction sample, reached the 5 percent level. This resulted in 26 predictor variables being available for the analysis. Gang membership, number of jobs since leaving school, type of victim, mental ability, last penalty, special conditions of probation, jurors index,** type of offense, and interval since last conviction were all included in the analysis. All splits were tested by means of Kass' statistic and all were found to be significant at the 5 percent level. The proportion of variance in the dependent variable explained by the AID analysis was found to be 0.29, and the prediction error 28 percent. This compares favorably with 0.17 and 33 percent obtained from PAA. The improvement is also evident from results of the risk classification (table 11.1): 155 probationers (compared with 92 for PAA) were identified as high or low risks. Conversely, more probationers were placed into categories with middle-range probabilities ($.3 < p < .7$) by PAA than by AID. γ increased from 0.58 for PAA to 0.71 for AID. However, the proportion of variance explained by replicating the AID analysis on the validation sample fell to 0.06 and γ to 0.22, which are both less than the values obtained by PAA. Furthermore, the prediction error increased to 42 percent, higher than that for PAA. Thus on the validation sample AID did not perform as well as PAA.

Other studies using AID

Two other studies have used AID. Fergusson et al. (1975) used AID to predict delinquency for ten-year-old boys in New Zealand. Large construction and validation samples (2,637 and 2,835) were available for analysis. AID did not produce better results than multiple regression or a point scoring method and the authors state

---

*Simon's prediction instrument was validated here by replicating the whole tree on the validation sample, whereas Simon herself replicated only those splits which were also found to be significant in the validation sample ($\chi^2 > 2.71$, 10 percent value, with one degree of freedom).

**Jurors index is the proportion of electors in an area eligible for jury service. At the time of this study eligibility depended partly upon the value of the elector's dwelling. It was, therefore, used as a measure of the economic status of an area.

"in addition, the AID results are considerably more cumbersome to use and interpret." However, the two dependent variables (appearance before the Children's Court and number of appearances before the court in a given period) were both highly skewed, and AID is known not to work well under such conditions. Schumacher (1973) compared AID, discriminant function analysis, and a point scoring method to predict reconvictions of offenders released from prison. The sizes of the construction and validation samples were 347 and 225, respectively. No method, as measured by prediction error, proved superior.

COMPARISON OF MULTIPLE REGRESSION AND RELATED TECHNIQUES

Multiple regression has been used extensively in criminological research, and Simon (1971) used it to build several prediction instruments. As this technique is familiar to many, only a brief description is given here.*

The fitted regression model is:

$$\hat{Y} = b_0 + b_1x_1 + b_2x_2 + \dots, \tag{11.2}$$

where $\hat{Y}$ is the dependent variable, b_0 is a constant, b_1 is the coefficient or weight attached to predictor variable x_1, b_2 is the coefficient or weight attached to predictor variable x_2, and so on. The coefficients b_i are obtained by the method of ordinary least squares, and a measure of how closely the data fits the regression equation is given by the multiple correlation coefficient R, which is the correlation between the observed and predicted values of the dependent variable (Y and $\hat{Y}$).

Multiple regression, as employed by Simon, required the predictor variables to be measured on at least an interval scale. But many of the variables available for analysis here are not of this kind. For example, last penalty, in this study, has the five categories: discharge, fine, probation, institution, and no previous convictions. Obviously it has no natural scale, and even an ordinal scaling of these categories would be open to criticism. Nevertheless Simon, in common with many other researchers faced with similar problems, assigned numerical values to each category. The value given to a category was in proportion to its rate of reconviction in the construction sample, and for last penalty this produced the following

---

*Further details can be found in any standard text, for example, Draper and Smith (1981). Note also that, in cases where the dependent variable is a dichotomy, multiple regression is equivalent to discriminant function analysis.

scale: discharge, 2; fine, 4; probation, 0; institution, 8; no previous convictions, 1. It should be remembered that Simon was fully aware of the implications of adopting this procedure.

A more appropriate way of handling categorical variables within regression analysis is to convert them into sets of "dummy variables" (Draper and Smith, 1981, pp. 241-57). We used an analogous technique: Yates's (1934) multiple classification analysis (MCA: Andrews et al., 1974).* Essentially, MCA is an analysis of variance model assuming fixed effects. The fitted model is:

$$\hat{Y}_{ijk} \ldots = \bar{Y} + a_i + b_j + c_k \ldots, \tag{11.3}$$

where $\hat{Y}_{ijk} \ldots$ is the dependent variable, a_i is the coefficient corresponding to the ith category of predictor A, b_j is the coefficient corresponding to the jth category of predictor B, c_k is the coefficient corresponding to the kth category of predictor C, and so on. The coefficients are, similarly, obtained by the method of ordinary least squares. The model assumes that an offender's probability of being reconvicted is equal to the grand mean $\bar{Y}$ (the overall probability of being reconvicted), plus additive coefficients or main effects (deviations from the grand mean) corresponding to the particular category or class in which he stands on each predictor. One requirement of MCA is that predictor variables are not highly intercorrelated (compare multicollinearity problems in multiple regression). Another is that the model fitted is additive, which means that there must not be any interactive effects between variables included in the model. Sonquist (1970) has suggested that AID can be used initially to determine whether additive assumptions appear warranted. If they are, MCA can be used directly, but if they are not, then information produced by the AID analysis is used to define the interactions to be incorporated into an additive model for MCA in place of the individual variables.

Results from Regression and MCA

Simon's best prediction instrument developed by a stepwise multiple regression procedure used all 62 variables available and was:

$\hat{Y}$ = -0.455 - 0.031 (jurors index) + 0.074 (victim) + 0.108 (companions) + 0.090 (probation officer's enquiry) + 0.034 (last penalty) + 0.033 (leisure interests) + 0.038 (gang membership) + 0.096 (school conduct) + 0.166 (whether last wages known).

---

*MCA is equivalent to "dummy variable" regression in which the weighted mean (weighted by the number in each category) of each set of coefficients is constrained to be zero, rather than making one of each set zero by excluding it.

In the construction sample, R was found to be 0.55, but it dropped to 0.17 in the validation sample, and the prediction error rose from 29 percent to 42 percent. The results of the risk classification are given in table 11.2. γ was found to be 0.72 in the construction sample, but it fell significantly to 0.24 in the validation sample.

An initial MCA was performed including all the 26 variables used in the AID analysis. Information provided by this and by the AID analysis was used to specify a more parsimonious model, which was then used to develop the final prediction instrument. The MCA calculated the proportion of the total sum of squares explained by each predictor (η^2), which provided a measure of the predictive power of each variable. The variables that had the highest η^2 were: interval since last conviction, leisure interests, gang membership, last penalty, mental ability, shortest interval between convictions, jurors index, number of jobs since leaving school, and type of victim. Most of these variables were prominent in the AID analysis.

The two predictors, interval since last conviction and shortest interval between convictions, were highly correlated ($r = .9$). Thus, only the interval since the last conviction was included. Examination of the results from the AID analysis suggested an interaction effect between gang membership and number of jobs since leaving school. Two analyses were performed: the first included only main effects, and the second included the interaction term "gang membership/number of jobs since leaving school" (the main effects of gang membership and number of jobs since leaving school being omitted). However, the results showed that the interaction term did not improve prediction. The η^2 values for each predictor were tested by means of an F-test, and all were found to be significant at the 5 percent level. In the construction sample, R was found to be 0.57, which is only a very slight improvement on R obtained for multiple regression (.55). Similarly, the prediction error fell slightly, from 29 to 27 percent. In the validation sample R was found to be 0.17 and the prediction error 41 percent, virtually the same as for multiple regression. Thus, there is little difference between the prediction instruments developed by the two techniques. This is shown clearly in table 11.2. The distribution over risk classes and the percentage reconvicted are similar. In the construction sample γ was found to be 0.76 (compared with 0.72 for multiple regression), but it fell significantly to 0.29 (compared with 0.24) in the validation sample. Although both methods produced a potentially useful discrimination between high and low risks in the construction sample, neither performed well on the validation sample.

Logistic Regression

The poor predictive ability of the two instruments developed by multiple regression and MCA may be due, in part, to the problems caused by a dichotomous dependent variable. One assumption underlying both these techniques is that the Y_i's are independently normally distributed with equal variance (homoscedastic). But, in the case of a dichotomous dependent variable, Y can take only one of two values (generally 0 and 1). Therefore, it is not normally distributed, and it can be shown that the variance of Y is equal to $p(1 - p)$, where p is the probability of being convicted. Since the variance of Y varies with the value of p, the requirement that Y_i is homoscedastic is also not met. However, this is likely to be an important problem only when p is near the extreme values of 0 and 1. Over the range of say, 0.2 to 0.8, $p(1 - p)$ remains relatively constant. In addition, when Y is a dichotomy, the method of ordinary least squares does not produce efficient estimates of the coefficients in the model. As a result, these estimates can lead to predicted probabilities of reconviction less than 0 or greater than 1, which are of course outside the range of permissible values. For further discussion of these points, see Cox (1970).

In this study multiple regression predicted 29 of the total sample of 539 probationers to have probabilities of reconviction less than 0 and 18 to have probabilities of reconviction greater than 1. Similarly, for MCA the numbers were 24 and 27 respectively. Probationers with predicted probabilities of being reconvicted of less than 0 were included in the risk class $0 < .3$, and those with predicted probabilities greater than 1 were placed in the risk class $.7 < 1.0$, but this is not an entirely satisfactory procedure.

A method that overcomes this difficulty is logistic regression. The fitted model is:

$$\hat{Y} = \log_e \frac{p}{1 - p} = b_0 + b_1x_1 + b_2x_2 \ldots, \tag{11.4}$$

where p is the probability of being reconvicted, b_0 is a constant, b_1 is the coefficient of predictor variable x_1, b_2 is the coefficient of predictor variable x_2, and so on. If p is the probability of being reconvicted, then $1 - p$ is the probability of not being reconvicted, $\frac{p}{1 - p}$ is the odds of being reconvicted, and $\log_e \frac{p}{1 - p}$ can be interpreted as the "log-odds" of being reconvicted. The probability of being convicted, p, can be calculated from the model by:

$$p = \frac{e^Y}{1 + e^Y} \tag{11.5}$$

For dichotomous dependent variables, therefore, logistic regression (11.4) is the analogue to multiple regression for continuous response variables. The form of the logistic model is also very similar to the more familiar loglinear model using iterative proportional scaling methods (see, for example, Fienberg, 1980, or Payne, 1977, for a description of loglinear models; Payne also outlines the relationship between the two techniques). In fact, when one dichotomous variable is considered as a response, loglinear models, appropriately specified, will produce the same inferences as the direct representation using the logit transformation.

Logistic regression is one of a class of general linear models discussed by Nelder and Wedderburn (1972), and their approach, using weighted least squares estimation procedures, was adopted in this analysis. Their method (as incorporated within the GLIM program) has the considerable additional advantage that both categorical and continuous independent variables can be included within the same logistic (or any other linear) model.

Results from Logistic Regression

The variables included in the logistic regression were selected from those already used in AID, MCA, and multiple regression. Several logistic models were fitted, and possible interaction effects were tested but none were found to increase predictive power. Variables included in the most powerful prediction instrument developed by logistic regression were: interval since last conviction, leisure interests, gang membership, last penalty, mental ability, jurors index, and number of jobs since leaving school. The correlation R between the observed and predicted probability of being reconvicted was found to be 0.56 in the construction sample and 0.19 in the validation sample; the prediction error was 27 and 42 percent, respectively. These results are similar to those obtained from multiple regression (0.55 and 29 percent versus 0.17 and 42 percent) and MCA (0.57 and 27 percent versus 0.17 and 41 percent).

The results of the risk classification are shown in table 11.2. In the construction sample logistic regression did identify more high- and low-risk probationers than the other two techniques, but the value of γ (0.75) was almost identical to that for MCA. In the validation sample the familiar pattern was repeated. Prediction was not good (γ fell to 0.26), and the instrument developed by logistic regression performed no better than the other instruments. Thus, from this comparison, logistic regression did not improve on either multiple regression or MCA.

Table 11.2 Risk Classification: Multiple Regression, Multiple Classification Analysis, and Logistic Regression

Risk Class p	Multiple Regression				Multiple Classification Analysis				Logistic Regression			
	Construction		Validation		Construction		Validation		Construction		Validation	
	Number of Offenders	Percent Reconvicted	Number of Offenders	Percent Reconvicted	Number of Offenders	Percent Reconvicted	Number of Offenders	Percent Reconvicted	Number of Offenders	Percent Reconvicted	Number of Offenders	Percent Reconvicted
0 to .3	83	12.0	79	31.6	90	8.9	75	29.3	103	10.7	84	29.8
.3 to .5	74	43.2	78	39.7	79	48.1	70	37.1	63	54.0	60	41.7
.5 to .7	69	55.1	57	43.9	51	58.8	74	48.6	45	57.8	60	45.0
.7 to 1.0	44	90.9	55	54.5	50	88.0	50	54.0	59	83.1	65	52.3
	$\gamma = .72$		$\gamma = .24$		$\gamma = .76$		$\gamma = .29$		$\gamma = .75$		$\gamma = .26$	
	se* $\gamma = .05$		se* $\gamma = .09$		se* $\gamma = .05$		se* $\gamma = .09$		se* $\gamma = .05$		se* $\gamma = .09$	

*se = standard error.

Other Studies Using Logistic Regression

A number of other studies have employed logistic regression (and further examples appear elsewhere in this book). Bottoms, McClintock, and Walker (1973) developed a prediction instrument to evaluate two different regimes within a borstal institution (Bottoms and McClintock, 1973). They found that logistic regression did not produce significantly better results than multiple regression. Furthermore, for each of the 651 boys in the sample, Bottoms, McClintock, and Walker compared the predicted probabilities of reconviction produced by the two methods and found that for only 22 boys did the estimates differ by more than 0.02.

Payne, McCabe, and Walker (1974) also compared logistic and multiple regression with a sample of 334 patients admitted to hospitals under criminal court orders. Although a better fit was achieved by logistic regression, the majority of offenders still fell into risk categories with middle-range probabilities of being reconvicted. Copas and Whiteley (1976) analyzed data for a broadly similar group: inmates of the Henderson hospital, a therapeutic community for the treatment of psychopaths. Although the prediction performed less well on a validation sample, the authors claimed that the instrument still gave a useful differentiation between the "poor" and "good" risk groups.

Among the American studies, Palmer and Carlson (1976) used logistic regression to develop a prediction instrument for males released from the Michigan prison system. The fitted model is given in their paper but, unfortunately, the authors do not comment on the usefulness of the instrument derived, nor give a risk classification that would enable the reader to judge it. Statistics are given, but without further information about their distributions, no proper assessment can be made.

It was not Solomon's (1976) explicit intention to compare different techniques but to demonstrate the application of logistic regression. Nevertheless, reanalyzing data from the Parole Decision Making Project (Gottfredson, Wilkins, and Hoffman, 1978), Solomon showed that more parsimony could be achieved by logistic regression than a point scoring method, even if predictive power was not increased significantly. A later study of parolees was undertaken by Van Alstyne and Gottfredson (1978), who also found that logistic regression (or its equivalent loglinear representation) did not improve prediction over a point scoring method. However, their analysis can be critized on the grounds that their predictor variables were dichotomized prior to formal analysis. This may have resulted in some loss of information, which in turn may have favored the point scoring method. Because of these restrictions placed on the data, the authors cannot be said to have fully explored the potential of logistic regression or to have subjected it to a fair test. Fuchs and Flanagan (1980) have since submitted this set of data to further analysis.

DISCUSSION

In this chapter prediction instruments were developed using AID, MCA, and logistic regression that, on statistical grounds, overcome the criticisms made against the techniques previously employed by Simon. Comparing results with those obtained by Simon using PAA and multiple regression, it was found for the construction sample that AID performed noticeably better than PAA, but MCA and logistic regression did not improve significantly upon multiple regression. All five prediction instruments identified groups of probationers with high or low probabilities of being reconvicted, but in every case there remained a large proportion for whom little discrimination was achieved. The proportion of probationers with predicted probabilities of being reconvicted between 0.3 and 0.7 ranged from 66 percent for PAA to 40 percent for logistic regression.

However, when tested on the validation sample, predictive power fell sharply in every case. This phenomenon, often referred to as "shrinkage", frequently occurs in prediction studies. Prediction instruments developed on one sample will capitalize on any source of variation and other chance relationships in the data that cannot be expected to exist in another sample. Some shrinkage could certainly have been expected, and Copas has recently subjected this problem to detailed investigation. (An account of his work appears in Chapter 12 in this book.) His findings enable researchers to estimate, at least for some prediction instruments, the amount of shrinkage that can be anticipated and also, if necessary, to correct for it by producing "preshrunk" prediction instruments [see equations (12.15) and (12.16)]. For ease of presentation his formula is reproduced here:

$$\hat{R} = \frac{(n-1)R_0^2 - p_0}{R_0^2(n - p_0 - 1)} R, \qquad (11.6)$$

where $\hat{R}$ is the estimated multiple correlation coefficient in a validation sample, p_0 is the number of possible predictor variables, R_0 is the multiple correlation coefficient with all p_0 variables included, R is the multiple correlation coefficient using a subset of the p_0 variables, and n is the sample size. It can be seen from equation (11.6) that the value of $\hat{R}$ will be higher in relation to R—that is, shrinkage is reduced—the larger the sample size (n) and the smaller the number of potential predictor variables from which the subset is preselected (p_0).

This formula was used to assess the actual shrinkage observed. For example, a multiple regression analysis was conducted including all 62 variables to obtain R_0, which was found to be 0.70. Simon's multiple regression, which selected 9 of these, produced an R of 0.55. With a sample size of 270, $\hat{R}$ is calculated to be 0.38. Therefore, in this study quite considerable shrinkage could have been anticipated but, importantly, shrinkage was always much greater than this, predictive power being approximately half the expected level. One possible reason that could not be ruled out was that Simon may have been "unlucky" in the division of her initial sample. Although the construction and validation samples were randomly chosen, the procedure, by chance, may have produced half-samples with very different underlying structures. And, of course, the shrinkage estimated by Copas's formula assumes that the construction and validation samples are replicas of the same population. Therefore, $\hat{R}$ can be regarded as an upper bound, in the sense that changes in the underlying structure of the data are likely to result in even greater shrinkage.

To test this hypothesis a new construction sample was constituted comprising half the existing construction sample and half the validation sample; the remainder forming a new validation sample. A limited number of prediction instruments were developed on the new construction sample, and these had comparable predictive power. However, when tested on the new validation sample, predictive power fell to the previous level (approximately $R = .19$). This additional analysis seemed to rule out the possibility that the results obtained by each of the prediction instruments were an artifact of the way the sample had been divided. Nevertheless, given this possible problem, it might be advisable to adopt a method based on the jackknifing or the bootstrapping principle, which by generating many subsamples, permits a further assessment of the prediction instrument.

On validation, then, no one statistical technique appeared to perform noticeably better than any other: all were equally disappointing on all the criteria employed to evaluate them. This study, in common with many others that have compared different techniques (despite the caveats that can be made against some of them) tends to support the conclusion reached by Simon: "it seems unlikely that the degree of power so far generally obtained can be greatly improved by further sophisticated techniques for combining variables."

But this does not imply that the choice of statistical technique is purely arbitrary. It is of course always to be recommended that the method to be employed should be appropriate for the data under consideration. Furthermore, the aims and purpose of the study and the application for which the instrument is needed could well have a bearing on the selection of the technique. If all that is required is some approximate measure that can be easily calculated, a point scoring method may have some administrative advantages. However, if what is wanted is some assessment of the relative strengths of the different factors and their conditional relationships, which would obviously be an important consideration in testing alternative theories, then a "modelling" approach such as multiple or logistic regression is much to be preferred. These methods have the additional advantage that Copas's procedures can help assess shrinkage. If the dependent variable is dichotomous, as in this and many other cases, logistic regression is preferable to multiple regression, since the strict assumptions underlying the latter are violated. If all that is needed is to identify relevant risk factors, multiple regression may work reasonably well; on the other hand, if the purpose is to estimate the actual magnitude of the parameters or the probabilities of events, multiple regression can yield misleading results.

The disappointing results were not due to weaknesses in the statistical techniques but, essentially, to the poor predictive ability of the available data, which may be due to several reasons. First, the type of offender given probation may be more homogeneous than those given custodial sentences, or the decision to award probation may be based on quite different criteria. For example, the relative predictive strengths of such factors as number of previous convictions was much weaker for this group of offenders, and the effect of age, also generally important, was minimized because this sample included only 17- to 20-year-olds. More important, this study relied mainly on pretreatment data, and models based on this are likely to be inadequate in explaining a large proportion of subsequent criminal behavior.

Simon, recognizing this deficiency, recommended that more attention should be paid to the treatment itself, and to the posttreatment environment in which the offender lives. Insufficient attention has been given to such potentially important factors as the nature of the supervision and the postsentence attitudes and experiences of the offender and much of the opportunistic nature of crime.

Some relevant empirical evidence has been provided by Schumacher (1973). In an attempt to account for the poor performance of her prediction instrument, she reexamined the files of those men who were incorrectly predicted. She could then identify aspects of the treatment—for example, being on a "release to work" scheme—or the posttreatment environment—for example, "met a good woman," "settled down in satisfying employment," or "summarily dismissed from his job when his criminal record was discovered"—that could have affected the outcome.

This supportive evidence suggests that prediction can be improved if criminologists incorporate within the models those aspects of the treatment and the posttreatment environment relating to criminal behavior. This is an issue for criminological theory, not statistical method.

ACKNOWLEDGMENT

The authors wish to thank Frances H. Simon for making her data available and for her help and assistance throughout the duration of this project.

REFERENCES

Aitchison, J., and Dunsmore, I. R. (1975). *Statistical prediction analysis.* Cambridge: Cambridge University Press.

Andrews, F. M.; Morgan, J. N.; Sonquist, J. A.; and Klem, L. (1974). *Multiple classification analysis.* Ann Arbor: Institute for Social Research, University of Michigan.

Blumstein, A.; Cohen, J.; and Nagin, D. (1978). *Deterrence and incapacitation: Estimating the effects of criminal sanctions on crime rates.* Washington, DC: National Academy of Sciences.

Bottoms, A. E., and McClintock, F. H. (1973). *Criminals coming of age.* London: Heinemann.

Bottoms, A. E.; McClintock, F. H.; and Walker, M.A. (1973). *Working papers and supplementary data relating to the study on "Criminals coming of age".* Cambridge: Institute of Criminology.

Brody, S. R. (1976). *The effectiveness of sentencing.* Home Office Research Study No. 35. London: Her Majesty's Stationery Office.

Brody, S. R., and Tarling, R. (1980). *Taking offenders out of circulation.* Home Office Research Study No. 64. London: Her Majesty's Stationery Office.

Carr-Hill, R. A. (1971). Review of "Prediction methods in criminology". *British Journal of Criminology* 11:402–03.

Copas, J. B., and Whiteley, J. S. (1976). Predicting success in the treatment of psychopaths. *British Journal of Psychiatry* 129:388–92.

Cox, D. R. (1970). *Analysis of binary data.* London: Methuen.

Draper, N. R., and Smith, H. (1981). *Applied regression analysis.* 2nd ed. New York: Wiley.

Eck, J. E. (1979). *Managing case assignments: The burglary investigation decision model replication.* Washington, DC: Police Executive Research Forum.

Efron, B. (1978). Regression and ANOVA with zero-one data: Measures of residual variation. *Journal of the American Statistical Association* 73:113–21.

Fergusson, D. M.; Donnell, A. A.,; Slater, S. W.; and Fifield, J. K. (1975). *The prediction of juvenile offending: A New Zealand study.* Wellington: A. R. Shearer, Government Printer.

Fielding, A. (1979). Binary segmentation: The automatic interaction detector and related techniques for exploring data structure. In *Exploring data structures,* Vol. 1 of *The analysis of survey data.* ed. C. A. O'Muircheartaigh and C. Payne. London: Wiley.

Fienberg, S. E. (1980). *The analysis of cross-classified categorical data.* 2d ed. Cambridge, MA: MIT Press.

Fuchs, C., and Flanagan, J. (1980). Stepwise fitting of logit models with categorical predictors in the analysis of parole outcomes: On the Van Alstyne and Gottfredson study. *Journal of Research in Crime and Delinquency* 17:273–79.

Gottfredson, D. M.; Wilkins, L. T.; and Hoffman, P. B. (1978). *Guidelines for parole and sentencing.* Lexington, MA: Lexington Books.

Kass, G. V. (1975). Significance testing in Automatic Interaction Detector (AID). *Applied Statistics* 24:178–89.

———(1980). An exploratory technique for investigating large quantities of categorical data. *Applied Statistics* 29:119–27.

Kirby, M. P. (1977). *The effectiveness of the point scale.* Washington, DC: Pretrial Services Resource Center.

Lancucki, L. B., and Tarling, R. (1978). The relationship between Mean Cost Rating (MCR) and Kendall's rank correlation coefficient tau. *Social Science Research* 7:81–87.

MacNaughton-Smith, P. (1965). *Some statistical and other numerical techniques for classifying individuals.* Studies in the Causes of Delinquency and the Treatment of Offenders, No. 6. London: Her Majesty's Stationery Office.

Maxwell, A. E. (1972). Review of "Prediction methods in criminology." *Journal of the Royal Statistical Society* A135:442–43.

Morgan, J. N., and Messenger, R. C. (1973). *THAID, a sequential analysis program for the analysis of nominal scale dependent variables.* Ann Arbor: Institute for Social Research, University of Michigan.

Nelder, J. A., and Wedderburn, R. W. M. (1972). Generalized linear models. *Journal of the Royal Statistical Society* A135:370–84.

Nuttall, C. P., et al. (1977). *Parole in England and Wales.* Home Office Research Study No. 38. London: Her Majesty's Stationery Office.

Palmer, J., and Carlson, P. (1976). Problems with the use of regression analysis in prediction studies. *Journal of Research in Crime and Delinquency* 13:64–81.

Payne, C. (1977). The log-linear model for contingency tables. In *Model fitting,* Vol. 2 of *The analysis of survey data.* ed. C. A. O'Muircheartaigh and C. Payne. London: Wiley.

Payne, C.; McCabe, S.; and Walker, N. (1974). Predicting offender-patients' reconvictions. *British Journal of Psychiatry* 125:60–64.

Phillpotts, G. J. O., and Lancucki, L. B. (1979). *Previous convictions, sentence and reconvictions: A statistical study of a sample of 5,000 offenders convicted in January*

1971. Home Office Research Study No. 53. London: Her Majesty's Stationery Office.

Press, L. I.; Rogers, M. S.; and Shure, G. H. (1969). An interactive technique for the analysis of multivariate data. *Behavioral Science* 14:26–34.

Schumacher, M. (1973). Predicting subsequent convictions for individual male prison inmates. *New Zealand Statistician* 8:26–34.

Sechrest, L.; White, S. O.; and Brown, E. D. (1979). *The rehabilitation of criminal offenders: Problems and prospects.* Washington, DC: National Academy of Sciences.

Scott, A., and Knott, M. (1976). An approximate test for use with AID. *Applied Statistics* 25:103–06.

Simon, F. H. (1971). *Prediction methods in criminology.* Home Office Research Study No. 7. London: Her Majesty's Stationery Office.

———(1972). Statistical methods of making prediction instruments. *Journal of Research in Crime and Delinquency* 9:46–53.

Solomon, H. (1976). Parole outcome: A multidimensional contingency table analysis. *Journal of Research in Crime and Delinquency* 13:107–26.

Sonquist, J. A. (1970). *Multivariate model building.* Ann Arbor: Institute for Social Research, University of Michigan.

Sonquist, J. A.; Baker, E. L.; and Morgan, J. N. (1973). *Searching for structure.* Ann Arbor: Institute for Social Research, University of Michigan.

Sonquist, J. A., and Morgan, J. N. (1964). *The detection of interaction effects.* Ann Arbor: Institute for Social Research, University of Michigan.

Tarling, R. (1982). Comparison of measures of predictive power. *Educational and Psychological Measurement* 42:479–487.

Van Alstyne, D. J., and Gottfredson, M. R. (1978). A multidimensional contingency table analysis of parole outcome: New methods and old problems in criminological prediction. *Journal of Research in Crime and Delinquency* 15:172–93.

Yates, F. (1934). The analysis of multiple classifications with unequal numbers in the different classes. *Journal of the American Statistical Association* 29:51–66.

CHAPTER 12

Prediction Equations, Statistical Analysis, and Shrinkage

JOHN B. COPAS

SUMMARY

The nature of probabilistic prediction and the use of statistical methods in criminological studies are discussed. By contrasting the validation fit and the retrospective fit of a prediction equation, I explore the phenomenon of shrinkage and propose methods whereby the amount of shrinkage can be anticipated in advance. Emphasis is given to the (not inconsiderable) effects of stepwise selection of predictive factors.

INTRODUCTION

The concept of prediction is central to all of science. A scientific theory is judged according to its ability to predict observable events. In science education, at least at the more elementary level, the assumption that predictions can and should be made exact is accepted without question. If x_A units of A react with x_B units of B, then the laws of nature see to it that x_C units of C will result. Even at the more advanced level, most scientific research is directed toward the goal of exact prediction, a goal that is assumed to be attainable, at least in principle, given enough theoretical knowledge and sufficiently powerful computing facilities. But in the behavioral sciences, as in biology and medicine, the whole idea of exact prediction has to be abandoned. A more or less substantial uncertainty has to be accepted as insurmountable, and the refusal of behavioral patterns to follow any preconceived formula becomes itself the object of study.

A more general concept of prediction comes about by noting the extraordinary similarity between the variability that is observed in nature and the realizations of games of chance: exact prediction is replaced by probabilistic prediction. In this more general concept, the focus of attention is not so much the characteristics of a given individual but, rather, the characteristics of a hypothetical population of like individuals. The success of prediction then corresponds to the degree of likeness characterizing such a population. At one extreme, the likeness is so strong that all individuals in the population are virtually identical, in which case probabilistic prediction is equivalent to exact prediction. At the other extreme, the likeness is no more than one would expect in a randomly chosen group of subjects, in which case no useful prediction has been achieved. Most cases, of course, fall somewhere in between.

The closer a given situation is to the second of these two extremes, the greater is the importance of the probabilistic aspects of prediction and, therefore, the greater must be the reliance on statistical methods. The prediction of crime and delinquency is a case in point. Judging from the empirical studies that have been undertaken in this area, only a very modest level of success in prediction seems to be possible, and the situation indeed appears to be much closer to the second extreme than to the first. The statistical problems associated with such studies are, therefore, correspondingly great, and it is some aspects of these problems that are to be discussed in this chapter.

It is useful to group the statistical questions arising in prediction studies in crime and delinquency under three broad headings: (a) design, (b) analysis, and (c) validation. The design heading includes such questions as whether a prospective or a retrospective approach is appropriate, how long the follow-up period should be, if sampling is involved how it should be carried out, exactly which variables should be measured, and so on. The second heading covers such questions as how the data obtained in the study are to be summarized and reported, which particular statistical techniques should be used, how the hypotheses of substantive interest can be tested, and so on. The validation heading concerns methods of testing the conclusions reached in (b) on information available on further subjects and how such conclusions should be modified in the light of such further experience.

Of these three, (a) is clearly the most important, as the decisions reached at this stage determine the whole course of the investigation and provide the baseline for (b) and (c). A good deal of the questions in (a) must be guided by common sense and practical constraints. Stage (b) is where the role of conventional statistical techniques is most apparent and where mathematical theory has the most to contribute. For this reason, (b) has received by far the greatest attention in the literature. Stage (c) is seldom given much emphasis by statisticians, but it corresponds to one of the tenets of the scientific method, namely, that research results should be reproducible, or amenable to independent verification. Criminologists, on the other hand, have attached considerable importance to the validation of prediction results, reflecting perhaps the rather high level of uncertainty and variability that is characteristic of research in this discipline.

Although these three headings are convenient, the first two of them being widely used in the titles of statistics textbooks, it would be wrong to think of them as entirely separate one from another. The link from (a) to (b) is obvious, as (a) provides the data that are analyzed in (b); imperfections in (a) will almost certainly limit the validity of conclusions in (b). Conversely, the choice of method in (b) must take account of the design in (a); failure to do so may render the statistical analysis completely invalid. The link from (b) to (c) is also obvious, since (b) provides the material to be tested in (c). The converse link, from (c) to (b), has not been explored very fully but is to be taken up in some detail in later sections of this chapter.

The fact that a study is called a *"prediction* study" indicates that the researcher will have in mind some particular response, say y, that is believed to be related to some or all of a number of predefined predictive factors, $x_1, x_2, \ldots, x_p$. The main objective in (b) will then be to distill all the information in the data pertaining to the value of y and propose a *prediction equation* which, in some sense, gives the most accurate possible forecast of y as a function of the x's. A prediction equation is, in fact, a probabilistic prediction in the sense described above: explicitly, the equation describes the probability distribution of y within a population of individuals defined by particular values of some or all of these predictive factors (the x's). From the practical point of view, a prediction equation can be useful in two different ways. First, it is an aid to management; for example, the screening of prisoners for parole (Nuttall et al., 1977) or the possible referral of individuals to a particular psychiatric institution (Copas and Whiteley, 1976). Second, it is a research tool in investigating the effect of changes in treatment or environment; for example, Mannheim and Wilkins (1955) used a prediction equation to define a small number of "risk groups" in the context of borstal training. More generally, the value of a prediction equation is that it provides a statistical covariate for use in further research work.

The relationship between prediction equations and some of the methods of data analysis used in stage (b) are discussed in the next section. In the third section, I go on to consider some of the methods of fitting prediction equations. The fourth section moves on to stage (c) and considers the validation performance of such predictors. Shrinkage, the statistical phenomenon whereby a prediction equation fits less well on validation than it does (retrospectively) on the original data, is explored in some detail. The fifth section describes the not inconsiderable effect on (c) of the empirical selection of predictive factors. The main result from these last two sections is that it is possible, and indeed desirable, to modify a prediction equation in the light of a forecast of its validation performance.

It is worth pointing out that although terms such as *prediction equation* and *validation sample* are part of the jargon local to criminology, the statistical problems underlying them are by no means specific to this particular discipline. Discriminant analysis (as understood by statisticians) is closely related to the theory of prediction equations when the response is binary or categorical, and the large statistical literature on that topic has a major contribution to make to prediction studies in crime and delinquency. Much of the more recent literature in discriminant analysis has, in fact, been stimulated by medical applications such as computer-aided diagnosis. Recent books are by Lachenbruch (1975) and Goldstein and Dillon (1978), with a useful reference to the medical applications being Titterington et al. (1981). In the case of a continuous or interval-scale response, prediction equations correspond to multiple regression analysis, which again is widely discussed in the statistical literature, albeit with slightly different terminology. A useful recent book here is by Daniel and Wood (1980).

DATA ANALYSIS AND PREDICTION

Since the primary interest in the results of a prediction study will usually be in the prediction equation itself, it is all too easy to gain the impression from published accounts of such studies that the numerical fitting of the prediction equation is the only statistical technique employed at the analysis stage. In practice, the choice of factors to use in a prediction equation will nearly always be based on an extended preliminary analysis of the data, aimed at both summarizing and understanding the information available to the researcher. The basic materials required for a preliminary analysis are readily available once the data are coded into a form suitable for a statistical package computer program such as SPSS (Nie, Bent, and Hull, 1970). It would be impossible to give an exhaustive list of the steps to be taken in this analysis, since much will depend on the practical context and quality of the data, but it is nearly always worthwhile to obtain printouts of each of the following:

1. The frequency distributions of each variable recorded in the data. This is useful in identifying missing observations and in "cleaning up" the data by isolating values that have been miscoded or mispunched.
2. The cross-classification of y with each of the x's. This will help

to identify those factors which are likely to be useful in prediction.

3. The three-way classifications between y and at least some of the possible pairs of x's. This will identify interactions between the effects of the individual predictive factors; strong interactions should normally be included as separate factors in the analysis.

4. The correlation matrix of all variables in the data. This will identify those pairs of factors which are highly correlated with each other and will possibly suggest how the number of factors can be reduced by appropriate redefinition and amalgamation.

5. A step-up multiple regression of y on all of the x's (assuming y is suitably coded). This is a guide (but not an infallible one) to the predictive value of combinations of x's taken several at a time.

Needless to say, progress at any one step should be influenced by any interesting findings at a previous step. For example, an interaction between two binary factors x_1 and x_2 suggests that a new factor defined as the product x_1x_2 should be added to the factors already recorded, or the discovery of a substantial number of missing readings on a factor may lead to the abandonment of that factor altogether. In a large study, a considered perusal of all these facets of the data may be time-consuming, but compared with the time and effort usually needed in designing the study and in collecting the data, time spent at the analysis stage is relatively trivial. The hope of developing a prediction instrument that is convincing from both an empirical and a substantive viewpoint can be realized only if that equation mirrors reality, a reality which can be revealed only by careful study of the data intermixed with whatever theoretical knowledge may be available to the researcher.

An example of a relatively simple prediction equation following a preliminary analysis of the data is reported in Copas and Whiteley (1976). This study was concerned with the treatment of psychopaths in a therapeutic community (Henderson hospital). The research material consisted of data pertaining to all patients admitted to the community during a specific period of time. The information covered social, psychiatric, and criminal history, together with a two- to three-year follow-up covering any subsequent criminal convictions and/or readmissions to a psychiatric institution. The response y was taken to be a simple dichotomy: success, if there were no reconvictions or psychiatric admissions; failure, if one or both of these were recorded in the follow-up information. The x's, about a dozen in all, corresponded to the information available for each subject at the time of admission. Thus, if an effective prediction equation could be developed, it could help to identify those subjects who are most likely to respond to the Henderson environment and, therefore, be a guide to referral agencies as well as to the hospital itself in its admission procedures.

Detailed examination of the x variables in this study revealed two quite marked interactions, both of which were subsequently included in the prediction equation described in the cited paper. One of these interactions is illustrated in table 12.1, which shows the rate of success cross-classified with recidivism (defined as more than one previous conviction) and previous psychiatric admission. The numerator and denominator of each fraction are the number of successful cases and the total number of cases, respectively; the numbers in parentheses are the corresponding percentages. As can be seen, there is a clear suggestion of a differential effect between the two factors. A psychiatric history is associated with a higher success rate among the recidivists but a lower success rate among the nonrecidivists. Note that the association between success and psychiatric history taken by itself is a very weak (53 percent against 42 percent); a superficial analysis that looks at the variables only one at a time is unlikely to judge psychiatric history a useful predictive factor.

The preliminary statistical analysis will doubtless suggest certain variables that are important and that should definitely be included in a prediction equation and certain others that can be eliminated from further consideration. However, there will often remain other variables whose contribution is modest or doubtful; the number of such variables may be large and can even exceed the number of subjects in the study. In the latter case, the fitting of a prediction equation using all the variables at once is impossible. Thus the major problem of selecting predictive factors remains.

The usual empirical guide to the importance of each individual variable is given by the level of significance, which assesses whether

Table 12.1 Success Rates in the Henderson Study

	Recidivist	Other	Total
Previous Admission	$\frac{13}{26}$ (50)	$\frac{14}{25}$ (56)	$\frac{27}{51}$ (53)
No Previous Admission	$\frac{3}{20}$ (15)	$\frac{14}{20}$ (70)	$\frac{17}{40}$ (42)
Total	$\frac{16}{46}$ (35)	$\frac{28}{45}$ (62)	$\frac{44}{91}$ (48)

Note: Numerator = number of successes; denominator = total number of cases; figure in parentheses = corresonding percentages.

the observed association between that variable and success (or whatever criterion is to be predicted) can reasonably be explained in terms of mere chance variation. The assumption has to be made, of course, that the subjects in the study have been randomly sampled from a relevant population of such subjects. Unfortunately, there are three technical difficulties with the repeated use of significance tests on the variables taken one after the other, and these are as follows.

(a) The tests are usually correlated with each other. Thus a spurious chance effect that upsets the conclusion of one test may also upset the conclusion of another test. This is a serious problem only if two or more of the variables are very highly correlated with each other in the original data; and this will have been checked already by examining the correlation matrix of all the variables. If two variables are found to be highly correlated (for example, $r = 0.9$), this will often be the result of an overlap between the definitions of those variables. In such a case, the problem can usually be removed by redefining one of the variables so that the information contained in them is more nearly independent or by combining them together into a single new variable. Failing this, the problem can only be alleviated by using more sophisticated multivariate significance tests.

(b) The results are difficult to interpret if the number of tests is at all large. For example, if 20 independent tests are carried out, then, by definition, one of them would be expected to give a significant result at the 5 percent level just by chance. Put the other way round, obtaining just one such significant result out of 20 cannot be interpreted as anything more than chance variation. A crude (but simple) way of overcoming this problem is to work to a much smaller significance level equal to the nominal level divided by the number of tests. For instance, in a series of 10 independent significance tests, a single result should be regarded as significant at the 5 percent level only if the level achieved by that particular test is five-tenths; or 0.5 percent. This is a rough approximation but serves to show that a significance level can be regarded only as a rough yardstick, and certainly the result of a significance test should never be taken as a definitive statement of proof.

(c) The extent of the contribution that a predictive factor makes to a prediction equation is only very indirectly related to the significance of that factor. It is frequently the case that factors that do *not* attain any reasonable level of significance in the data are still useful as predictors. Conversely, a factor may be highly significant in the data but contribute minimally to a prediction equation.

The nature of difficulty (c) is exemplified by the simplest nontrivial prediction situation, in which a dichotomous response is to be predicted from one dichotomous prediction factor. To take a specific example, suppose we are predicting the chance of reoffending within a given period of time (R_T) on the basis of whether or not the subject's criminal record includes sexual assualt (Sa). For the moment, let us put to one side the contribution any other predictive factor may make. Thus the data can be arranged in the frequency table shown in table 12.2. The table shows that, of n_s sexual offenders, a reoffend and n_s - a do not; of n - n_s nonsexual offenders, b reoffend and n - n_s - b do not. If all available information is used, the predicted probability of reoffending is

$$\hat{p}_1 = \begin{cases} \dfrac{a}{n_s} & \text{for sexual offenders,} \\[2em] \dfrac{b}{n - n_s} & \text{otherwise.} \end{cases}$$

If, however, the information on sexual assault is ignored, then the predicted probability is

$$\hat{p}_2 = \frac{a + b}{n} \qquad \text{for all cases.}$$

Now the significance of the association between sexual assault and reoffending is given by the value of χ^2:

$$\chi^2 = \frac{n[a(n - n_s - b) - b(n_s - a)]^2}{n_s(n - n_s)\,(a + b)\,(n - a - b)},$$

with the data attaining significance at the 5 percent level if $\chi^2 \geq 3.84$ (with one degree of freedom). Hence, a third, and perhaps more realistic, prediction equation is given by

$$\hat{p}_3 = \begin{cases} \hat{p}_1 & \text{if} \quad \chi^2 \geq 3.84, \\[1em] \hat{p}_2 & \text{if} \quad \chi^2 < 3.84. \end{cases}$$

Suppose now that these prediction equations are to be validated on a large future sample of offenders of whom the present sample can be considered representative. Let the rates of reoffending in the

Table 12.2   Data for Simple Prediction Problem

	Reoffend (Ro)	Not Reoffend	Total
Sexual Assault (Sa)	a	$n_s - a$	n_s
No Sexual Assault	b	$n - n_s - b$	$n - n_s$
Total	$a + b$	$n - a - b$	n

future sample be p_s for the sexual offenders, p_n for the nonsexual offenders, and p_t in the total sample. Then the squared errors of any predicted probability $\hat{p}$ are $(p_s - \hat{p})^2$ and $(p_n - \hat{p})^2$ for sexual and nonsexual offenders, respectively. Since these arise in the ratio $n_s:(n-n_s)$, the overall prediction mean squared error of $\hat{p}$ is approximately

$$\frac{1}{n} \{n_s \, E[(p_s - \hat{p})^2 \mid \text{sexual offender}] + (n - n_s) \, E[(p_n - \hat{p})^2 \mid \text{nonsexual}$$

offender]}, where E denotes expectation or average. It is fairly easy to show that for $\hat{p} = \hat{p}_1$ the mean squared error equals

$$\frac{2p_t(1 - p_t)}{n} \tag{12.1}$$

and for $\hat{p} = \hat{p}_2$ it equals

$$\frac{p_t(1 - p_t)}{n} (1 + \gamma^2), \tag{12.2}$$

where

$$\gamma = \frac{p_s - p_n}{\sqrt{p_t(1 - p_t) \left(\frac{1}{n_s} + \frac{1}{n - n_s}\right)}}.$$

The parameter γ is equal to the difference between the reoffending rates for sexual and nonsexual offenders expressed in standard deviation units, the standard deviation being that pertaining to the difference between these two rates as estimated from the original data. The prediction mean squared error for $\hat{p} = \hat{p}_3$ is much more complicated to evaluate but can be shown to be approximately

$$\frac{p_t(1 - p_t)}{n} A(\gamma) \tag{12.3}$$

where

$A(\gamma) = 2 + [(\Phi(\gamma + 2) - \Phi(\gamma - 2)] (\gamma^2 - 1) + (\gamma + 2) \, \phi \, (\gamma + 2) - (\gamma - 2) \, \phi \, (\gamma - 2),$
the functions ϕ and Φ in this expression being defined by

$$\phi(x) = \frac{1}{\sqrt{2\pi}} e^{-x^2/2},$$

$$\Phi(x) = \int_{-\infty}^{x} \phi(t)dt,$$

the density function and cumulative probability function, respectively, of the standard normal distribution. The function $A(\gamma)$ is shown in figure 12.1. Since (12.1) and (12.2) are equivalent to (12.3) if $A(\gamma)$ is replaced by 2 and $1 + \gamma^2$, respectively, the prediction mean squared errors of $\hat{p}_1$ and $\hat{p}_2$ have also been represented on the same diagram. The percentage scale along the bottom of this diagram gives the median significance level one would expect from a true difference equal to the corresponding value of γ. Thus 5 percent corresponds to 2 standard deviations ($\gamma = 2$) and is placed in the center of the scale. Situations for which one would expect higher levels of significance in comparing the rates of reoffending between sexual and nonsexual offenders are to the right of the center; situations where the difference is unlikely to be significant are to the left of the center.

Since the vertical coordinate in figure 12.1 is proportional to average prediction squared *error*, the lower the curve, the more accurate the corresponding prediction equation. It is immediately clear that none of the three prediction equations is uniformly best for all situations. Although $\hat{p}_2$ is best (as one would expect) if the difference between the two groups is very small (that is, if γ is small), it becomes rapidly worse as γ increases. The fact that the researcher has felt it worthwhile to separate his subjects into sexual and nonsexual offenders suggests that there is at least some prospect of detecting a difference between the two groups (that is, some prospect of γ being large), and so it seems that $\hat{p}_2$ (always omitting sexual offending from the prediction equation) cannot be considered sensible. Conversely, $\hat{p}_1$, which always takes account of the sexual assault factor, is worst for very small values of γ but best for all moderately large and large values of that parameter. The third predictor, $\hat{p}_3$, which includes the sexual assault factor if and only if it is statistically significant, is a compromise between $\hat{p}_1$ and $\hat{p}_2$ and might have been expected to predict well under all circumstances. But figure 12.1 shows that, unless γ is very small, $\hat{p}_3$ is *worse* than $\hat{p}_1$ and sometimes considerably so. Evidently, the risk of possibly omitting a factor that is important more than outweighs the advantage of having a more parsimonious prediction equation. Although it is not possible to make a definitive choice without more information as to the likely size of γ, the example does show that it is wrong to suppose that only factors that are statistically significant should be included in a prediction equation.

This example with just one predictive factor is obviously a gross oversimplification. However, it can be generalized to studies with several predictive factors, provided these factors are independent of each other. In such a study the average prediction squared error is proportional to the average of several curves of the kind shown in figure 12.1, one curve for each factor. Thus any qualitative conclusion reached in the single-factor case extends to the multi-factor situation. In practice the predictive factors are unlikely to be independent of each other, but the situation does not seem to be markedly different unless the interfactor correlations are large.

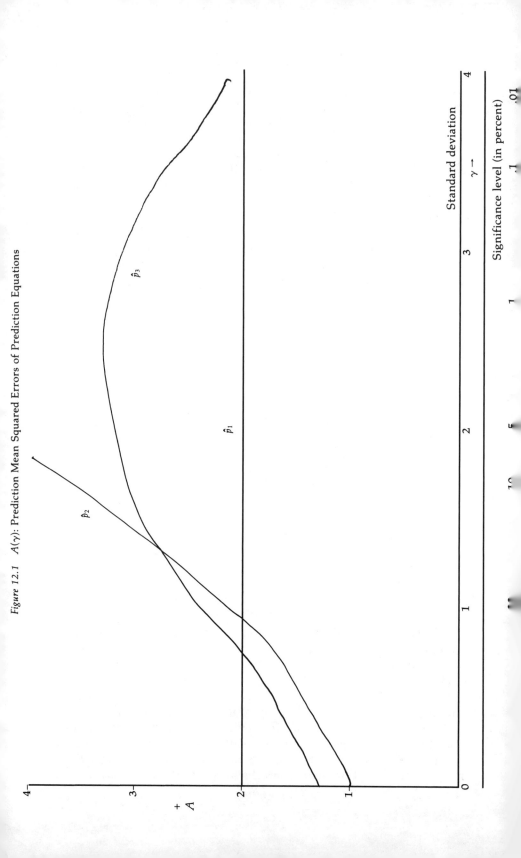

Figure 12.1 A(γ): Prediction Mean Squared Errors of Prediction Equations

PREDICTION EQUATIONS

In the example considered at the end of the previous section, we saw that a prediction equation specifies the probability of reoffending (probabilistic prediction) rather than forecasts whether the event of reoffending will actually occur (which would be exact prediction). More generally, if the response y is to be predicted from predictive factors $x_1, x_2, \ldots, x_p$, it is accepted that y is not actually determined by the x's, but that y is a random variable whose distribution is indexed by those x's. Essentially, this is a mathematical model in which y is likened to the outcome of a game of chance whose rules are set by the particular values of $x_1, x_2 \ldots, x_p$. Thus any characteristic of the probability distribution of y will be a function of the x's, the simplest being the expected value, or average, which we write as

$$E(y \mid x_1, x_2, \ldots, x_p) = H(x_1, x_2, \ldots, x_p). \qquad (12.4)$$

where H is some general function of the x's.

The precise definition of y is one of the most important considerations in the design of the study. The two most important cases are described next.

Binary Prediction

The case already considered, when y takes one of just two values according to the presence or absence of some event, is an example of binary prediction. In the earlier example, the event was defined to be reoffending within a given period of time, R_T. By convention, y is taken to be 1 if R_T occurs and 0 if R_T does not occur, so that the expectation in (12.4) is just the probability of R_T, $P(R_T)$.

Continuous Prediction

In continuous prediction, y is a quantitative factor taking values over a given range of possibilities. For example, y might be defined as the time period to first offense, the variety of offenses (number of different types of conviction), or the number of convictions in a given time period. The number of possible values is assumed to be sufficiently great so that the approximation of y as a continuous (interval-scale) variate is reasonable. Here, an actual value of y is taken to be

$$y = H(x_1, x_2, \ldots, x_p) + \epsilon, \qquad (12.5)$$

where ϵ is a "random error" with expectation 0. The standard deviation of ϵ is a measure of the accuracy of the prediction equation. The assumption that ϵ has a normal distribution is often made, but is not really necessary in most applications.

For the estimation of the function H to be a feasible proposition, it is nearly always necessary to assume in advance some simple structure so that the problem reduces to the estimation of a fairly small number of constants or coefficients. A linear structure, or a transformation of a linear structure, is usually assumed. Corresponding to the above cases, the standard models are

for binary prediction,

$$P(R_T) = \frac{e^{\alpha + \beta_1 x_1 + \beta_2 x_2 + \ldots + \beta_p x_p}}{1 + e^{\alpha + \beta_1 x_1 + \beta_2 x_2 + \ldots + \beta_p x_p}},$$ (12.6)

where α is a constant and β is a coefficient.

and for continuous prediction,

$$y = \alpha + \beta_1 x_1 + \beta_2 x_2 + \ldots + \beta_p x_p + \epsilon.$$ (12.7)

Equation (12.7) is the usual model of multiple regression of y on $x_1, x_2, \ldots, x_p$ and can be fitted by using one of the many statistical package computer programs such as SPSS (Nie, Bent, and Hull, 1970). Equation (12.6) is known by statisticians as "logistic regression" and can be fitted by a more specialized computer program such as GLIM (Baker and Nelder, 1978).

The assumption of linearity and additivity of the effects of $x_1, x_2, \ldots, x_p$ in (12.6) and (12.7) may seem unduly restrictive. However, as noted earlier, it is possible to allow for interactions between these effects by defining new predictive factors or by fitting separate equations to different subsets of the data. Nonlinear effects can be accommodated similarly. In practice, the available sample size imposes a severe constraint on the sophistication of the equations it would be realistic to fit, and it is usual to allow for interactions and nonlinear effects only if their importance is clearly evident from the data.

Although equations (12.6) and (12.7) can be regarded as standard procedures, there are several other methods of fitting prediction equations that have been discussed and used (with varying degrees of success) in the literature. Space does not permit a detailed survey of all these methods, but two of them are particularly useful and should be mentioned.

Fitting the Predictive Factors One at a Time

Here the method is equivalent to fitting a series of simple prediction equations of y based on x_i taken one at a time and then combining these simple prediction equations together in some appropriate way to obtain the full prediction equation. Such a method is used in the Home Office Parole Study (Nuttall et al., 1977).

In this study a prediction score is calculated as the sum of a series of increments in the percentage rates of reoffending defined over the various levels of each predictive factor taken in turn. The method is quite intuitive and does not seem to be based on any clearly defined statistical principles. However, the procedure works tolerably well because the unusually large sample size available (over 2,000 male prisoners) admits a direct calibration of the prediction score in terms of observed rates of reoffending. The method of taking the x_i's one at a time can be put on a firm mathematical basis if it is assumed that the predictive factors are statistically independent of each other. The most useful case here is in the binary prediction situation when it can be shown that

$$P(R_T) = \frac{e^\delta}{1 + e^\delta},$$

where δ is a prediction score given by

$$\delta = \log \frac{q}{1-q} + \log \frac{f_1(x_1)}{g_1(x_1)} + \log \frac{f_2(x_2)}{g_2(x_2)} + \ldots + \log \frac{f_p(x_p)}{g_p(x_p)}.$$

In this equation q is the overall observed rate of reoffending, $f_i(x_i)$ is the proportion of the reoffending cases for whom the ith predictive factor takes the particular value of x_i, and $g_i(x_i)$ is the same as $f_i(x_i)$ but calculated for the cases who do *not* reoffend. All these quantities are easy to work out from the data. The main advantage of the method is that, since all reference to the simultaneous distribution of the predictive factors is avoided, the prediction equation can be fitted with a much smaller sample size than would be required for a more sophisticated model. The obvious disadvantage of the method is the underlying assumption of independence, an assumption which is usually in blatant violation of reality. However, experience shows that, unless the sample size is quite large, the advantage in the ease and precision of the estimation of the necessary coefficients more than offsets the disadvantage implied by the unrealistic assumption of independence.

Discriminant Analysis

In discriminant analysis y is again assumed to be binary, but a very different model is assumed for the structure of the data. The subjects who reoffend and those who do not are supposed to be two separate populations each characterized by a multivariate probability distribution of the predictive factors $x_1, x_2, \ldots, x_p$. The object of the method is to allocate rather than to predict; a future subject with given values of $x_1, x_2, \ldots, x_p$ is to be assigned as belonging to either the reoffending population or the nonreoffending population.

Assignments are made by using a "discriminant score," z, together with a suitable cut-off value, k, such that a subject is allocated as a reoffender if $z \geq k$ and a nonreoffender if $z < k$. Details of the method can be found in many statistics textbooks (for example, Maxwell, 1977). It can be shown that if z is assumed to be a linear function of x_1, $x_2, \ldots, x_p$, then the usual method of estimating the discriminant score is mathematically equivalent to fitting the multiple regression equation (12.7) to all the data with y taken to be 1 if R_T occurs and 0 otherwise. But this equivalence does not justify the use of (12.7) as an actual prediction equation in the binary case, although many of the earlier empirical prediction studies did, in fact, do so (Mannheim and Wilkins, 1955; Simon, 1971). First, (12.7) may in fact be negative or exceed 1 for certain values of $x_1, x_2, \ldots, x_p$, which is, of course, impossible if the prediction is to be interpreted as a probability; and second, the assumptions about the error term ϵ implied in multiple regression analysis cannot possibly hold if y is confined to equal 0 or 1. Nonetheless, there is at least one circumstance in which the application of (12.7) to binary data gives a tolerable approximation to the more informative prediction equation (12.6), that is, when the level of uncertainty is so high that $P(R_T)$ never becomes close to 0 or 1 (say, is always between 0.1 and 0.9). In such a case the use of (12.7) is adequate in view of the relative ease with which it can be fitted, as compared with equation (12.6), this being an important consideration if a number of different combinations of predictive factors is to be explored.

SHRINKAGE

Any formal method of fitting a statistical model must involve some criterion of accuracy or goodness of fit. In the case of prediction equations it is important to distinguish between two different senses in which fit can be assessed—retrospective fit and validation (or prospective) fit. Retrospective fit concerns the comparison of the predicted values of y given by a prediction equation and the actual values of y observed in the data on which that prediction equation is based. Validation fit, on the other hand, looks forward to a new and independent sample of cases (the validation sample) and compares the predictions calculated for these new cases with the corresponding values of y that are subsequently observed. It is clear that conventional statistical principles like least squares and maximum likelihood are designed to optimize retrospective fit; equally clear is the fact that it is validation fit that is the important consideration in judging the practical value of a prediction equation.

Since, in the retrospective fit, any unusual chance effects in the data will influence both the prediction equation and the information on which its performance is judged, the success of any prediction equation when measured retrospectively will tend to be too optimistic and its performance on a validation sample will almost always be worse. The amount by which validation fit falls short of retrospective fit has been termed "shrinkage." Judging from the relatively small number of studies in which validation samples have been obtained, the degree of shrinkage can be very considerable. This has been interpreted by some as amounting to a condemnation of the whole procedure of fitting prediction equations. In still more studies, only the retrospective fits have been reported and no attempts at all have been made to assess validation performance.

The more complicated the model being fitted, the more influence random fluctuations in the data will have on the coefficients of that model, and so the greater the shrinkage. The point is illustrated by the following artificial example. Suppose the names of the subjects in a study are arranged into two lists, the first being for the reoffenders and the second being for those subjects who did not reoffend. Now define the prediction equation that assigns the probability of reoffending to 1 if the subject's name is in the first list and 0 if his name is in the second list. This prediction equation will give a perfect retrospective fit (R = 1) but clearly will be useless (R = 0) when judged on a validation sample. Although the use of subjects' names is taking the argument to the point of absurdity, the fact remains that if the number of predictive factors can be increased without limit then a stage will be reached when each subject in the study can be described uniquely by a pattern of of vlaues of $x_1, x_2, \ldots, x_p$. If this happens, the use of these patterns of predictive factors will be exactly equivalent to the use of names, with equally devastating shrinkage.

A more realistic example of shrinkage is reported in the study already cited, by Copas and Whiteley (1976). Table 12.3 shows the retrospective and validation fits of the binary prediction equation (12.6) using an initial sample size of 91 and a validation sample size of 75. In each case the subjects have been divided into four groups according to the values of the predicted probability of success, and

Table 12.3   Retrospective and Validation Fits of Prediction Equation

Predicted Probability of Success	Retrospective (N = 91) Number of Cases	Percent	Validation (N = 75) Number of Cases	Percent
0 to .3	14	21	12	33
.3 to .5	33	36	21	43
.5 to .7	19	63	29	52
.7 to 1.0	25	80	13	77

the observed percentages of subjects who were in fact successes are calculated as shown. The table confirms that there is good retrospective agreement between the proportions of successful cases and the corresponding ranges of predicted probabilities; indeed, this must be so because of the optimization method used in fitting the model. However, the agreement on validation is evidently worse, with the observed proportions in all four groups being moved toward the center. The differentiation between high- and low-risk groups, as given by the prediction equation, is less marked on validation than it might appear to be from the retrospective assessment.

Another manifestation of shrinkage relates to the correlation coefficient between the observed and predicted values of y. This correlation when calculated over a validation sample (validation correlation) is always expected to be smaller than its value calculated over the original data (retrospective correlation). Obviously, it is the validation correlation that gives an appropriate measure of the practical value of a prediction equation; the retrospective correlation is always too optimistic. (When calculating these correlations the product-moment formula is usually adequate, provided y is suitably coded.) This shrinkage of correlation is often quite marked, a halving of its value from original data to validation sample being not uncommon. For instance, for the figures shown in table 12.3 the retrospective correlation of 0.52 falls to 0.27 on validation. Some similar situations are also reported in Simon (1971). If certain technical assumptions are made (which are usually reasonable in practice) it is possible to predict the size of the validation correlation from that of the retrospective correlation by the formula

$$\frac{(n-1)R^2 - p}{(n-p-1)R},\qquad(12.8)$$

where R is the retrospective correlation, n is the sample size, and p is the number of predictive factors. If practical constraints prohibit obtaining a validation sample, then the use of this formula can give some idea of the amount of shrinkage to be expected. For example, if a prediction equation based on 50 cases with 5 predictive factors gives a retrospective correlation of 0.50, then the formula predicts a shrinkage in this correlation to 0.33, that is, a reduction of 34 percent.

The validation fit shown in table 12.3 suggests that the prediction equation tends to give values that are too extreme and that a better approximation to the future values of y would be obtained if the predicted values were all adjusted toward the overall mean value. This, along with inspection of validation fits in other studies, suggests that the prediction equations (12.6) and (12.7) would be improved if the expression

$$\alpha + \beta_1 x_1 + \beta_2 x_2 + \ldots + \beta_p x_p, \tag{12.9}$$

which appears in both equations, were to be replaced by

$$\alpha + \beta_1 \bar{x}_1 + \beta_2 \bar{x}_2 + \ldots + \beta_p \bar{x}_p + K[\beta_1(x_1 - \bar{x}_1) + \beta_2(x_2 - \bar{x}_2) + \ldots + \beta_p(x_p - \bar{x}_p)]. \tag{12.10}$$

Here, $\bar{x}_1, \bar{x}_2, \ldots, \bar{x}_p$ are the average values of the predictive factors and K is a "shrinkage constant" between 0 and 1. For an "average" subject for whom $x_1, x_2, \ldots, x_p$ are equal to the average values just mentioned, (12.9) and (12.10) are identical and so the predicted value is unchanged. For other cases, however, the value of (12.10) is closer to this overall average than is the value of (12.9). Such prediction equations might be said to be "preshrunk," because the shrinkage effect is anticipated in advance. For the multiple regression case in (12.7), Stein (1960) and Stone (1974) give mathematical arguments for the modification given in (12.10); a number of related techniques are also reviewed in Draper and Van Nostrand (1979). A simpler treatment of the validation behavior of both (12.6) and (12.7) is given in Copas (1983), who proposes the following values of the shrinkage constant K:

$$K = \begin{cases} 1 - \dfrac{p-2}{\chi^2} & \text{for binary prediction equation (12.6),} \\[2em] 1 - \dfrac{p-2}{pF} & \text{for continuous prediction equation (12.7),} \end{cases} \tag{12.11}$$

where F is the usual F-statistic for assessing the significance of the multiple regression and χ^2 is the corresponding chi-squared statistic for assessing the significance of the binary regression. If the value of K in (12.11) is negative or greater than 1, then it is truncated to 0 or 1, respectively: this value of K is therefore always in the range [0, 1], as required.

Although it is impossible to guarantee that the modification to a prediction equation implied by (12.10) and (12.11) will necessarily result in an improvement in validation fit for all conceivable sets of data, it can, nonetheless, be expected to do so on the average. Naturally, the retrospective fit of such a modified prediction equation will be worse, since, by the nature of the fitting process, the original equations (12.6) and (12.7) are precisely those which optimize the retrospective fit over all possible such prediction equations.

EMPIRICAL SELECTION OF PREDICTIVE FACTORS

The use of the validation correlation to indicate the practical value of a prediction equation has already been mentioned. In the case of continuous prediction, modelled in equation (12.7), a more direct measure of prediction accuracy is given by the average of the squared prediction errors,

$$E(y - \hat{y})^2, \qquad (12.12)$$

where the expectation is taken over a validation sample in which observed values y are predicted by corresponding values $\hat{y}$. The more accurate the prediction, the smaller is this quantity and vice versa. Clearly, the value of (12.12) must depend on the characteristics of the validation sample to which the prediction equation is applied, but if the (not unreasonable) assumption is made that the validation sample is a statistical replication of the original data, then (12.12) can be shown to equal

$$\sigma^2(1 + \frac{p+1}{n}), \qquad (12.13)$$

where, as before, p and n are the number of predictive factors and sample size, respectively, and σ is the (theoretical) residual standard deviation of y or, equivalently, the standard deviation of ϵ in equation (12.7).

Expression (12.13) shows both the potential advantage and disadvantage of using a large number of predictive factors. As the number of such factors increases, the better will be the retrospective fit of the prediction equation and so the smaller will be the value of σ; therefore, the first component of (12.13) will decrease while the second component will increase. The behavior of (12.13) will, therefore, depend on the rate of decrease of σ with p, a matter that can be assessed only in the light of the details of any particular study.

Since σ^2 is an unknown parameter, a more useful form of (12.13) is obtained by replacing σ^2 by its estimate based on the retrospective correlation R, giving

$$\frac{S^2(1 - R^2)(n - 1)(n + p + 1)}{n(n - p - 1)}, \qquad (12.14)$$

where S is the overall standard deviation of y. Again the effect of increasing p can be seen: $(1 - R^2)$ will decrease whereas $(n + p + 1)/(n - p - 1)$ will increase. Evidently, the selection of predictive factors must involve a compromise between choosing p to be large enough so that the prediction equation is informative and yet not so large that the prediction error becomes inflated.

When a relatively large number of potential predictive factors is available, this selection can be made on either substantive (*a priori*) or empirical grounds or, of course, a mixture of both. If it is possible to isolate a relatively small number of interesting subsets of the predictive factors, then a multiple regression equation can be fitted for each such subset and the final choice made on the basis of the corresponding values of (12.14). For this purpose, the terms $S^2(n-1)/n$ in (12.14) can be ignored because they will be the same whichever subset is used.

It is not often recognized, however, that when a subset of predictive factors is chosen by some empirical method such as stepwise regression, the quantities in (12.8), (12.11), (12.13), and (12.14) are *invalid*, since the regression coefficients for an empirically selected subset will always be biased. For example, in stepwise regression the worth of each variable is judged on the basis of its contribution to the overall fit; typically, a variable will be accepted if its regression coefficient is large and rejected if its regression coefficient is small. But regression coefficients are only statistical estimates subject to random errors, and so it follows that the coefficients of those variables selected by the stepwise procedure will be more likely to be overestimated than underestimated. In consequence, the usual theory based on least squares and unbiased estimation does not apply. The tendency for the coefficients in an empirically selected subset of predictive factors to be overestimated leads to a tendency for the resulting predictions, $\hat{y}$, to be too extreme in either the positive or negative direction. This adds to the effect of shrinkage discussed above; a prediction equation based on an empirically selected subset of predictive factors will be expected to shrink more (often substantially more) than will a similar equation based on a predetermined set of predictive factors.

The amount of this additional shrinkage is very difficult to predict in advance unless some assumption is made about the configuration of the true values of the regression coefficients of the predictive factors. One such assumption, which leads to a Bayesian analysis, is given in Copas (1983). Using a statistical test developed in that paper, it is suggested that the assumption is reasonable in many practical applications of prediction equations and that, even when the assumption does not hold exactly, the ensuing analysis can give at least some guide to the shrinkage that might be expected when the prediction equation comes to be validated.

Suppose that the total number of potential predictive factors is p_0 and that an empirically selected subset of size p is taken. Let R_0 be the retrospective correlation for a prediction equation based on all p_0 variables, and R ($\leq R_0$) be the corresponding quantity for the selected subset. Then, according to the analysis in Copas (1983), the validation correlation for the prediction equation useing only the p selected factors is estimated to be

$$RL \tag{12.15}$$

where

$$L = \frac{(n - 1) R_0{}^2 - p_0}{R_0{}^2 (n - p_0 - 1)} \tag{12.16}$$

This formula is illustrated in table 12.4, which relates to a recent study concerning a sample of patients in a maximum security hospital. The variable being predicted is the "variety of offenses," defined as the number of different types of offenses in the patient's criminal record; the $p_0 = 10$ predictive factors relate to social history together with a number of psychometric and psychophysiological measures. Multiple regression equations were fitted using stepwise regression starting with one predictive factor and working up to the full complement of 10 predictive factors. The values of R (retrospective correlation), expression (12.8) (validation correlation ignoring empirical selection), and expression (12.15) (validation correlation allowing for empirical selection) are shown in this table for each step. At the final step, when no empirical selection is in fact invoked, (12.8) and (12.15) agree, as one would expect. But, at the earlier steps, it is clear that (12.8) considerably overestimates (12.15). Evidently, if these prediction equations were to be validated on an independent sample of subjects, substantial shrinkage would be expected.

The corresponding formula for the prediction mean squared error defined in (12.12) is equal to

$$S^2 \left\{ \frac{n - 1}{n - p_{0-1}} \left[\frac{n + 1}{n} (1 - R_0{}^2) + \frac{LD}{(n - 1)R_0{}^2} \right] + R^2 \left[\frac{p_0(1 - R_0{}^2)}{(n - p_0 - 1)R_0{}^2} \right]^2 \right\} \tag{12.17}$$

where

$$D = [(n - 1)R_o{}^2 - p_0])(R_o{}^2 - R^2) \mid p_0 R_0{}^2 (1 - R_0{}^2)$$

Table 12.4 Correlations for Stepwise Prediction Equations

Numbers of Predictive Factors	1	2	3	4	5	6	7	8	9	10
Retrospective Correlation	.31	.41	.47	.50	.52	.53	.55	.55	.56	.56
Validation Correlation (12.8) (ignoring selection)	.26	.33	.38	.38	.38	.37	.37	.34	.33	.29
Validation Correlation (12.15) (allowing for selection)	.16	.21	.24	.26	.27	.28	.29	.29	.29	.29

and L is defined in (12.16). This formula is the appropriate modification to (12.14) allowing for empirical selection of the predictive factors. The values of (12.17), but omitting the constant multiple S^2, are calculated for the maximum security hospital data and shown in table 12.5, along with the corresponding values of (12.14). Since S is the overall standard deviation of y, a value of 1.00 in this table can be interpreted as the result one would obtain if one simply predicted y as the overall average regardless of the values of the predictive factors. Thus, a value greater than 1.00 is *worse than useless*, in the sense that one would be better off omitting the predictive factors altogether. This is seen to be precisely the case for all the prediction equations fitted in the stepwise regression, despite the fact that the first two predictive factors are "statistically significant" as judged by the usual significance tests of the regression coefficients. Clearly, the contribution made by these two predictive factors is more than outweighed by the empirical selection effect. Note that (12.14), which makes no allowance for selection, is much too optimistic.

The possibility of modifying a prediction equation in the light of anticipated shrinkage has already been discussed in connection with expressions (12.10) and (12.11). Naturally, if empirical selection is used, the value of the shrinkage constant K must take account of this fact. Continuing the analysis leading to the equations quoted above, it is shown in Copas (1983) that K should in fact be the same whichever empirically selected subset is used and that this common value should be obtained from the formula (12.11) as applied to the regression on *all* the predictive factors. The prediction mean squared error for the corresponding "preshrunk" prediction equation in (12.10) is, on average, less than that for the original equation with the same predictive factors, the difference being estimated as

$$S^2 R^2 \left[\frac{p_0(1 - R_0^2)}{(n - p_0 - 1)R_0^2} \right]^2. \tag{12.18}$$

Thus the prediction mean squared error of a "preshrunk" prediction equation is given by (12.17) minus 12.18 or, equivalently, (12.17) with the last major term in that expression omitted. For the maximum security hospital data, K comes to be 0.52, and the corresponding mean squared error of (12.10) is shown in the lower row of table 12.5 (again omitting the constant multiple S^2). These figures suggest that, although ordinary regression equations are useless as predictors in this case, some modest predictive power is obtained by the "preshrunk" prediction equations.

Finally, we return to the binary prediction study of Copas and

Whiteley (1976). The prediction equation quoted in that paper was based on an empirical selection procedure that selected a subset of 6 out of a set of 14 variables (including two interactions) that were considered relevant. The value of K in (12.11) for the regression on all 14 variables came to 0.51; the actual validation fit of the corresponding "preshrunk" equation following (12.6) and (12.10) is shown in table 12.6. In this table, the sample frequencies are the same as for the validation fit given in table 12.3, but the boundaries defining the groups in terms of the predicted probabilities have shrunk towards the center. Although the validation sample is too small to admit any very precise estimates of the success rates, there is a tendency for the four percentage rates shown in table 12.6 to agree more closely with the modified ranges of predicted probabilities than with the original ranges used in table 12.3.

The remark has already been made that it is very difficult to predict the shrinkage caused by empirical selection and that progress can be made only if certain assumptions are made about the underlying statistical model. It goes without saying that, in any practical situation, such assumptions should be subjected to examination and, if possible, empirical verification. Although the assumptions leading to the formulae quoted in this section appear to be reasonable in the small number of studies in which they have been tested (Copas, 1983), they cannot possibly apply in all situations; further research is needed to evaluate the sensitivity of the proposed methods to violations in these assumptions. Further research is also needed in the monitoring of shrinkage under alternative and more general assumptions. However, the fact that empirical selection *does* lead to additional shrinkage cannot be denied, and failure to allow for

Table 12.5 Prediction Mean Squared Errors for Stepwise Prediction Equations

Number of Predictive Factors	1	2	3	4	5	6	7	8	9	10
Multiple Regression (12.14) (ignoring selection)	.95	.91	.88	.88	.89	.90	.91	.94	.97	1.01
Multiple Regression (12.17) (allowing for selection)	1.02	1.01	1.01	1.01	1.01	1.01	1.01	1.01	1.01	1.01
Preshrunk Prediction Equation [(12.17) – 12.18)]	.99	.97	.96	.95	.94	.94	.94	.93	.93	.93

Table 12.6 Validation Fit of Preshrunk Prediction Equation

Predicted Probability of Success	Number of Cases	Percent
0 to .4	12	33
.4 to .5	21	43
.5 to .6	29	52
.6 to 1.0	13	77

this fact can result in seriously misleading conclusions. It can be argued that, given the lack of more general methods, it is at least better to explore the shrinkage implied by somewhat inadequate assumptions than to ignore it altogether.

REFERENCES

Baker, R. J., and Nelder, J. A. (1978). *The GLIM system*. Oxford: Numerical Algorithms Group.

Copas, J. B. (1983) Regression, prediction, and shrinkage (with discussion). *Journal of the Royal Statistical Society, Series B.*, 45:311–54.

Copas, J. B., and Whiteley, S. (1976). Predicting success in the treatment of psychopaths. *British Journal of Psychiatry*, 129:388–92.

Daniel, C., and Wood, F. S. (1980). *Fitting equations to data: Computer analysis of multifactor data*. 2d ed. New York: Wiley.

Draper, N. R., and Van Nostrand, R. C. (1979). Ridge regression and James-Stein estimation: Review and comments. *Technometrics* 21:451–66.

Goldstein, M., and Dillon, W. R. (1978). *Discrete discriminant analysis*. New York: Wiley.

Lachenbruch, P. A. (1975). *Discriminant analysis*. New York: Macmillan.

Mannheim, H., and Wilkins, L. T. (1955). *Prediction methods in relation to borstal training*. Studies in the Causes of Delinquency and the Treatment of Offenders No. 1. London: Her Majesty's Stationery Office.

Maxwell, A. E. (1977). *Multivariate analysis in behavioural research*. London: Chapman and Hall.

Nie, N. H.; Bent, D. H.; and Hull, C. H. (1970). *Statistical package for the social sciences*. New York: McGraw-Hill.

Nuttall, C. P. et al. (1977). *Parole in England and Wales*. Home Office Research Study No. 38. London: Her Majesty's Stationery Office.

Simon, F. H. (1971). *Prediction methods in criminology*. Home Office Research Study No. 7. London: Her Majesty's Stationery Office.

Stein, C. (1960). Multiple regression. In *Contributions to probability and statistics in honour of Harold Hotelling*, ed. I. Olkin. Stanford: Stanford University Press.

Stone, M. (1974). Cross validatory choice and assessment of statistical predictions. *Journal of the Royal Statistical Society, Series B*, 36:111–47.

Titterington, D. M.; Murray, G. D.; Murray, L. S.; Spiegelhalter, D. J.; Skene, A. M.; Habbema, J. D. F.; and Gelpke, G. J. (1981). Comparison of discrimination techniques applied to a complex data set of head injured patients. *Journal of the Royal Statistical Society, Series A*, 144:145–75.

VI
Conclusions

CHAPTER 13

Criminological Prediction: The Way Forward

DAVID P. FARRINGTON AND ROGER TARLING

SUMMARY

This final chapter summarizes both the implications of this book for criminological prediction and the latest developments in this field. Progress has been made in measuring predictor variables, in defining criterion variables, in selecting and combining predictor variables into a prediction instrument, in measuring predictive efficiency, and in establishing validity.

INTRODUCTION

One of the aims of this final chapter is to summarize the implications of this book for criminological prediction. The chapters demonstrate the uses of prediction methods in a wide variety of contexts: in probation and parole, in institutions, with unconvicted persons, with dangerous or mentally disordered offenders, and with a complete criminal justice system. They also demonstrate how similar issues arise in many applications: problems of research design, the choice of predictor and criterion variables, methods of selecting and combining variables into a prediction instrument, measures of predictive efficiency, and external validity or generalizability. Many of these issues were reviewed in our introductory chapter, but we will return to them here in order to draw conclusions and make recommendations.

Another aim of this chapter is to summarize some of the latest developments in criminological prediction and to speculate about how prediction can be improved in the future. The chapters in this book show the extent to which behavior can be predicted—not perfectly, but much better than chance. They help in determining whether the accuracy of prediction justifies its use in criminal justice decisions, and they discuss some of the ethical problems involved. We hope that this book will help to reduce the number of exaggerated claims made about the accuracy of criminological prediction. A recent example is the following (Fischer, 1983, p. 13):

> Those familiar with past efforts in recidivism prediction should appreciate the significance of the results of our validation study. Rates of accuracy in the neighborhood of 85–90% have previously been unattainable for a variety of reasons, some dealing with the quality and breadth of research data bases, and some with the types of analytic tools available. Only the test of time will show whether or not the Iowa system foreshadows a new era in the application of statistical methods to prediction problems in the social sciences.

On the basis of data presented so far, the Iowa system does not, in our opinion, foreshadow a new era in criminological prediction. One of the most basic problems is that, despite the use of the term *validation*, no true validation study has yet been published. The "validation" samples are essentially new construction samples. Also, the proportion of correct identifications is rather unsatisfactory as a measure of predictive efficiency, as it is greatly affected by the base rate and selection ratio (see below) and gives equal weight to all kinds of errors and successful identifications. It would be nice if our book would foreshadow a new era of sophistication in criminological prediction, in which researchers learn from the mistakes of the past half-century and do not repeat them.

USES OF PREDICTION IN CRIMINOLOGY

The emphasis in this book is on methods of selecting and combining predictor variables to produce a prediction table or risk groups. In chapter 2, Leslie Wilkins defended the use of such methods in predicting recidivism, although he said that he would not use them to predict offending in unconvicted groups. He essentially argued that persons found guilty by due process of law have lost their right to protect personal information, but that unconvicted persons have a right to privacy. He took issue with a strict "just deserts" approach to sentencing, pointing out that many such approaches allow previous convictions to be taken into account and that even when criminal justice decisionmakers deny that they take note of likely future events, they take cognizance of the same items of information as they would if they were doing so. In other words, there may be very little difference in practice between sentencing based on past events and sentencing based on predicted future events, since the past events predict the future events.

Stephen and Don Gottfredson in chapter 3 and William Wilbanks in chapter 4 compared the efficiency of five methods of constructing parole prediction tables. Interestingly, both found that all the prediction devices tended to identify the same people and hence would tend to lead to the same recommended decision for each person. Both also, ingeniously, studied the effect of introducing random error ("noise") into the data, and both found that the simplest (Burgess and Glueck) techniques were least affected. As Wilbanks pointed out, researchers should be cautious about using techniques that make heavy demands on the quality of the data, because the data employed in the criminal justice system are notoriously "noisy."

In chapter 5, Gillian Hill presented a detailed review of the literature on the extent to which measures of personality or behavior taken in institutions after sentencing add to the efficiency of predictions of recidivism that could be made at the time of the sentence. In the interests of cumulative knowledge, such attempts to bring together in a convenient form the wealth of experience and information from a large body of research need to be completed more often. Loeber and Dishion (1983) have recently provided an extensive, detailed review of the prediction of delinquency that advances our knowledge of that field. Hill concluded that institutional misconduct seemed to be the most reliable institutional predictor, but she drew attention to the need for more research to establish whether misconduct adds significantly to the efficiency of known predictors such as previous criminal record. She also discovered that institutional staff were able to predict the likelihood of reoffending, suggesting that research was needed to establish how and why they could do this and whether some types of persons were better at predicting recidivism than others. There have been several recent attempts to predict institutional adjustment (for example, Hanson et al., 1983; Louscher, Hosford, and Moss, 1983).

Continuing the theme of custodial prediction, David Thornton and Sheila Speirs in chapter 6 studied the important practical problem for institutional management of predicting absconding. Although some previous research had suggested that the characteristics of inmates did not predict the risk of absconding, Thornton and Speirs found that factors such as age, race, previous offense type, and employment status were predictive. While, as expected, the best predictor of future absconding was past absconding, predictive efficiency was improved by taking account of inmate characteristics. The national system for allocating incarcerated young offenders in England and Wales is now based on this research, showing its practical usefulness.

The research described by Eric Cullen in chapter 7 also had important practical implications. Self-injury by female offenders was predicted by previous self-injury (of course), but also by previous psychiatric treatment, high neuroticism, low self-esteem, high aggressiveness, and low happiness. A prediction scale was constructed and validated and then used to identify potential self-injurers for preventive treatment. Cullen found a significant decrease in self-injuries after this system was introduced.

David Farrington in chapter 8 investigated the prediction of delinquency, as measured by self-reports and official records. He found that it was difficult to identify a group with more than a 50 percent chance of delinquency and, conversely, to identify more than 50 percent of the delinquents. Although a group of "chronic" offenders could be identified (6 percent of the sample, who accounted for 49 percent of all convictions) and predicted to a considerable extent, the incapacitation of these offenders would not lead to a significant reduction in the crime rate.

Tony Black and Penny Spinks in chapter 9 attempted to predict future convictions and psychiatric admissions of a sample of dangerous, mentally abnormal offenders. Whereas half had previously killed someone and a further quarter had committed other violent offenses, only about 10 percent were reconvicted for violence during a five-year follow-up period. Nevertheless, using background variables, such as the type of offense and the number of previous convictions, and psychological test variables, Black and Spinks were able to divide the sample into groups differing markedly in the risk of reconviction. These results could help in deciding whether and when "dangerous" offenders should be released into the community. As mentioned in our introductory chapter, very few studies of the prediction of dangerousness have attempted to develop prediction scales.

In chapter 10, Gordon Cassidy described the development of a model of the Canadian criminal justice system. Such models are very important because they can be used to predict the effects of policy changes on different parts of the system. Many researchers concentrate on only one element of the system, such as police discretion or sentencing in court, but changes in one area can have important implications in another. Ideally, the effects of new laws or policy changes should be investigated before they are brought into effect, and one of the easiest ways of doing this is to use a computer model. Cassidy's model is especially useful in estimating the cost of processing a given number of persons at each stage.

Chapter 11, by Roger Tarling and John Perry, and chapter 12, by John Copas, were primarily methodological rather than substantive.

The remainder of this chapter will review the implications of this book for statistical and methodological issues.

MEASURING PREDICTOR AND CRITERION VARIABLES

It has been emphasized in this book that the choice of predictor variables to measure should depend on theoretical considerations (which theoretical constructs affect the criterion variables), rather than on what is available in institutional records. This was true in chapter 8 by Farrington. Variables were measured from a variety of sources: not only records, but interviews and tests given to the subjects, their parents, their peers, and their teachers. Studies based only on records are vulnerable to the accusation that predictive efficiency is low because important predictors have not been measured. Also, using variables measured from a variety of sources makes it more possible to establish reliability and validity. It is plausible to argue that the best hope of improving predictive efficiency is to measure more relevant variables more reliably, more validly, and more sensitively.

Wilkins in chapter 2 and the Gottfredsons in chapter 3 both discussed the problem of unethical or discriminatory predictors such as race. Wilkins argued that what it was ethical to study in prediction research diverged from what it was ethical to use in decisions affecting individuals. The Gottfredsons studied the order of entry of different types of predictor variables into prediction equations and concluded that the variables that were most vulnerable to ethical or legal attack often added very little to predictive efficiency. Clearly, what is needed is a careful study to establish the extent to which different types of variables nevertheless identify the same people. It seems probable that those who would be identified by "unethical" predictors would also be identified by "ethical" predictors. The problem of "unethical" predictors is discussed in the extensive review of sentencing guidelines by the National Academy of Sciences Panel on Sentencing Research (Blumstein, et al., 1983).

In most studies in this book, as in most prediction research, the criterion variable is official recidivism within a fixed follow-up period, measured as a dichotomy. This has many known disadvantages. From a statistical viewpoint, it wastes information, because it does not take into account time to reoffending, only whether or not the person has reoffended within a fixed period. There is a further problem caused by censoring: that is, some persons may recidivate after the end of the follow-up period or censoring point. There is also the conceptual problem that a variable may predict official recidivism either because it is related to offending behavior or because it is related to the probability of being arrested following offending behavior. Chapter 8 by Farrington tried to overcome this problem by studying the prediction of both official and self-reported delinquency. Interestingly, it was easier to predict convictions than self-reports of offending, suggesting that more may be known about the correlates of police selection than about the correlates of offending.

What is needed in the future are studies of the prediction of more basic criterion variables. Little is known at present even about differences between the prediction of convictions and the prediction of recidivism. Farrington's chapter shows that adult convictions could be predicted better than juvenile ones because of the efficiency of juvenile convictions as a predictor of adult ones. It might therefore be expected that recidivism could be predicted more efficiently than convictions, because of the efficiency of prior convictions as a predictor of recidivism.

Unfortunately, the occurrence of convictions or recidivism is difficult to interpret theoretically. Currently, a National Academy of Sciences panel is studying criminal career research, chaired by Alfred Blumstein. One of the major contributions of this panel is expected to be the clarification of the elements of a criminal career. It is clearly necessary to distinguish the participation rate (the proportion of persons who are active offenders) from the individual crime rate (the average rate of offending of those who are active). It is hard to know whether a group with a high recidivism rate is higher on participation, on individual crime rate, or both. One of the important contributions of Greenwood (1982) and Chaiken and Chaiken (1982) was to try to disentangle and predict the individual crime rate.

Other elements of criminal careers also need to be distinguished. In particular, it is important to study the predictors of onset, duration, and termination. In estimating incapacitation effects, for example, it is essential to predict residual career length. In addition, it is important to predict not only the individual crime rate but also the types of crimes committed and transition probabilities (for example, from less serious to more serious crimes). Furthermore, there are many reasons for trying to predict the rates of arrest, conviction, and incarceration at different stages of a criminal career.

Careful analysis of criminal careers as well as statistical considerations forces attention to the time dimension, which has important implications for statistical methods. Once the criterion is not a dichotomy but a series of events occurring at different times, stochastic point process models can be used. If the interest is in time to failure, failure rate regression or survival models should be used. These can accommodate censored data (Cox and Oakes, 1984). An emphasis on the time dimension requires a more careful specification of the times at which offenses are committed, of the time at risk of committing offenses, and of the time incarcerated than has been usual in the past.

In the future, we expect the criterion variable in prediction research to change from recidivism to criminal career parameters such as participation rate, individual crime rate, residual career length, transition probabilities, and times to failure.

SELECTING AND COMBINING PREDICTORS

One of the major contributions of this book lies in the careful, systematic comparisons of different methods of selecting and combining predictors to produce a prediction table or risk groups. In chapter 1, we noted that little was known about the efficiency of the newer loglinear and logistic methods in comparison with the more traditional techniques. These newer methods have been used in most of the chapters in this book, and we are now in a good position to evaluate them.

Unfortunately, the detailed comparisons of different methods with the same data, often involving large samples, in a variety of criminological contexts shows that no method is consistently better than any other in validation samples. The loglinear and logistic techniques, in common with multiple regression and predictive attribute analysis, often prove to be more efficient in construction samples than the simpler Burgess and Glueck techniques. However, the more sophisticated techniques are more prone to shrinkage, so that no method is better than Burgess and Glueck in validation samples. Nevertheless, as Tarling and Perry pointed out in chapter 11, with a dichotomous criterion variable there are good statistical reasons for preferring a technique like logistic regression, which makes it possible to estimate the independent contributions of the predictor variables. In addition, Copas and Tarling (1984) have recently shown how the Burgess and Glueck methods can be incorporated within the statistical framework of general linear models. Burgess and Glueck are not separate and distinct models but are, in fact, simple loglinear models in which all the predictors are treated as independent, that is, not correlated.

Chapter 12 by Copas is noteworthy because of his description of how to set about a predictive analysis. We hope his thoughtful approach will act as an antidote to the mindless "throw-it-all-into-SPSS-and-turn-the-handle" technique, which is depressingly common in this and other fields. Copas recommends a thorough initial exploration of the data to study significant relationships and interactions (although Farrington in chapter 8 found very few in his study) and a good deal of data reduction, by amalgamation or redefinition, to avoid highly correlated variables. All this should be done *before* selecting and combining variables to construct a prediction instrument.

An interesting recent approach to the development of prediction instruments is the "multiple gating" technique of Loeber, Dishion, and Patterson (1984). Multiple gating is essentially a hierarchical clustering technique, but it takes account of the different costs of different kinds of screening. The researchers were interested in predicting delinquency in order to apply prevention methods to a vulnerable group. Initially, they applied an inexpensive screening measure (teacher ratings) to a population of youths to identify a relatively high risk group; they then applied more expensive measures (such as assessment of parenting skills) to identify a successively smaller, higher-risk group they could eventually treat.

Since most prior prediction research has been based on institutional records, researchers have been able to ignore the relative cost of collecting different kinds of data. However, where the treatment is expensive and can be given only to the most needy cases, and where different predictor variables are differentially expensive and differentially efficient, the approach described by Loeber, Dishion, and Patterson seems worth developing. It is to be hoped that it can be properly validated.

MEASURING PREDICTIVE EFFICIENCY

As stated in our introductory chapter, there is a need for more standardized, comparable, and comprehensible measures of predictive efficiency. It is often valuable to show the full relationship between risk groups and outcomes, as Wilbanks did in chapter 4, in addition to summary measures of efficiency. Doing so may reveal different relationships within different risk groups that are hidden by the summary measure. The appropriate measure of predictive efficiency obviously depends on the nature of the predictor and criterion variables. One advantage of our book is that, although different chapters use different measures, the chapters that compare different prediction techniques use the same measure of predictive efficiency to evaluate each one. For example, Wilbanks used the total number of errors and also the proportional reduction in error.

Another measure of predictive efficiency has recently been proposed by Loeber and Dishion (1983)—the relative improvement over chance. Relative improvement can be calculated from 2 x 2 tables, such as those presented by Wilbanks, relating predicted success and failure to actual success and failure. For example, using the Glueck method in the validation sample, Wilbanks predicted 147 successes, of which 96 were actual successes; 280 were predicted to be failures, of which 234 were actual failures. The total number of correct identifications was 330, in comparison with 97 errors (false positives or false negatives).

Unfortunately, although the total number of errors is intuitively easy to understand, it is greatly dependent on the base rate (the total number of actual failures in the above example) and the selection ratio (the number of predicted failures). These two quantities determine the number of correct predictions expected by chance (235.8 in the above example) and the maximum number of correct predictions which could possible be achieved (422). Every person in a sample could be predicted correctly only if the base rate is equal to the selection ratio (as it was, approximately, in the Wilbanks study). The maximum possible number of correct predictions decreases as the base rate and selection ratio diverge.

The Loeber-Dishion measure of predictive efficiency is designed to eliminate the effects of the base rate and selection ratio but nevertheless to be stated in an understandable form. In their formulation,

$$RIOC = \frac{AC - RC}{MC - RC} \times 100\%$$

Where RIOC is the relative improvement over chance, AC is the actual number of correct predictions, RC is the randomly expected number of correct predictions, and MC is the maximum possible number of correct predictions. In the above example,

$$RIOC = \frac{330 - 235.8}{422 - 235.8} \times 100\%$$

$$= \frac{94.2}{186.2} \times 100\% = 50.6\%.$$

A closer examination of RIOC by Copas and Tarling (1984) casts doubt on the measure's invariance. They showed that RIOC increases as the selection ratio increases, and they suggested that care should be exercised when using RIOC. They also discovered one other interesting property of the measure. When the base rate equals the selection ratio, RIOC equals ϕ.

Another problem with the Loeber-Dishion measure of predictive efficiency is that equal weight is given to the different kinds of errors and correct predictions. However, in many applications of prediction techniques, it is desirable to take account of the social costs and benefits of the different outcomes in assessing the adequacy of the technique. Blumstein, Farrington, and Moitra (1985), using decision theory, have provided a way of doing this. They developed a prediction score for identifying chronic offenders at the time of their first convictions and were interested in determining the optimum cutoff point. Identifying this cutoff point, they pointed out, depends on the benefits associated with correct labeling and on the concern over mislabeling. The authors developed a "civil-libertarian ratio" that summarized the relative concern over false positives compared with false negatives and plotted a graph to show how the optimum cutoff point varied with this ratio.

In determining the adequacy or desirability of any prediction technique, it is clearly necessary to take into account not only predictive efficiency but also the costs and benefits associated with the different possible outcomes.

EXTERNAL VALIDITY

Any prediction instrument constructed on one sample needs to be validated on another, as explained in chapter 1. Any practical use of a prediction instrument involves essentially a prospective longitudinal design: the prediction is made before the outcome and in ignorance of it. In contrast, much prediction research is essentially retrospective, beginning after the outcomes of interest are known. In this book, as in much research, the construction and validation samples were usually randomly chosen halves of a larger total sample. Ideally, a prediction instrument should be constructed on one sample and then validated prospectively on another one. In addition, further validation studies should be carried out to establish how well the predictions hold up over time, place, and different samples.

An interesting recent paper on this topic was completed by Wright, Clear, and Dickson (1984), who were concerned to evaluate the Wisconsin system for estimating probation risk. The Wisconsin system had been designated as a model system by the National Institute of Corrections, which was undertaking a large project to implement it on a nationwide basis. Although it was recommended that the instrument should be revalidated in each new setting, this was rarely done. Wright, Clear, and Dickson applied the instrument to probation cases in New York City and found that it did not hold up very well.

In moving from a construction to a validation sample, there is always some shrinkage, even when both are randomly chosen halves of the same total sample. The chapters in this book show the extent of shrinkage and show that it is just as great a problem with loglinear or logistic methods as with other sensitive techniques such as multiple regression. Chapter 12 by Copas is useful in providing a way of estimating the likely shrinkage in advance and in developing "preshrunk" measures of predictive efficiency from the construction sample. He shows how the amount of shrinkage depends on the sample size and on the number of predictor variables. These ideas are extended in Copas and Tarling (1984).

CONCLUSIONS

Prediction in criminology has always been an important topic, and it will continue to be important in the foreseeable future. However, there will be new developments, of course. We expect prediction methods to be used increasingly in new areas—for example, by the police in deciding how to allocate resources in crime investigation. Whereas prediction methods in the past have been used mainly in the area of treatment, we expect their use in prevention and in theoretical analysis to increase in the future.

We expect that predictor variables will be measured more reliably, validly, and sensitively and that they will not depend so much on what is available in records. We expect that more adequate criterion variables than recidivism will be measured, especially criminal career parameters that take account of the timing of offenses. We expect that more sophisticated methods of selecting and combining variables into a prediction instrument will be used, despite our demonstration that, with existing data, existing methods are about equally efficient in validation samples. Certainly, different methods will be needed to predict criminal career parameters and time intervals. We also expect that better methods of measuring predictive efficiency will be developed, especially those taking account of financial and social costs and benefits of different outcomes.

Prediction in criminology has made significant progress since the pioneering work of Burgess (1928), and the pace of progress has accelerated since the landmark studies of Ohlin (1951) and Mannheim and Wilkins (1955). We are optimistic about further progress, and about cumulative knowledge, in this field of endeavor.

REFERENCES

Blumstein, A.; Cohen, J.; Martin, S. E.; and Tonry, M. H., eds. (1983). *Research on sentencing: The search for reform.* 2 vols. Washington, DC: National Academy Press.

Blumstein, A.; Farrington, D. P.; and Moitra, S. (1985). Delinquency careers: Innocents, desisters, and persisters. In *Crime and justice,* vol. 6, ed. M. Tonry and N. Morris. Chicago: University of Chicago Press, in press.

Burgess, E. W. (1928). Factors determining success or failure on parole. In *The workings of the indeterminate-sentence law and the parole system in Illinois,* ed. A. A. Bruce, A. J. Harno, E. W. Burgess, and J. Landesco. Springfield, IL: Illinois State Board of Parole.

Chaiken, J. M., and Chaiken, M. R. (1982). *Varieties of criminal behavior.* Santa Monica, CA: Rand Corporation.

Copas, J., and Tarling, R. (1984). *Some methodological issues in making predictions.* Paper prepared for the National Academy of Sciences Panel on Research on Criminal Careers.

Cox, D. R., and Oaks, D. (1984) *Analysis of survival data.* London: Chapman and Hall.

Fischer, D. R. (1983). *The use of actuarial methods in early release screening.* Paper presented to the 113th Congress of the American Correctional Association.

Greenwood, P. W. (1982). *Selective incapacitation.* Santa Monica, CA: Rand Corporation.

Hanson, R. W.; Moss, C. S.; Hosford, R. E.; and Johnson, M. E. (1983). Predicting inmate penitentiary adjustment: An assessment of four classificatory methods. *Criminal Justice and Behavior* 10:293–309.

Loeber, R., and Dishion, T. (1983). Early predictors of male delinquency: A review. *Psychological Bulletin* 94:68–99.

Loeber, R.; Dishion, T. J.; and Patterson, G. R. (1984). Multiple gating: A multistage assessment procedure for identifying youths at risk for delinquency. *Journal of Research in Crime and Delinquency* 21:7–32.

Louscher, P. K.; Hosford, R. E.; and Moss, C. S. (1983). Predicting dangerous behavior in a penitentiary using the Megargee typology. *Criminal Justice and Behavior* 10:269–84.

Mannheim, H., and Wilkins, L. T. (1955). *Prediction methods in relation to borstal training.* London: Her Majesty's Stationery Office.

Ohlin, L. E. (1951). *Selection for parole.* New York: Russell Sage.

Wright, K. N.; Clear, T. R.; and Dickson, P. (1984). Universal applicability of probation risk-assessment instruments: A critique. *Criminology* 22:113–34.

Author Index

Subject Index